JOSEPHUS

JOSEPHUS

The Historian and His Society

Tessa Rajak

FORTRESS PRESS   PHILADELPHIA

First published in 1983 by
Gerald Duckworth & Co. Ltd., London, England

First Fortress Press edition 1984

Library of Congress Cataloging in Publication Data

Rajak, Tessa, 1946–
  Josephus, the historian and his society.

  Includes index.
  1. Josephus, Flavius. De bello Judaico. 2. Jews—
History—Rebellion, 66–73. 3. Jews—History—168 B.C.–
135 A.D. I. Title.
DS122.8.J83R34 1984   933′.05   83–16538
ISBN 0–8006–0717–1

K468H82   Printed in the United Kingdom   1–717

Contents

Remercie humblement aussi ton Createur
Que t'a donné Iosephe, un si fidele auteur,
Certes qui tousiours semble avoir de Dieu guidée
La plume, en escrivant tous les faits de Iudée:
Car bien qu'il ait suyui le Grec langage orné,
Tant s'en faut qu'il se soit à leurs moeurs adonné,
Que plutost au vray but de l'histoire il regarde
Qu'il ne fait pas au fard d'une langue mignarde.

Pierre Tredehan, au peuple françois, 1558.

Preface

This book is a re-interpretation of Josephus' history and of the war which he described, rather than a general introduction either to the author or to first century Palestine. It is, none the less, intended for, among others, readers who are not specialists in this period, and I have borne their needs in mind, along with those of scholars. Thus, while the arguments are fully documented and (it is hoped) substantiated, the supporting texts are translated into English, and unfamiliar concepts, whether Greek, Roman or Jewish, are explained. Occasional Greek, Hebrew and Aramaic words are transliterated, and this is done according to simple, largely phonetic principles.

I have incurred debts over a long period of time. Without Fergus Millar's vision, advice and encouragement, this book could hardly have been written; and he has also commented on various versions of its chapters. I am much indebted to Alan Wardman who has improved both substance and style and given generous assistance with proof reading. I am grateful to Peter Brunt and David Lewis, the examiners of the Oxford D.Phil. thesis out of a section of which the book has grown, for many detailed and acute corrections; to Geza Vermes, Arnaldo Momigliano and Miriam Griffin for support and useful suggestions; to my parents for their help and constant interest; and to my husband, Harry Rajak, for perceptive criticism and for loving concern of every kind, of which this book is one result and one acknowledgment.

This work reached its final form at the Center for Hellenic Studies, Washington D.C.; I must thank the Trustees of Harvard University, and especially Bernard Knox, the Center's Director, who presides over a stimulating and tranquil writing environment. A year's leave of absence granted by the University of Reading enabled me to benefit from this, as also did a Fulbright Scholarship.

I have been further assisted by grants from the Memorial Foundation for Jewish Culture and from the Wolfson Foundation. Doreen Janes typed a difficult manuscript with tolerance. My publishers waited patiently for the book and then looked after it admirably.

London, 1982.   T.R.

Abbreviations

I have generally followed the *Oxford Classical Dictionary* (2nd edition) for Classical works, *Année Philologique* and Schürer-Vermes-Millar for the titles of periodicals, and the *Encyclopaedia Judaica* for Jewish sources. Book titles are normally given in full, but 'Schürer-Vermes-Millar' is used throughout to refer to the new English Edition of Emil Schürer's *History of the Jewish People in the Age of Jesus Christ* (1973 and 1979). Of Josephus' works, *BJ* is the *Jewish War*, *AJ* the *Antiquities*, *V* the *Life* and *CA* is *Against Apion*.

Table of events

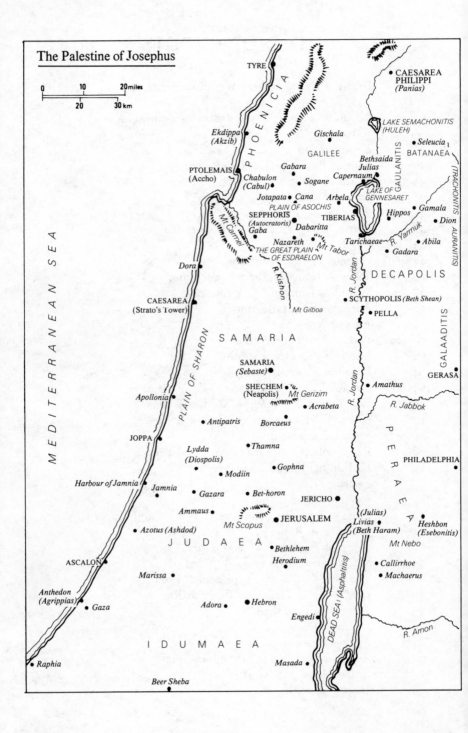

The Palestine of Josephus

0   10   20 miles
0   20   30 km

TYRE

CAESAREA
PHILIPPI
(Panias)

P
H
O
E
N
I
C
I
A

LAKE SEMACHONITIS
(HULEH)

Ekdippa
(Akzib)

Gischala

GALILEE

Seleucia

BATANAEA

Gabara

Bethsaida
Julias

G
A
U
L
A
N
I
T
I
S

(T
R
A
C
H
O
N
I
T
I
S)

PTOLEMAIS
(Accho)

Chabulon
(Cabul)

Sogane

Capernaum

Jotapata   Cana
PLAIN OF ASOCHIS

Arbela

LAKE OF
GENNESARET

Gamala

SEPPHORIS
(Autocratoris)
Gaba

Dabaritta

TIBERIAS

Hippos

Dion

A
U
R
A
N
I
T
I
S

Abila

Mt Carmel

Nazareth
THE GREAT PLAIN
OF ESDRAELON

Mt Tabor

Tarichaeae

R. Yarmuk

Gadara

M
E
D
I
T
E
R
R
A
N
E
A
N

S
E
A

Dora

R. Kishon

Mt Gilboa

DECAPOLIS

CAESAREA
(Strato's Tower)

SAMARIA

R. Jordan

SCYTHOPOLIS (Beth Shean)

PELLA

G
A
L
A
A
D
I
T
I
S

SAMARIA
(Sebaste)

Amathus

GERASA

Apollonia

P
L
A
I
N

O
F

S
H
A
R
O
N

SHECHEM
(Neapolis)   Mt Gerizim
Acrabeta

R. Jordan

R. Jabbok

Antipatris

Borcaeus

P
E
R
A
E
A

JOPPA

Thamna

PHILADELPHIA

Lydda
(Diospolis)

Gophna

Harbour of Jamnia

Modiin

Jamnia

Gazara   Bet-horon

JERICHO

Ammaus

Mt Scopus

JERUSALEM

(Julias)
Livias
(Beth Haram)

Heshbon
(Esebonitis)

Azotus (Ashdod)

JUDAEA

Bethlehem
Herodium

Mt Nebo

ASCALON

Marissa

Callirhoe

Machaerus

Anthedon
(Agrippias)   Gaza

Adora   Hebron

Engedi

D
E
A
D

S
E
A (Asphaltitis)

R. Arnon

I D U M A E A

Raphia

Masada

Beer Sheba

Introduction

I

Josephus was a Jewish priest of royal descent and Pharisaic persuasion, born in Jerusalem in A.D. 37, just after Pontius Pilate had ceased to govern the province. He took a leading but reluctant part in the great anti-Roman revolt of A.D. 66–73, and after he had been defeated in Galilee and had surrendered himself to the Romans he witnessed the later stages of the revolt from the Roman camp. He saw the fall of Jerusalem and the burning of the Temple. He was at Alexandria with the Roman general Vespasian shortly after the legions there had declared their leader emperor. Josephus was made a Roman citizen; and the second half of his life was spent at Rome, where, still a Jew, he seems to have devoted himself to writing historical works, usually in Greek, on Jewish subjects.

Josephus was thus intimately connected with some of the most significant events of the first century. His books constitute our only continuous source for the history of Palestine in the time of the Herods and the Roman procurators, of the Dead Sea Scrolls and the formation of the oral tradition on which Rabbinic Judaism would be based, of John the Baptist and of Jesus Christ. Also, his career embodies in a distinct way the principal themes and conflicts of the Roman middle east during this period: the tension between local patriotism and the claims of the imperial order, between native culture and the allure of Greco-Roman civilisation, between Semitic languages and Greek, between pragmatic flexibility and committed sectarianism, between class loyalty and group loyalty.

Through the ages, Flavius Josephus has, for one reason or another, attracted considerable attention from the reading public. Now perhaps, the respect granted him by Christians as the author of the foremost 'testimony' to Jesus and as the witness to the punishment of the Jews through the loss of their temple has faded from general consciousness. And Jews may be less dismayed than they

used to be by what could be judged a betrayal of nation and religion.
Instead, Josephus has evoked other kinds of interest—as the writer
who had made it possible for us to understand the remarkable
discoveries of Qumran, and as the surprisingly careful reporter of
what was built and what was done on the rock of Masada. All these
fragmentary views, while serving the invaluable purpose of keeping
our author's reputation alive, have at the same time detached him
from his historical context, to which I hope to restore him. A career
as full of variety and vicissitudes as his was makes him a personality
of unusual interest. At the same time, this diversity is not unexpected in a world like his, with its many cross-currents. Palestinian
Jews were subject to a number of different influences, and they
could expect to have to make difficult choices.

By the first century A.D., the relationship between Jews and
Greeks, and even between Jews and Romans, had had a history of
some length and complexity. Alexander the Great with his Mace-
donian army had marched through Phoenicia, Egypt and Syria
nearly four hundred years before Josephus was born. Even before
that event, there had been some Greek influence in the region. After
Alexander's death, Palestine fell under the control of the Greek
dynasty of the Ptolemies who ruled from Egypt, and it later passed
to the Seleucid kings of Asia. Unique in some ways, it was none the
less a part of the Hellenized orient. Meanwhile, the Jewish Diaspora
grew, with communities becoming established in many Greek cities,
and this meant that Jews were often living together with Greeks,
whether harmoniously or otherwise. In Palestine, the revolt of Judas
Maccabaeus against the Seleucid king Antiochus IV Epiphanes
(175–165 B.C.) was provoked not only by the establishment of a
heathen cult in the Jerusalem temple and the king's attack on
Jewish practices, but also by a party of Hellenizers among the Jews,
represented first by the high priest Jason, and then by the more
extreme Menelaus, who ousted him. The outcome of the successful
revolt was virtual political independence for Palestine under its own
Maccabean kings; but this did not go hand in hand with the expulsion of all things Greek from Jerusalem. Rather, a sort of cultural
compromise evolved. External Hellenization was recognised as
being there to stay. But the religious core of Judaism was protected:
the Temple cult and the study of the Torah continued unchallenged
at the centre of national life. In another way, too, Judas Maccabaeus
marks a turning point, for he, and his successors after him, sent

ambassadors to the Roman senate, and brought back a treaty between the Jewish people and the growing power in the west.

The Hasmonean (Maccabean) dynasty ruled for a century, acquiring the high priesthood, and becoming worldly and expansionist. But eventually, in 63 B.C., during the period of weakness, and conflict between two Hasmonean brothers, Jerusalem fell to the Roman conqueror of the east, Pompey the Great. So began a new era, that of subjection to Rome, either direct or indirect. Some welcomed this; indeed a delegation of Jews is said to have met Pompey at Damascus and invited him to take over their country. On the other hand, there were sectarian circles, probably including certain Pharisees, who were bitterly hostile, especially to his intrusion into the Holy of Holies. By this time, then, there have emerged two distinct tendencies – a cosmopolitan, outward-looking approach, and a reaction of fierce resentment against alien domination and foreign influence.

The Hasmonean monarchy was propped up for some twenty years after Pompey's conquest. But then Rome's own political upheavals following on the assassination of Julius Caesar, in particular the eventual war between Octavian and Antony, made an opening for a new power in Palestine, the client kingship of the Herods. Antony was associated both with Herod's father and with Herod himself; but Octavian, when he became Augustus, pardoned his former enemy, who was able to rule, with some Roman assistance, for almost as long as his Roman patron. The division of Palestine into three smaller kingdoms after his death in 4 B.C. led, by predictable stages, to the re-establishment of direct Roman rule, first in Judaea and later in Galilee.

Now Herod, who was of an Idumaean family but one which had converted to Judaism, called himself not only *Philorōmaios*, a lover of Rome, but also a lover of the Greeks, and his pride in his own Greek culture expressed itself in such acts as the founding of Greek cities, and benefactions to the Olympic games. It was not confined to the pagan world, but made an impact also within Palestine. As a result, the cleavage among the Jews was intensified. Herod had violent arguments with the Pharisees, the Qumran sect, the adherents of the 'fourth philosophy'; and there were also other elements favouring dissidence who became active under Herod, and then continued to flourish under the Roman prefects, spurred on by the latter's misgovernment.

Josephus and his family, though unswerving, it seems, in their devotion to Jewish law and cult, belonged very definitely among the conformists and the cosmopolitans. Though forced to rebel for a short time, he was in general accepting of Roman power and, equally, must always have been competent in Greek and ready to mix with Greeks. His varied career can be seen as an expression of the ambivalences and conflicting forces to which prominent Jews of this kind were increasingly subject under Roman rule, until the great revolt transformed the situation, if only by the physical elimination of the greater part of them. What makes our author different from others is essentially just his capacity for survival, a capacity which we may dislike, but cannot regret.

II

This, then, is a book about a man who was for a short time a politician, for a shorter time a soldier (of dubious merit), but in the end, and principally, a writer. As a writer, his first subject, to which he later returned, was the war in which he had been involved in various ways—the Jewish revolt against Rome starting in A.D.66, together with the civil troubles which were a part of it. Where he had not been a combatant, he had often been an eyewitness, or at least was close to what happened and reacted strongly, deploring especially the rebels' excesses. He also developed good relations, while the fighting was still on, with his former enemies, the father and son who commanded the Roman imperial army; and this patronage continued when Vespasian and Titus themselves became emperors.

Josephus' writings raise many questions; but there is one central problem. They prompt us to ask about the value of history which emerges from such circumstances; and about the relation between what was done and what was written. The author's own participation in what took place makes it likely that what he produces will be, on the one hand, especially informative, on the other, in some ways distorted. That is obvious. But how are we to read behind the distortions, and unravel the intricate interaction between author and subject?

I have used the technique of interpreting Josephus in the light of what can be known about his contemporaries and their attitudes. Since Josephus' testimony is a basic source of information about them, the problem is doubly delicate. Yet to tackle it promises the reward of understanding not only the individual writer but also the Jews and Romans of his day.

Interesting reflections on the process of history-writing are also provoked, especially about the effects of a historian's prejudices on his grasp of his subject, and about the kinds of misrepresentation to which he is prone because of his personal interest in what he writes. Today, history is most often produced by professionals. But the ancients thought that men with experience of action were the best qualified to describe it: 'For how is it possible,' Polybius asked, 'to cross-examine someone properly about a battle or a siege or a sea-fight, or to understand the details of his account, if one has no acquaintance with what is being talked about?' Following Thucydides, contemporary history was a highly respected genre (and some have even maintained that it always occupied the centre of the historiographical stage). So Thucydides' insistence on the superiority of eye-witness testimony lent a special cachet to this kind of evidence. Indeed Josephus himself claimed in the preface to the *Jewish War* that it was much better to write a history of recent events, like his, and to present material that was new, than to do as others did, merely dressing familiar themes from antiquity in new clothes. As a result it was not at all unusual for political histories to be written by people who had themselves been party to the controversies they reported, or, at the very least, dependent upon previous partisan accounts. This was true of Herodotus and Thucydides, of Polybius and of Sallust, to name but a few. At the same time, Greek and Roman historians were fully aware of the dangers of bias in a committed writer, and there was scarcely one who did not profess to be setting out the truth, with an entire lack of 'ira et studium'. But what they actually did tended to be rather different. The detachment, or apparent detachment, which Thucydides achieved was rare indeed.

Some kinds of modern historical narration, especially the records and memoirs produced by politicians, are subject to the same hazards. The principal difference is simply that, as a rule, a large number of dissimilar accounts is available from other sources, making it easier for the reader to correct the picture. More generally, these cases are extreme instances of the broader problems of subjectivity in writing history. Few would dispute that it is virtually impossible for good history not to be to some degree partisan in one way or another. But where should the limits be drawn? This analysis of Josephus' partisanship explores the shady borderline area between genuine commitment and irresponsible bias. Furthermore, since Josephus' *Jewish War* was also influenced by another personal factor, his connection with the emperors, it raises also a related issue, making us reflect on the various ways in which patrons might influence the literature which they support.

To disentangle a historian's prejudices—the sentiments that arise from his personal position and interests—is to see him as a social agent, to relate his writings to their social and political environment. My interest is in the intersection of culture, politics and society. This book, therefore, does not adopt one single style of historical investigation: it is not political, social, or literary history, but each of these in turn, as appropriate. Josephus' personality, and his writings, are the focus of the argument and its connecting link. This book might have become a biography, if such a thing had been possible; but too little is known about the life of Josephus. Even as an intellectual biography, it remains fragmentary and is often conjectural. Yet there is a biographical thread. This is both because he is interesting enough as a man to stimulate curiosity and engage attention, and because to concentrate in this way on a single member of an élite, one about whom we do have at least a fair amount of knowledge, is an obvious way of getting closer to a world of which so much has sunk into oblivion.

I have been mainly concerned with Josephus' early life and writings, for, after that, information on his activities disappears almost entirely and, in any case, what he did must have become less significant and less dramatic. Also, the intimate connection between word and action was lost in his later years. None the less, the later works have been useful: not only the *Life*, a partial autobiography (though not of the interior modern kind) which deals in a new way with the events of A.D. 67, but also sections of the twenty-book *Antiquities*, and occasionally even the apologetic, pro-Jewish polemic, *Against Apion*, published in the mid-nineties. In the end, my interpretation of the first stages of his career has some consequences also for my reading of Josephus' development and of the kind of changes that he underwent—changes which, in my view, were rather limited.

Josephus belongs equally to Jewish and to Greco-Roman history; while the light he casts on the era of the Gospels and his adoption by the Church Fathers into Christian tradition also gives him an important role in the history of Christianity. In fact, it soon becomes apparent how interdependent these areas are. The lives of Jews, Greeks, Romans and Christians touched each other at many points. Thus, in the first century A.D., the Jews, as I have said, were constantly reacting to the Greek language and culture; and they lived for the most part either within the Roman empire, or, if among the Parthians, then in its shadow. Again, it was the fusion of Jewish with pagan elements which allowed Christianity to mature. And if it is the Romans we are considering, then it is clear that their empire was an amalgam of peoples, and contained, beneath a more or less uniform Greco-Roman veneer, diverse local cultures. This is especially true of the 'Greek' east; and in the eastern patchwork, the Jews are a far from insignificant part.

In essence, my aim has been to cast light on the cultural and social history of the Roman empire. Josephus belonged to the Jewish élite of first-century Jerusalem, and that group, apart from its own intrinsic interest, can provide illuminating comparisons with similar groups elsewhere in the empire, groups which included many local dynasts and their followers, priests of provincial and city cults, councillors, civic benefactors and large landowners throughout the east. Others (less well documented) reveal a comparable concern for political accommodation with the ruling power and a similar grasp of the benefits which could come from this. Yet the Jews were also different, and this difference can be summed up in the fact of their indigenous cultural life, which seems more vigorous than that of others and was intimately associated with a demanding and tenacious set of religious beliefs. This had some effect on the upper classes, by limiting the hold which Greek culture could have even over them, and a greater effect on the lower orders, whose loyalty was needed by those in control. So we find no uprising in any eastern province equal to the Jewish revolt. It is through both the similarities and the distinctions between Jewish society and other native societies that we discover important aspects of the imperial system's operation at the local level.

But Josephus moved from the periphery to the centre, for he later lived in Rome, where he wrote his books. He is an important Flavian writer and a principal source on the Flavian dynasty's rise to power. In his flattery of the emperors he is quite in tune with the spirit of the age. Thus in looking at what he has to say about them and at the relationship between the historian and his patrons, I have been concerned again with Roman problems, though from a rather different angle.

At the same time, this has been an exploration of the character of first-century Judaism, not so much as a system of belief and ritual, but as a social and intellectual phenomenon. It is evident that Josephus, not only through the information he offers, but in his own person, fills a void in our knowledge of the Jews. Through his early life, we can learn from the inside about the upper échelons of the Palestinian priesthood, an outward-looking, flexible group, yet strict in its religious practices and prescriptions; a group which vanished with the fall of the Temple in A.D. 70. The Gospels, and some sections of Talmudic literature, provide a different kind of view, and one which is complementary. Subsequently, Josephus belongs to the Jewish Diaspora, to the world of Greek-speaking urban Jews, with its great communities at Alexandria, Antioch, Sardis, and its numerous smaller ones, of which the community at Rome was one, dotted over much of the empire, and beyond. This Diaspora had been in existence since well before the conquests of Alexander, and the Palestinian élite had long had personal and public links with it. It would contain enough dynamism to produce, some twenty years after Josephus' death, its own great revolt in several centres, against both the local administration and the Roman emperor (Trajan). It was within this Diaspora that Christianity grew; but this is a subject on which Josephus chooses to remain silent. The internal development of the Jewish Diaspora in the second half of the first century A.D. is extremely obscure; when, in the following century, the Trajanic revolt breaks out, it seems to spring almost out of nothing. In fact, Josephus is the only major figure from this context of whom anything much is known, so that in this way too he is important.

My interest in Josephus as a representative of those two Judaisms originated in a desire to disentangle Greek from Jewish within them. This is a distinction which has dominated, sometimes to good effect, investigation of Josephus' forerunner in Greek-Jewish writing, the Alexandrian philosopher Philo. I am now less convinced of the value of systematic attempts of this kind. In dealing with an age when ideas had a very wide diffusion and circulation, at all levels of society, it is rarely possible to assert with confidence that such and such an idea is Greek or non-Greek, except perhaps where the influence of a particular writer is detectable, as Plato's is in the case of Philo. Nevertheless, there are times when this polarity is a useful and practical tool of analysis. Thus, an assessment of Josephus' education is relevant to any attempt to understand why he became a Greek writer. Again, his linguistic background must be grasped if we are to appreciate how much effort and adjustment this decision cost him—and, indeed, whether he would have been at all capable of writing Greek histories without assistance. Yet again, we often find ourselves asking about the relation between form and content in Josephus' work, about how far the classical exterior of his history, features such as the imaginary speeches ascribed to protagonists, or the Greek terminology used for concepts like freedom or chance, have disguised the real, non-Greek nature of what was said or meant at the time.

In talking of non-Greek aspects of his work, I do not mean to suggest that Josephus requires some excuse as a Greek historian. While the *Jewish War* is patently not among the very greatest of Greek histories, it is a perfectly respectable one. In addition, it can make a distinctive and useful contribution, hitherto insufficiently exploited, to our knowledge of the development of the genre. It is the only complete surviving example of a Thucydidean history of a war from the early imperial period; and this, as we learn from Lucian's satire *How to Write History*, represented a prominent historiographical fashion of the time. Josephus' *Jewish War* also contains some of the best instances we can find in Greek of the 'tragic' manner of writing history, that tendency to the emotive, pathetic and grotesque which was popular from the Hellenistic period on, and which also was mocked by Lucian. Then again, Josephus' book is by far the most readable and appealing in the line of Greek histories written by immigrants from the east who spent time in Rome and became associated with Roman politics, a line which contains Polybius and the *Roman Antiquities* of Dionysius of Halicarnassus, as well as Appian, Arrian and Cassius Dio. Josephus was also more original than the others, for he took, quite consciously it would seem, the bold step of introducing a Jewish notion of God's role in the historical process into a conventional history. Literary technique has not in itself been my theme; but Josephus' ideas cannot be discussed without attention to the way they are expressed; and I hope that through the discussion some impression has emerged of his quality as a historian.

I have been reluctant to spend time refuting the views of others.

Unfortunately, the literature on Josephus abounds in received opinions and inherited assumptions concerning matters both great and small. It was often not possible to make positive points without first clearing away old notions. It is often said, for example, that because, as a general, Josephus was not always entirely trustworthy, it is unwise ever to believe him as a writer. Another established doctrine – this one has commanded almost universal assent—is that the *Jewish War* was composed as official history, or propaganda, commissioned by the Flavian emperors, and therefore having their interests and those of the Roman state at heart. Only when the Flavian influence has been put in its place, is it possible to understand Josephus' Jewish partisanship. In other ways, interpretations of Josephus have been coloured by the widespread conviction that the Jewish revolt against Rome was in truth an expression of Messianic frenzy, arising largely out of a heightened sense of religious expectation; Josephus, then, is taken not only to be concealing this, but to give an entirely misleading picture of what happened. These ideas and their like have made it very difficult for readers to notice what Josephus actually says about the war and about his fellow Jews, and to consider in a broader perspective his possible reasons for speaking as he does.

That, quite simply, is what I have tried to do. In the process, it became increasingly clear that Josephus meant much of what he said to have an immediate political application, whether or not he gave it also a religious dimension; the most notable case is his interpretation of the disturbances in Palestine in terms of *stasis*, the Greek word for civil dissension. And when, to explain Josephus, I turned to look at the character of the Jewish war as a whole, it emerged that only a political analysis, which viewed this event in the comparative light of other revolutions, could make sense of the complicated interplay between external revolt and internal social struggle. The presence of powerful religious feelings, and the use of the religious terminology habitual to first-century Jewry, does not alter the truth of this. There is nothing more difficult, in writing about the Palestine of this period, than to form an adequate conception of the relation between religion and other spheres of life. It scarcely needs saying that religion is interfused with almost every activity. But a proper reading of Josephus shows us that it was not the only dynamic factor in any situation, that Jewish behaviour was governed also by other instincts and other influences.

CHAPTER ONE

Family, Education and Formation

Josephus' life falls physically into two sharply divided halves. Born in Jerusalem, in A.D.37 (V 5), he had been outside his native country only once on an embassy, by the time the Jewish revolt of A.D. 66 broke out. He was then about 28 years old. After the fall of Jerusalem in 70, he left for Rome together with Titus; and there the emperor Vespasian, Titus' father, arranged for him to live in his own former house. Although Vespasian also gave him two tracts of land in Judaea, to compensate for losses in the war, and Josephus still held these under Domitian, there is no evidence that he ever returned to his homeland.[1] The rest of Josephus' life, some quarter of a century,[2] was spent in Rome. In this period, as well as being the protégé and client of emperors, Josephus was part of Diaspora Jewry. The only contacts with Palestinian Jewry about which we hear are hostile ones: Palestinians are likely to have been among those men who went on making attacks on his conduct during the war.[3]

Josephus was always a Jew, and, throughout his writing life, was preoccupied with Judaism; yet he was also for some time a politician who had constantly to be looking Romewards; and after that, when he became a writer, it was in Greek that he wrote. Thus, his thinking is subject to a variety of different pressures. And yet there can be no doubt that the influence of Jerusalem was of overwhelming importance. Any man is, naturally, shaped by his upbringing and

---

[1] On the Roman emperors' benefactions to Josephus, see V 422–3, 425, 429.

[2] We have no date for Josephus' death. On the dating of his later works, see pp. 237–8.

[3] V 425. It was conjectured by Graetz, 'Zur Geschichte und Chronologie Agrippa II's, der Procuratoren und die Hohenpriester seiner Zeit', *MGWJ* 26 (1877), p. 355, that the 'philosopher' (in *Derekh Eretz Rabbah* 5) who welcomed the patriarch Gamaliel and his three companion rabbis in Rome during the 90s A.D. was Josephus. Cf. H. Vogelstein and P. Rieger, *Geschichte der Juden in Rom* (1896), vol. 1, p. 29.

his education. And Josephus did not, in his literary career, reject
that basis: he did not try to become a Roman (though he had
Roman citizenship (*V* 423)) or a Greek, in such a way as to exclude
his previous concerns. Indeed, in the *Jewish War*, his first work, he
had expressed, in a speech which he put into his own mouth, the
intention of remaining loyal to his race and his people's tradition
as long as he lived. And in his last, the *Antiquities*, he still speaks of
the Jews as his compatriots (*BJ* 6.107; *AJ* 20.263). The Jewish client
king Agrippa I had been credited by Philo, in a letter directed to
Gaius the emperor, and clearly meant to appeal to Romans, with
saying that 'love of one's country and acceptance of its native laws
is natural to all men' (*Leg.* 277). Josephus may be doing no more
than self-consciously claiming credit for this variety of laudable
sentiment; if so, that does not lessen the significance of the self-
identification he chooses to adopt.

And so we ask, simply, what Josephus might have learnt, and
become, during those years which he spent in Jerusalem. Evidence
of various kinds will contribute. The starting point will be Josephus'
own brief remarks about himself in the work known as his *Life*,
together with a few scattered allusions in his other works. Setting
these against what we know of the background, we can try to
ascertain what position Josephus and his family occupied in Jerusalem society, and what were the implications of that position.
Using inference and imagination, it is possible to succeed fairly well
in sketching Josephus' early years. But, lest the reader expect too
much, it must be stressed that the account can only be superficial
and incomplete; and that is the case in spite of the fact that Josephus
is the only classical author to have produced a surviving work
known as 'autobiography'.

For Josephus' fourth work (if we are to count the lost Semitic
original of the *Jewish War* (see Chapter 7) as a separate endeavour)
is commonly known as the *Vita*, his *Life*. Unfortunately it is not
quite as valuable for our purpose as such a title might suggest. The
Vita is not really an autobiography in our sense of the word. Nor is
it quite a *bios* (a life) in the ancient sense, that is, an account of a
man's moral qualities.[4] Most of it is concerned with refuting certain

---

[4] As Nicolaus of Damascus' *Autobiography* to a great extent was, even though it
dealt with politics as well. See Jacoby, *FGH* F136 and IIA Comm., 288ff. On
Josephus' work as contrasted with Nicolaus', G. Misch. *A History of Autobiography in
Antiquity* (1949–50), vol. 1, pp. 315ff.

accusations which had been made, some twenty years after the Jewish revolt, about Josephus' war career. Some six months of the year 66 occupy most of the space. There are only a brief introduction and conclusion about Josephus' family and the rest of his life. And these passages are influenced by the work's overall purpose.

There is, in fact, no evidence that Josephus ever called the work his *Life* at all. It seems to have been issued as a kind of appendix to his *Antiquities*, and to have carried straight on from them.[5] In the manuscripts, it appears after the *Antiquities*.[6] It has no introduction of its own, and opens with a connecting particle.[7] It would therefore not have needed any other title, and the fact that the Church historian Eusebius (*Church History* 3.10), when he quotes from the *Life*, calls it the *Antiquities* suggests that it had no other title in his day.[8] The title *Life of Josephus* would quite naturally have been added in later manuscripts, since for many readers of the *Antiquities* the interest of the *Life* was precisely that it told them who Josephus was; and the rest of the narrative would often have been ignored. Josephus gives his own description of the work in a sentence at the end of the *Antiquities*, which heralds what follows: 'Perhaps it would not be invidious, and will not seem inept to most people, if I give a brief account both of my origins and of the events of my life.'[9]

More informative about its character, however, is what we discover in the course of the work, where Josephus' purpose in composing it emerges: he is defending his reputation. His person and his career had been under attack. When he tells of his family, he is vindicating it against his detractors. To smear the opponent's family was virtually *de rigueur* in ancient invective. The *Life* was directed against a literary adversary who, as well as making specific political charges, had launched a variety of conventional assaults on Josephus,[10] and his family was certainly one target.

[5] On the view that there were two editions of the *Antiquities*, see p. 237.

[6] See Niese, *Josephi Opera I* (1887), *praef.* v. Niese asserts, without demonstration, that *Life of Josephus* was Josephus' own title.

[7] The particle '*de*'.

[8] In the MS tradition, as reported by Niese, M and W give a different title, 'On Josephus, his family and his nation'. The Tours MS (that of Peirescius) of the tenth-century *Excerpta Constantiniana* has this, and an additional explanation. There is no reason to prefer the tradition of PRA.

[9] *AJ* 20. 266. Though it is possible to hold that this refers to some work which Josephus projected, and then changed his mind about (under the pressure, say, of attacks on him) the description fits the *Life* adequately. And the more complicated theory is only attractive if it be believed that there were two editions of the *Antiquities*.

[10] See T. Rajak 'Justus of Tiberius', *CQ* 23 (1973), p. 357.

From the *Life*, we know a certain amount about Josephus' leading
opponent. He was Justus of Tiberias, a Jew who had also been
involved in the revolt. The principal charge was that Josephus had
been an irresponsible warmonger, and brought ruin on his people
(see p. 153). It was important for Josephus to indicate, therefore,
not only the distinction of his lineage, but, more generally, the
respectability of his Jewish upbringing and education, and his early
concern for the common good. At the same time, he writes in Greek
and, if the same readership is intended for the *Life* as for the
Antiquities, for Greeks; so some Greek patterns are naturally imposed
on his account of his early life.

This, then, will be the character of Josephus' account of himself.
The *Life* is a polemic. But if we bear in mind the kind of work we
are reading, there should be no difficulty in interpreting what we
read. It is not likely that Josephus would try to get away with
outright fabrications on this subject. What he does tell us is very
valuable, in spite of its limitations; and we should have known a
good deal less of our author if he had not been goaded into writing
the *Life*.

That the family of Josephus was a highly respectable one is
beyond doubt, even if it is from so polemical and tendentious a
work as the *Life* that we learn about it. Josephus opens by challenging men who had cast aspersions on his background and origins:
'My family is not undistinguished, but is descended from priests
from a long way back.' He supports this with an assertion that, in
Judaea, priests constitute the social élite: 'With us participating in
the priesthood is a proof of distinguished descent.' Josephus, as will
emerge, was somewhat attached to a picture of Judaea as a hiero-
cracy. And even if the Jewish state was in fact rarely, if ever, a pure
example of one, all the evidence suggests that the prominence of
the priesthood, and its culmination the high priesthood, was for a
long period a distinguishing feature of Jewish society.[11] Josephus
himself assumes it when he divides a group of people of whom he
writes into those who are of priestly and those who are of lay
descent, calling the latter 'men of the people' (*V* 196–7). Philo puts
into the letter of Agrippa I which we have already noticed the claim
that his ancestors had been kings (he refers to the Hasmoneans),
but most of them also high priests, and that the latter is so much

[11] See the comments of F. Millar, 'The background to the Maccabean revolution',
JJS 29 (1978), pp. 1–21.

the more prestigious status as God is greater than man (*Leg.* 278).
From what would seem to be a quite different Jewish environment,
we have information that the Qumran sect distinguished in its
members between priests and laity, so that the priests (however
defined by the community), were always to occupy a separate and
prominent position at gatherings (*Community Rule* 6).

Josephus goes on to claim that he belongs to the first of the
twenty-four courses of priests (who managed the Temple service in
rotation); in other words (not spelled out) that of Jehoiarib (I
Chron. 24.7). This goes together with the next and second most
important claim; that of membership of the most distinguished
Jewish ruling dynasty in many centuries. Herod's family, not truly
Jewish in any case, could not match the lustre of the Hasmonean
house, with its origins in the Maccabean heroes. 'In addition, I am
of royal blood on the mother's side' is what Josephus says. He goes
on to sketch a family tree according to which his *father's* grandfather
married the daughter of 'Jonathan the high priest, the first of the
sons of Asamoneus to have been high priest'. Critics have pounced
on this as a clear instance of Josephus' blatantly contradicting
himself, at the most elementary level, within a few sentences.[12] But
it is possible to give perfectly good sense to what he says. By 'from
the mother' he may mean the matriarch of his family, his Hasmonean great-great-grandmother. It is she who must be referred to
when he goes on in the same sentence to say: 'For the sons of
Asamoneus, whose child she was, were for a long time high priests
and kings of our nation.' [13] Such a curious use of the word 'mother'
can be paralleled from the Hebrew sources: the Mishnah,[14] asserting
that, if a priest wishes to marry the daughter of a priest, he must
look into her pedigree for four generations, writes: 'If a man would
marry a woman of priestly stock, he must trace her family back
through four mothers, which are in fact eight.' In fact, the application of 'mother' to a wide range of related females is a
phenomenon well-known to social anthropologists. Writing our passage, Josephus would be likely to have in mind traditional Jewish

---

[12] See e.g. Hölscher in *RE* 9 (1916), 1935.

[13] Reading '*ekgonos*'—child—and not (with Niese) '*eggonos*'—descendant.

[14] *Kidd.* 4. 4. But not, it seems from Greek sources: see M. Radin, 'The pedigree
of Josephus', *CPh* 24 (1929), pp. 193–6, who anticipated my interpretation. Cohen's
attempted refutation, *Josephus in Galilee and Rome* (1979), pp. 107–8, n. 33, by examination of other genealogical uses of 'mother' in Josephus, does not succeed.

rulings on matters of pedigree, and to be thinking in their terminology.

Josephus' father's family, then, traced its descent from a Hasmonean princess; and the family consciousness of this origin is surely indicated by the existence of a 'Matthias', or 'Mattathias', named after the famous father of the Maccabees, in virtually every generation.[15] Both Josephus' father and his brother had that name.

The family tree which Josephus gives for his father, and which he says he found in the records, has also been impugned by his modern detractors,[16] who say it contains impossibilities. It is necessary to enter into some detail in order to clear Josephus, as I think we can. For, while there are some features which are improbable, there are none which are impossible; and, as long as what Josephus tells us is *possible*, we have no right to correct it. What we are told requires that Josephus' grandfather be 73 when Josephus' father was born, while his great-grandfather be 65 when his grandfather was born. And why not? We are told that the grandfather of Josephus' great grandfather, Simon Psellus, was a contemporary of the Hasmonean king John Hyrcanus (135/4–104 B.C.), while his son married the daughter of Hyrcanus' uncle, Jonathan. In other words, the woman married into a generation below herself. This would be quite possible if Simon Psellus was active during Hyrcanus' rule but was rather older than the ruler, or even if Jonathan's daughter was born to him late in life and Simon Psellus' son early in his, as the diagram shows.

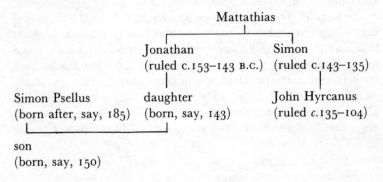

If, on the contrary, we decide that by 'Jonathan the High Priest' Josephus must in fact have meant the later king Alexander Jannaeus (103–76 B.C.), who was also so called on his coins, we find ourselves in new and greater difficulties and have to perform various contortions.[17] Not the least difficulty is that Josephus himself speaks of the Jonathan in question as the first of the Hasmoneans to be high priest. Certainly, nothing is gained by juggling with Josephus' data. At most, we may believe, if we please, that the historian inadvertently omitted a generation or two;[18] if he did, the matter is of no importance.

Now the Hasmoneans were priests of the course of Jehoiarib, which is the one to which Josephus attaches himself (I Macc. 2:1; 14:29). The suspicion immediately arises that it may be by virtue of his Hasmonean connection that Josephus claims association with the priesthood, which would then have come to him through a woman, his Hasmonean ancestress, Jonathan's daughter. What could otherwise be at best an idle suspicion seems to be confirmed, unexpectedly, by a passage in Book 16 of the *Antiquities* in which Josephus is evidently talking *in propria persona*.[19] In a polemic against Herod's historian, Nicolaus of Damascus, he writes that Nicolaus cannot be blamed for omitting some of Herod's wrongdoings, since the historian wrote to serve the king; he himself, however, could have a more objective attitude: 'being of a family close to the Hasmonean kings, and on account of this carrying honour and the priesthood' (*AJ* 16.187). Josephus' priesthood, he says, came to him from the Hasmonean side of the family. Strictly speaking, that status could, of course, only be transmitted through the sons of Aaron.[20] Yet we must accept that the menfolk of Josephus' family

[17] Witness the complication of Schürer and Hölscher's discussions.

[18] So J. Jeremias, *Jerusalem in the Time of Jesus* (English translation 1969), p. 214, n. 212.

[19] Hardly, as Hölscher would have it, copying mindlessly from an anonymous Jewish author. We shall find throughout that there is no justification for such a view of Josephus' relationship with his sources.

[20] Ex. 40. 15; Num. 16. 40; 18. 1–20; Lev. 21. 1ff.; *AJ* 20. 225–6. In these texts, no allowance is made for the possibility of transmission of the priesthood through a woman. But some curiosities are worth noting: (1) The accession of Alexander Jannaeus' widow to the throne. But her son, Hyrcanus II, became high priest. (2) A family in which seven brothers were high priests and they were known each by his own name and, instead of his father's, by what seems to have been his mother's— Kimhit. See *TJ Meg.* 1. 72a; *TJ Yoma* 3. 47d and 5. 42b; *TB Yoma* 47a; *Lev. Rabbah* 20. 164a; J. Levy, *Wörterbuch über die Talmudim und Midraschim* vol. 4 (1924). Josephus has a high priest named Simon, son of Kamith (*AJ* 18. 34) and one named Joseph Kami (20. 16), which may be distortions of the same name.

did actually minister as priests, for Josephus claims that on one occasion during the war he freely gave up the tithes due to him (*V* 80).

In various contexts Josephus talks of himself as a priest, and what always stands out is the value he places on this attribute. In introducing his *Jewish War* he is 'Josephus son of Matthias, a priest from Jerusalem'. In *Against Apion* (his last work) Josephus writes (of his *Antiquities*): 'I have translated the *Antiquities* from the sacred texts, being a man who was born a priest by descent' (*CA* 1.54). In both these cases, of course, it suited Josephus to call himself a priest, for it served to give his non-Jewish readers the impression that their author had some special expertise. In the *Against Apion* passage, the juxtaposition of 'priest' with 'sacred writings', cognate words in Greek (*hiereus* and *hierōn*) is purposeful. Again, in the *Life*, Josephus talks of his priesthood, in order to place himself on an equal footing with two other priests (*V* 198). It is not function, but status, which is in each case suggested.[21] Still, although it had propaganda value for Josephus to emphasize his priesthood, he could hardly have done so if this did not mean anything to him. For all their limitations, the passages in which he discusses it provide valuable and even unique testimony to a priest's own attitude to his role in the days when the Temple still stood.

On only one occasion—but a highly significant one—does Josephus say something more about his priesthood and explicitly suggest that it entails a particular form of activity. Explaining how he decided to surrender to the Romans after the failure of his defence of the stronghold of Jotapata, he maintains that through his skill in the interpretation of dreams he had been able to understand visions which he had had about the future of the Jews and of Rome, while through his being a priest and descended from priests he could interpret various prophecies in the sacred books.[22] In this passage, Josephus is explaining the most difficult moment of his career. At the time, it cannot have been easy for him to secure the confidence of the Romans. It was even harder, in retrospect, to justify his survival and his reception to Jews, probably to others, and perhaps even to himself. His assumption of prophetic status certainly served

---

[21] In just the same way the label 'high priest' operated as a status-indicator. See Schürer, *GJV³*, vol. 2, 274–7. Jeremias' criticisms of Schürer's view (op. cit. (n.18) pp. 175–81) are not weighty.

[22] *BJ* 3. 352. On this whole episode, see pp. 169–72; 185–92.

both to explain himself to the Romans and to account for his behaviour. This occurs in no other context except Jotapata, and we may suspect that here, if anywhere, there is an element of pretence or at least exaggeration.

The suspicion is strengthened when we remember that on the whole priests were not especially renowned in Jewish tradition for their interpretation of the Holy Scriptures. From the time of Ezra, this had been the province of the scribes, and of those shadowy figures, the Men of the Great Synagogue;[23] and we do not even hear of the priests themselves claiming any special relationship with the Torah. When, in A.D. 66, priestly experts were brought forward to support the view of those who disapproved of the cessation of the Roman sacrifices in the Temple (*BJ* 2.417) the question was exclusively about the Temple cult. It is in eastern pagan traditions that priests are characteristically interpreters of dreams and of sacred texts.[24] Therefore, it is doubtful whether this particular claim of Josephus would have been taken seriously by his fellow Jews. At any rate, caution demands that we do not build upon it in interpreting the implications of Josephus' priesthood.

In general, however, Josephus' emphasis on his being a priest can be taken as seriously meant. That he did in truth identify himself with the upper strata of the priesthood is apparent from his attitude to the high priests and to priestly rule throughout his writings, a more significant fact than the technicalities of his family's credentials. He repeatedly talks of the Jews as a nation ruled by priests,[25] and asserts the superiority of such a system: 'And what constitution could be finer or juster than that which makes God the ruler of all things, and puts into the hands of the priests as a body

[23] J. Blenkinsopp, 'Prophecy and priesthood in Josephus', *JJS* 25 (1974), pp. 239–62, assembles interesting instances of connections between prophecy, priesthood and exegetical activity in Biblical and post-Biblical Judaism, and especially among the Essenes. But the causal connection claimed by Josephus remains in a class apart.

[24] See A. D. Nock, *Conversion* (1933), pp. 54 and 89. For priests as keepers of records, see, for example, the Egyptian priests from whom Hecataeus of Abdera learned: Diod. 1. 46. 7–8. In Judaism, there is something approaching this phenomenon in the Court of the Priests, which is empowered to pass sentence in Biblical law (Deut. 17. 9); and in Malachi's castigation of the priests (Mal. 2. 7), where he says that men seek 'knowledge and correction from them'.

[25] See H. Mantel, *Studies in the History of the Sanhedrin* (1961), ch. 2, pp. 67–8. It has also been noted that there are points in the Biblical narrative of Josephus' *Antiquities* where he appears to play up the importance of priests: H. W. Attridge, *The Interpretation of Biblical History in the Antiquitates Judaicae of Flavius Josephus* (1976), pp. 176–7, n. 1, and references cited there.

the control of the most important matters, and again entrusts the highest priest of them all with the control of all the other priests?' (*CA* 2.185) For Josephus this was no abstract matter, for on one of the rare occasions when he offers his own judgment on a political question, he expresses his approval for the Hasmonean system, where the high priest had been the ruler of the state:[26] 'the throne, which had previously been assigned to the hereditary high priests, became the privilege of ordinary men' (i.e. the Herodians).

Certainly, the respectability of Josephus' family would not have been in question—except to those whose purpose was to denigrate him. In the *Jewish War* (5.419), when he quotes his own long address to the people, he himself talks of his 'not undistinguished lineage and a family which had for many years been prominent', as though these were known facts; had they not been, he would have made himself look ridiculous. The family records were kept in the public archives, as was required of priests, as well as of families which wished to marry into the priesthood.[27] That Josephus, in *Against Apion*, gives a detailed discussion of this very phenomenon, telling what strict rules there are concerning the marriage of priests, and how the records have to be compiled afresh in case of destruction in war, might suggest to us that it was something which he had heard discussed in his own home (*CA* 1.30–6).

It must be admitted that at one point in his life Josephus does seem to have acted in a manner inadmissible for a priest, but the amount of special pleading with which he relates the episode, suggests that he knows all is not well. The case in point is his first marriage, to a captive Jewess, when he was a prisoner of Vespasian. In Jewish law, priests were not allowed to marry anyone who was, or had been, in captivity. Josephus says first that Vespasian ordered

[26] Again, at *AJ* 14. 41, the Jews, appealing to the conqueror Pompey, are made to ask for the replacement of the Hasmoneans by their traditional form of government, rule by priests. J. C. H. Lebram, 'Der Idealstaat der Juden', *Josephus-Studien* (ed. O. Betz, K. Haacker, M. Hengel), 1974, pp. 233–53, argues that here Josephus echoes pagan assessments, deriving ultimately from Hellenizing Jews, of the Jewish constitution. But the texts he cites, Diodorus and Strabo, make scarcely anything of this idea.

[27] *Sifrei Num.*, Korah, 116; *M Kidd.* 4. 5; *M Midd.* 5 etc. At Ezra 2. 61–3 = Neh. 7. 63–5, families which claim to be priestly are debarred from office because they cannot produce their genealogies. See Jeremias, op. cit (n.18) pp. 213ff. A. Büchler, *Family Purity and Family Impurity in Jerusalem before A.D.70* (ed. Brodie and Rabbinowitz, 1956), p. 68.

him to do it.[28] Next, he maintains that the woman was a virgin; and this is obviously aimed at rebutting the presumption that such a woman must have been raped, the presumption which constituted the reason for the original legal prohibition.[29] Thirdly, he insists that he divorced her as soon as he was free. The lengths to which he goes in his attempt to exonerate himself stand out.

But the priesthood was not all. In comparison with parvenu high priests of the Herodian and procuratorial periods,[30] Josephus' family had substance and antiquity. For, in spite of the unpopularity of the last Hasmonean monarchs, respect for the Hasmonean house never really died in Judaea. Even Herod had felt constrained to appoint the Hasmonean Aristobulus III high priest, before he murdered him and instituted a new high priest of his own choosing (*AJ* 15.30ff. and 56–7). In sum, even though Josephus' family was by no means one of those from whom, in the years before 70, 'the high priests were in turn appointed' (*BJ* 4.148), it was one which could mix with this new aristocracy, and was perhaps even superior, especially as the latter's dependence on external support was made constantly manifest by frequent replacement of the serving high priest. Josephus was to become a commander of the Jewish revolt at a young age; similar positions were held by a number of men of high priestly families, and one of the two supreme commanders was an ex-high priest. Whatever Josephus' talents, it is improbable that he would have been appointed, especially before he had proved his ability, unless he was of equal social standing with these men.

It has been argued by some that (in this period) the label 'high priests', which evidently was not ascribed exclusively to holders of that office, was in actual fact the name of a social group which contained members of the upper échelons of the priesthood as well.

[28] D. Daube, 'Three legal notes on Josephus after his surrender', *Law Quarterly Review* 93 (1977), pp. 191–2, argues that there was no order involved: the Greek word used is a Latinism, drawn from the normal Roman marriage ceremony. But it is unlikely that Josephus would have had enough Latin at this stage to pick up the formula, and questionable whether he would have been married according to Roman law.

[29] Correctly analysed by Daube.

[30] On the emergence of this new élite, see M. Stern, 'Herod's policy and Jewish society at the end of the Second Temple Period'; *Tarbiz* 35 (1966) pp. 235ff (Hebrew). And now, in English, 'Aspects of Jewish society: the priesthood and other classes' in *The Jewish People in the First Century: Compendia Rerum Iudaicarum ad Novum Testamentum*, section 1, vol. 2 (1976), pp. 561–630.

Whether or not this be a correct explanation of the terminology,[31] the category in question is precisely that into which Josephus falls.

Josephus relates that his father received special recognition in Jerusalem society because of his personal merits, principally the thoroughly Jewish virtue of justice (*V* 7); this may well have been so, and, by choosing to stress it, Josephus shows himself, once again, attached to those values which were traditional for him. At the same time, his family's position would need to have been buttressed with substantial wealth. Although its members will not have had the same access to the Temple funds as high priests, they perhaps inherited something from the Hasmoneans; and, unlike those in office, they will not have needed to lavish bribes on procurator and people.[32] The élite to which they belonged was known for its wealth. Just as Herod's Temple, in which, 'in expenditure he surpassed his predecessors' (*AJ* 15.396), dominated the city, opulent and 'adorned with goodly stones and gifts' (Luke 21.5), so the prosperity of its managers impressed itself on the other inhabitants. All the available types of source material conspire to give us the same picture. Archaeological discoveries testify that those very clans whose nepotism, cruelty and corruption are said by the literary sources to have made the inhabitants groan, put the proceeds of their misdemeanours into conspicuous—and, presumably, pleasurable—consumption.

The most eloquent and informative testimony of all to the high priests' oppressiveness is provided by what is certainly a contemporary document, even though it is embedded in later texts—the complaint made by one Abba Saul, in the name of an earlier authority:

Woe unto me because of the house of Baitos,
  Woe unto me for their lances [or 'evil speaking']!
Woe unto me because of the house of Hanin,
  Woe unto me for their whisperings [or 'calumnies']!
Woe unto me because of the house of Katros;
  Woe unto me because of their reed pens!
Woe unto me because of the house of Ishmael ben Phiabi,
  Woe unto me because of their fists!
For they are high priests and their sons are treasurers,

[31] For the suggestion, J. Jeremias, op. cit. (n. 18), pp. 175–9.
[32] See e.g. Josephus on Ananias, son of Nebedaeus, *AJ* 20. 205.

And their sons-in-law are Temple overseers,
And their servants smite the people with sticks.[33]

A cautious reconstruction, from the information in Josephus, of
the list of twenty-eight high priests between 37 B.C. and A.D.70,
shows eight from the first family castigated, that of Boethus (cf. p.
55), eight from the second, that of Ananias, and three from that of
Phiabi.[34]

The second- or first-century B.C. monumental tomb in the Kedron
Valley, of priests of the watch of Hezir, is substantial and impressive. The style is a curious mixture of Greek, with pure Doric
columns, and eastern, with a side-monument surmounted by a
pointed roof. The inscription is in Hebrew (which, of course, does
not mean that the family could not have known Greek), and simply
names those buried there and the watch, or section of the priesthood, to which they belonged.[35] An old attempt to identify in the
inscription three sons of Boethus is now generally rejected, on the
grounds that the inscription talks of 'sons of Joseph' and that we do
not know that the family of Boethus was in the watch of Hezir.
However, the association still seems extremely attractive, since we
are dealing with names typical of the house of Boethus, or of that
of Ananus, which intermarried with it. The monument must have
been a landmark in Jerusalem, and it is hard to believe that it
belonged to an ordinary priestly family which has left no record.[36]
The two monuments which stood near it, today nicknamed the
tombs of Zachariah and of Absalom, must also belong to Second
Temple families, but we have no indication which these were, or
indeed whether or not they were priestly.[37] Josephus at one point
mentions as a landmark the tomb of Ananus the high priest in the
Siloam Valley. This was no doubt another such family tomb:

[33] *Tos. Men.* 13. 21; *TB Pes.* 57a. The Tosefta text, though earlier, appears to be
inferior.
[34] List in Jeremias, op. cit. (n. 18), pp. 377–8 (based on Schürer). There is some
doubt about the identification of the fourth family.
[35] 'This is the tomb and monument of Eleazar, Haniah, Joezer, Judah, Simon,
Johanan, sons of Joseph, son of Obed; Joseph, Eleazar, sons of Haniah, priests of
the watch of Hezir.'
[36] Full discussion in N. Avigad, *Ancient Monuments in the Kedron Valley* (1954;
Hebrew), pp. 37ff.
[37] See N. Avigad in *Jerusalem Revealed: Archaeology in the Holy City, 1968–1974* (1975),
p. 18.

Ananus the elder (son of Seth) was the father of five sons, all of whom became high priests (*BJ* 5.506; *AJ* 20.197–8).

Excavations in the old Jewish quarter of Jerusalem have in recent years brought to light the lower floor of a burnt house. This had an entrance, four rooms, a kitchen and a bath. The upper storey was completely ruined; but the house was clearly built on quite a large scale. Objects discovered in it include small scent bottles, and many large and small vessels. The date of its destruction is indicated by coins of years two to four of the revolt. An iron weight found in one of the rooms reads 'Bar Katras'—'son of Katras', in Aramaic; and thus the weight and probably the house can be associated with the second of the houses mentioned in the complaint. Thus we would see the burnt house as one of the typical, large high priests' houses in the upper city. Ananias' house was burnt down at the outbreak of the revolt.[38] In the Gospel of John, we read of the house of Annas with its large court and its doorkeeper; and in two of the Gospels, of Caiaphas' home, which was on the same level, and was alleged by Luke (albeit probably falsely) to have accommodated a special meeting of the Sanhedrin.[39]

The moral story of Martha, daughter of Boethus and widow of the high priest Joshua ben Gamala (see p. oo), speaks clearly enough about the opprobrium which the wealth of such families incurred. Martha was, as other traditions about her also suggest, one of the richest women in Jerusalem. During the siege of the city, she repeatedly sent out her servant to buy flour, unable to understand why money could not obtain what she needed. Eventually, she threw away her gold and silver, she went out into the street, dung stuck to her foot, and, being—we must suppose—unusually delicate, she died (*TB Gittin* 56a). On a previous occasion, when she had wanted to watch her husband officiating for the Day of Atonement, a day during which all walked barefoot, she had a carpet stretched out for her all the way from her house to the Temple gate (*Lam. R.* 1.16.47).

The Temple cult was a principal source of the wealth of such families. But Josephus also held land in the territory of Jerusalem. It is only in a different context (*V* 422) that he lets slip this information, and we can well understand that he should have regarded

---

[38] N. Avigad, *IEJ* 20 (1970), pp. 6–7: Ananias' house: *BJ* 2. 426.

[39] John 18.16—Annas; Matthew 26.57, Mark 14.53—Caiaphas. Cf. Jeremias, op. cit. (n. 18), p. 96.

it as irrelevant to an account of his background and family: a priest's prestige was derived in the first instance from other sources, while the Torah insisted that priests were not to be landowners.[40] On the other hand, there is no cause for surprise in the fact that Josephus was one. The Bible itself contains exceptions.[41] For the Greco-Roman period, while the assertion of the pagan observer Hecataeus of Abdera that the Jerusalem priests had bigger allocations of land than the ordinary settlers may not be worth much,[42] we do know of one landowning priest who could have been active before 70. This was the extraordinarily rich, and at the same time studious Eleazar ben Harsum, whose father left him one thousand hamlets, or perhaps farmsteads, in 'the king's mountain', and the same number of ships—though all was ultimately destroyed.[43]

What we also know is that the ownership of land, or at any rate of extensive land, and control of the crowd of labourers employed on it,[44] was in itself also a source of status in Jerusalem society. While Josephus could match himself with kings and high priests, he would also have been at home with men like the father of R. Eliezer ben Hyrcanus, who had many ploughmen on his territory outside Jerusalem, and who was able, as one of the 'great men of Jerusalem', to invite all the city's notables to his son's circumcision.[45] Other associates might have been those three famous magnates, Nakdimon ben Gorion, ben Kalba Savua, and ben Zizit ha-Keset (or ha-Kasaf), who between them could keep the city fully supplied for three years with wheat and barley, wine, oil, salt and wood.[46] The first could well be the Nicodemus of the Gospel of John, a prominent Pharisee (the Talmud too presents him as learned and pious), who asked Jesus how it was possible for a man to be 'born again', and who later brought plentiful myrrh and aloes for Jesus' burial. After the revolt, however, his daughter was found

---

[40] Deut. 10.9; 12.12; 18.1; Num. 18.24. Cf. M. Stern (n. 30), p. 587.

[41] Stern, loc. cit.

[42] *Ap.* Diodorus Siculus 40. 3. 7 = Stern, *Greek and Latin Authors* no. 11, p. 28.

[43] Probably in the first revolt: see *TJ Ta'an.* 4.8; *Lam. R* 2.2; *TB Yoma* 35b; *Kidd* 49b.

[44] As in some Gospel parables: e.g. Matth. 20.1–16; Matth. 21.33–43 = Luke 20.9–18; Luke 16.1–8; cf. S. Applebaum, in *Compendia* etc. (n. 30), pp. 659; see pp. 119–20, n. 40, on the status of these labourers.

[45] *ARN* a6 (Schechter 15bf.; Goldin 43f.); *ARN* b13 (Shechter 15b–16a) *Pirkei de Rabbi Eliezer* 1–2, and parallels.

[46] For this trio, the refs. given in the previous note, and, most extensively, *TB Gittin* 56a ff, together with *Lam.R.* 1. 5. 31 and *Eccl.R.* 7.12.

picking grains of barley out of the dung.[47] The second had a house of splendid dimensions, with a gold-covered roof. The third was variously said to derive his name from his cushion, which had trailing fringes, or from his seat—the fact, that is, that his seat was among those of the nobility of Rome. These are surely but the extreme instances of a type apparently common in Palestinian society, the (presumably landowning) householder, with his many servants, who figures in the Gospel parables;[48] or again the so-called 'house-owner' of a somewhat later period, who is central to many legal debates in Talmudic literature.[49] Such men may have lived in town, but they evidently owned country estates.

Wealth and learning were not co-extensive in Jerusalem society. But Josephus insists that he had a thorough Jewish education, and excelled in it: 'Educated together with Mattathias, my full brother by both parents, I progressed to an advanced level of education and was regarded as being first class in memory and perceptiveness. While I was still a mere boy, aged about fourteen, I was praised by all for my love of letters, and the high priests and leading men of the city used to come to me to gain more accurate knowledge of some point related to the laws' (*V* 8ff.).

A few details given by Josephus are echoed in various remarks in the Jewish literature which expose the Rabbinic approach to the instruction of the young. Josephus' education was traditional. Thus, he seems to suggest that he was educated by his parents, for he sees fit to mention no outside teachers, saying only that he studied together with his brother, and then going on to speak of his attainments. And, of course, that a child's instruction is first and foremost the responsibility of his parents, goes right back to Deut. 11.19— 'And thou shalt teach them to thy children . . .' In the Babylonian Talmud (*Kidd.* 29a) there is a discussion of whether the various obligations which the father has to the son might be binding upon women as well as men, and one of the duties discussed is that of giving instruction.

---

[47] John 3.1; 7.50; 19.39. On his daughter, *TB Ket.* 66b; *Lam.R.* 1.16.48; *Mekhilta on Exodus* 19.1 (where she is unnamed).

[48] e.g. Matth. 24.43ff. = Luke 12.39ff.; Matth. 22.2.16 = Luke 14.17–20; Luke 12.39ff. On landowners, cf. H. Kriessig *Die sozialen Zusammenhänge des judäischen Krieges* (1970), pp. 19ff.

[49] See the concordances, s.v. *Ba'al Ha-bayit*. None of the evidence can be securely attached to our period, but a plausible case for its relevance has been argued by G. S. Gibson, *The Social Stratification of Jewish Palestine in the First Century of the Christian Era* (unpubl. diss., London 1975), pp. 74–82.

It would not be surprising if Josephus attended no elementary school. The scholar Simon ben Shetah (the brother-in-law of king Alexander Jannaeus who ruled in the early first century B.C.) was responsible for some pronouncement about the schooling of young children; but the laconic and enigmatic statement about this in the Jerusalem Talmud,[50] which occurs quite out of context, does not tell us much about the position either before or after Simon. The tradition was that schools had at first existed in Jerusalem, and their spread to the various districts was associated with the name of the high priest and scholar Joshua ben Gamala, Josephus' father's friend and his own (*TB BB* 21a; *V* 204). In spite of these measures, which were long remembered, we cannot tell how universal the system was, and whether all classes of the population took to the schools with equal alacrity. Aristocrats in many societies prefer to educate their children at home. The Talmudic account which we have just referred to, about Joshua ben Gamala's reform and the emergence of the school in Palestine, implies that such things were necessary because not all fathers were in a position to teach their children themselves. Dicta like Rabbi Akiba's—'When you teach your son, teach him out of a corrected scroll' [51]—whose appearance in Hebrew in the Aramaic text of the Babylonian Talmud may be some guarantee of authenticity, would seem to imply that parental instruction was still the ideal in his day.

Although Mishnaic and Talmudic statements about education, even if linked with pre-70 individuals, carry with them the possibility of anachronism, it is reasonable to assumed that the general attitude and the approach expressed in them did not suddenly spring into being after 70, but were the product of tradition and slow evolution. Whether taught at home or at school, the rudiments would not vary much. It is clear that the Bible was to be mastered first, only then the interpretations. The training of memory was very highly valued, as is to be expected in a tradition where much is transmitted orally. In the Mishnah (*Avot* 2.8), Rabbi Eliezer ben Hyrcanus, who grew up in pre-70 Jerusalem, is praised for being 'like a plastered cistern, which loses not a drop'. And it was said

---

[50] Simon ben Shetah ordained three things: 'that a man may do business with the marriage contract; that children should go to school; that glassware be subject to contamination'. *TJ Ket.* 8.11.

[51] *TB Pes.* 112a. For the many Talmudic statements on the father's obligation to teach his son, see W. Morris, *The Jewish School: an Introduction to the History of Jewish Education* (1937), pp. 21 and 249, n. 17.

that 'he who had repeated a chapter 100 times is not to be compared with him who has repeated it 101 times' (*TB Hag.* 9b). So it is interesting that Josephus singles out memory as one of his two principal endowments.[52]

But when Josephus, at the age of fourteen, solved problems for the high priests and the city leaders, he had obviously gone beyond the stage of mere memorising, and was able to apply the intelligence which was his second main asset to the analysis of complex problems. The use of the distinctive Greek word, *to philogrammaton*—love of grammar— which might evoke a Greek literary education, clearly has no special significance here. There is a traditional schema (*M Avot* 5.21), which has a child studying the Bible at eight, Mishnah at ten and Talmud at fifteen (as well as marrying at eighteen). In Josephus' day, Mishnah and Talmud did not yet exist, but the oral material which went to make them up was already current. The schema may have little relation to an untidier reality, but the endorsement of academic precocity in it is reminiscent of Josephus' claim that he was a repository of learning by the time he was fourteen. We are also reminded of another very similar claim: 'they found him in the temple, sitting in the midst of the doctors, both hearing them and asking questions. And all that heard him were astonished at his understanding and answers' (Luke 2. 46–7). Here the word used for 'understanding' is the same as that applied by Josephus to himself. The phenomenon of the *Ilui*, the youthful genius, has been not uncommon in Judaism through the ages. In the eighteenth century, the young Elijah, Gaon of Vilna, read the Bible and the Talmud without a teacher at six, and at six and a half delivered in the Great Synagogue of Vilna a learned discourse taught him by his father—and, when tested, proved that he could have done it unaided.[53] It is true that the motif of early intellectual brilliance can be found also in classical biographies—witness Suetonius on the young Titus, or Nicolaus of Damascus on himself.[54] But the Jewish parallels are much closer here, in that the youth is

---

[52] Memory was, of course, valued in Greek education too; and it was said of the wonder-worker Apollonius of Tyana that, when he reached the age at which letters had to be learned, 'he showed great strength of memory and the power to learn through repetition' (Philostr. *VA* 1. 7).

[53] L. Ginzberg, *Students, Scholars and Saints* (1928), p. 127.

[54] Jacoby, *FGH* 90. F132. 1. On the motif, see S. J. D. Cohen, op. cit. (n. 14), p. 105, n. 23, who gives a list of classical examples; he, however, sees Josephus simply as repeating a Greek commonplace.

represented as already proficient among, and in the same sphere of study as, his elders, and as outshining them.

Talmudic sources generally represent the Rabbinic tradition as having always been the mainstream of the nation's religious and cultural life. Since pre-70 Palestine contained many sectarian groups, there must have been other educational systems too. Those Qumran texts which are distinctively sectarian show unequivocally how far their producers had established their own self-contained system, with rival rulings on purity, on the Temple ritual, and on the calendar, and different views on knowledge, salvation and eschatology, sharing with other Jews only respect for the Biblical texts and the exegetical process, together with the view of the past enshrined in them. We shall shortly find Josephus himself attesting diversity in 'higher education'. But Josephus' sketch has, in its attitude, enough in common with the Talmudic picture of Palestinian education for us to take it that they are referring to the same thing. What is more, by far the greatest number of educational institutions—whether in the narrow sense or whether in a wider sense of gatherings in men's houses (as are referred to in the injunction of a second-century B.C. Rabbi quoted in the Mishnah, 'Let your house be a meeting-house for wise men' (*Avot* 1.4))—were certainly under the auspices of the sages, the *hakhamim*. These people, the creators and transmitters of the Rabbinic tradition, spiritual ancestors of the compilers of Mishnah and Talmud, are to be identified with the Pharisees: about that there is now scarcely any doubt.[55] In the first century A.D., they were not so much an organized group as the body of the nation's religious mentors and scholars, or so it has seemed to those who have given some attention to the picture offered by Rabbinic literature.[56] Even Josephus says

---

[55] On who the sages were, see E. Urbach, 'Class status and leadership in the world of the Palestinian sages', *Proc. Isr. Acad. of Sciences and Humanities* 2 (1968). For the identification of sages with Pharisees, see already R. Travers Herford, *The Pharisees* (1924), ch. 1; cf. E. Rivkin, 'Defining the Pharisees, the Tannaitic sources', *HUCA* 40–1 (1969–70), pp. 205ff. (who, however, complicates the matter); R. Marcus, 'The Pharisees in the light of modern scholarship', *Journal of Religion* 23 (1952), p. 152.

[56] I do not entirely share the extreme scepticism of J. Neusner, in *The Rabbinic Traditions about the Pharisees before 70* (1971). Josephus' information is misleading, both because of his tendency to describe them as a philosophical sect, (see pp. 36–7), and because the part which he assigned to them in Palestinian life is small. Johanan ben Zakkai, for example, is never even mentioned by him. But if we grant that they were cultural and social rather than political leaders, that is no more surprising than, say, Thucydides' failure to mention Euripides or Aristophanes. Josephus does

that the Pharisees had the greatest following among the people and
that Pharisaic concepts were dominant in Palestine. According to
him, all worship—and that must include the Temple cult—was
conducted in Pharisaic style (*AJ* 18.15 and 17; 13.298). Talmudic
passages point in exactly the same direction, talking of the Sadducees' fear of the Pharisees, and illustrating (naturally) the superiority of Pharisaic contentions about certain activities of the high
priests and priests.[57]

It is also worth bearing in mind that their studies may have done
more to unite than to separate Pharisees and Sadducees. The differences over matters of practice, and even the divergent attitudes
to the status of the oral law, need not have precluded much common
ground.[58] Again, thoroughgoing Pharisees and Sadducees were
probably quite rare, and the bulk of the population may well have
occupied an ill-defined central territory, under the guidance of those
leaders who happened at any time to make the most impact.

It seems best to hold that Josephus' early education was, broadly,
Pharisaic. That, after all, is what his abbreviated account suggests.
Confirmation may be found in a passing remark made by him in a
different context in his *Life*. An embassy of four had been sent out
from Jerusalem to enquire into Josephus' activities as commander
of the Galilee; it included three Pharisees, while the fourth was a
young man of a high priestly family. Josephus writes of them as
'men who differed in their origins, but were equal in learning: two
of them were laymen, Jonathan and Ananias of the sect of the
Pharisees, the third, Joazar, was from a priestly family, and also a

---

mention such rabbinic figures as play an important part in the political events he
describes: the Samaias and Pollio of *AJ* 14 and 15, who are active critics of Herod,
are almost certainly the Shemaiah and Avtalion of Talmudic literature; Simon b.
Gamaliel and Eleazar b. Avkilus are involved in the Jewish revolt.

[57] First, whether the high priest should scatter incense inside or outside the Holy
of Holies: *Tos. Yoma* 1. 8; *TB Yoma* 19b. Secondly, on the ritual state of purity
required of priests for the ceremony of the burning of the red heifer: *Tos. Parah* 3. 8;
cf. 3. 6; *M. Parah* 3. 5. That the wives of the Sadducees were afraid of the Pharisees
is stated in *TB Niddah* 33b. It has been pointed out, however, that some items of
Sadducean *Halakhah* and *Aggadah* may be incorporated in the teaching of the *Tannaim*
and *Amoraim*. See *Dict. de la Bible*, ed. L. Pirot, A. Robert, H. Cazelles and A.
Feuillet, *Suppl.* 7 (1966), pp. 1022ff.

[58] Cf. G. Alon, 'The attitude of the Pharisees to the Roman government and the
house of Herod', *Scripta Hierosolymitana* 7 (1961), pp. 65–7, who suggests that,
throughout the Hasmonean period, there was much co-operation, in spite of bursts
of antagonism.

Pharisee, while the youngest, Simon, was of high priestly stock'.[59] He goes on to say that the ambassadors were experts in the law just as he was. Later (*V* 274) he refers to the group as his 'teachers and fellow citizens'. This special relationship which he claims with the Pharisees (he can hardly be including the fourth and youngest member) is not likely to have originated in that period when, as we shall see, Josephus explored all three Jewish sects. It could stem from his eventual and final alignment with the Pharisees (see p. 27), but by that time he was no longer, by his own account, being taught by any teachers. So it is most likely that it is the main part of his education which is in question. And it is interesting to note that, in the third member of the group, we have a figure comparable to Josephus, another example of a priestly Pharisee.

The family friendship with Joshua ben Gamala, that founder of schools praised in Rabbinic tradition, but at the same time a high priest (see p. 27), might point in the same direction (though far from conclusive evidence in itself). While Sadducees were to be found mainly among the high priests, not all hereditary high priests will have chosen to be Sadducees. Joshua ben Gamala is an example of one who was not, and there were others.[60] In the Babylonian Talmud, we meet a high priest, the landowning Eleazer ben Harsom, who cared for nothing but studying the Torah—a Pharisaic trait par excellence. Provisions in Mishnah and Talmud make it clear that the level of education of the high priests varied greatly: it is laid down that during the night before the Day of Atonement, if the high priest is able to do so himself, he expounds the book of Daniel; if not, someone should do it for him.[61] Therefore, even if Josephus' family moved among high priests, that is no reason to take them to have been Sadducees.

[59] *V* 197. The members of the embassy are also listed at *BJ* 2. 628 (with a slight variation), but there Josephus says nothing of their religious affiliations, describing them only as excellent speakers.

[60] See J. Wellhausen, *Die Pharisäer und die Sadducäer* (1924), pp. 43ff., and J. Le Moyne, *Les Sadducéens* (1972), pp. 21ff. (though Le Moyne takes Josephus' family to have been Sadducean). For evidence that there were Pharisaic priests, see also the discussion by J. Lightstone of a controversy between Pharisees and Sadducees about purifying the Sanctuary candelabrum in 'Sadducees versus Pharisees: the Tannaitic Sources', *Christianity, Judaism and Greco-Roman Cults: Studies for Morton Smith at Sixty*, vol. 3 (1975), pp. 207–8. Note that Josephus never says that the Sadducees were mainly high priests.

[61] *M Yoma* 1. 6. Cf. *M Hor.* 3. 8: a bastard learned in the law is of higher status than a high priest who is ignorant!

Josephus says that at the age of nineteen he began to adhere to the Pharisaic sect. He gives no reason for having done so (*V* 12), and describes it as a matter-of-course decision. It would make good sense if we supposed that in the end he fell back upon the views with which he had been brought up.

Josephus does not speak of any studies undertaken after the age of nineteen. The knowledge and conception of Judaism shown in his works must therefore stem from what he acquired before that time, even if it was refreshed in synagogue and Temple. We can obtain some indication of the kind of familiarity with the Bible which was part of Josephus' mental furniture before he came to write the *Antiquities* from the speech, already mentioned, in which he urges the people of Jerusalem to surrender before the Romans press the siege any further. He gives a series of Biblical illustrations showing God's intervention to save the Israelites on occasions when they themselves would not have recourse to violent action. The incidents quoted are not all particularly popular Bible stories, for example the punishment of the Philistines for the theft of the ark. Josephus even remembers the number of men of Sennacherib's army to perish before Jerusalem—185,000—and the number of retainers possessed by Abraham. That he is working from memory is suggested by the presence of a small mistake, where he states that Zedekiah actually witnessed the fall of Jerusalem, whereas in fact the king had previously fled, and had his eyes put out by the Babylonian monarch. When Josephus, working from the text, comes to deal with the episode in his *Antiquities*, the error has gone. Once, a traditional embellishment is blended, perhaps unconsciously, with what is to be found in the Bible, when Josephus tells how Pharaoh invaded Palestine to steal Sarah, but returned her to Abraham untouched as the result of a vision.[62] All these incidents were probably brought together by Josephus himself, although the form—a catalogue of God's great deeds—is a popular one: there are several examples in the Passover text, the *Haggadah*.

When it comes to the *Antiquities*, few would deny that Josephus' conceptions are on the whole Pharisaic. It is enough here simply to recall that in many small points of *halakhah* (law) and *aggadah*

---

[62] See *BJ* 5. 379–391, and, for the Biblical episodes, I Sam. 5–6; II Kings 19.35; Gen. 12.10–20; II Kings 25.7–11. Zedekiah: *AJ* 10. 135–50.

(extra-legal tradition) Josephus agrees with the Rabbis.[63] Although their texts are all later in date than Josephus, the natural assumption where there is agreement is that the tradition found in the later texts was already current in Josephus' day.

It must be admitted that for the purpose of his argument in the *Life*, and at the date at which he wrote, it would have suited Josephus to *present himself* as a Pharisee. After 70, Sadducees and Essenes disappeared, and the consolidation of Judaism undertaken by Rabban Johanan ben Zakkai at Yavneh[64] was based upon Pharisaism: so to say that one was a Pharisee would be to say that one was a respectable Jew, and that, in a sense, was precisely what his critics had said that Josephus was not. Josephus would, then, have a motive for falsification; but a recent attempt to pin him down by showing that in his later works his view of the Pharisees is substantially different from that in the *War* cannot be deemed a success.[65] For we may admit that in the early account they are described as a political party, and as just one of several Jewish philosophies, and are treated on occasion with a distinct lack of sympathy; while in the *Antiquities* they tend to be represented more favourably, as the most powerful body in Judaism, holding the allegiance of the mass of the population. But we are not entitled to deduce a difference in attitude from this change. First, there is the real change in the situation, which Josephus accurately reflects. Secondly, he is not always hostile in the *War* (see e.g. *BJ* 2.166). And last, the Pharisees only crop up in the *War* in the context of a relatively short conspectus of pre-66 history, which forms a kind of introduction to the

[63] For a collection of comparative halakhic (legal) material, see still M. Olitski—*Flavius Josephus und die Halacha* (Diss. Berlin, 1855); cf. M. Duschak, *Josephus Flavius und die Tradition* (1864). There are naturally some points of difference between Josephus and Rabbinic statements. More worthy of consideration than the possibility that *halakhot* (rulings) known to Josephus may have disappeared by the Rabbinic period, or that Josephus was deliberately expressing personal dissension, is the observation of B. Revel, in 'Some anti-traditional laws of Josephus', *JQR* 14 (1923–4), pp. 293–30: Josephus repeatedly gives just the plain meaning (*peshat*) of a Biblical ordinance, and this may be either because he has forgotten the *halakhah* on the subject, or because, for his expected pagan audience, it was not worth discussing it. Later, Karaite *halakhah* shows strikingly similar treatment of many points. It cannot be excluded, however, that in these limited cases Josephus was influenced by Sadducean interpretation. Direct connections between Sadducees and Karaites have been posited: see S. Sandmel, *The First Christian Century in Judaism and Christianity* (1969), p. 94, n. 1.
[64] J. Neusner, *A Life of Rabban Johanan ben Zakkai* (1970), ch. 8.
[65] J. Neusner, following Morton Smith, in 'Josephus' Pharisees', *Ex Orbe Religionum, Studia Geo Widengren Oblata* (1972), vol. 1, pp. 224–44.

work: it would be natural for the Pharisees only to be mentioned in connection with specific activities of political importance there. And, in any case, since there is good reason to think that most of the conspectus comes directly from the historical work of Nicolaus of Damascus, it is not evidence for Josephus' own ideas. He himself may well have inclined towards the Pharisees even before 70: and to do so would not have constituted an unconventional choice.

What is surprising is that Josephus did not take the obvious road, that of Pharisaism, until he had experimented with other forms of Judaism. He says: 'At about the age of sixteen, I decided to gain personal experience of our sects: they are three, the Pharisees are the first, the Sadducees the second, and the third are the Essenes, as we have often said. I thought that if I was familiar with them all, I should be able to select the best. So I toughened myself up, and, by working very hard, went through all three' (*V* 10–11). He continues by telling how, finding this insufficient, he spent three years in the wilderness as the devotee of a man named Bannus, subsisting on natural foods and washing himself in cold water, to achieve purity. What exactly Josephus means by 'going through' all the sects is hard to tell. Presumably, he received some instruction from masters, and learnt the principles of each sect's interpretation of the Bible and regulations for life. Among the Pharisees, for example, he might have attended the disquisitions of two famous authorities, Johanan ben Zakkai and Simon ben Gamaliel.[66] We do not know whether any Essenes were to be found in Jerusalem, or whether Josephus had to seek them elsewhere.

This claim that he explored the sects has been treated as another of our author's supposed lies: it is maintained that if Josephus spent three years in the wilderness between the ages of about sixteen and about nineteen, he would have had no time for the other activities he mentions.[67] But it is a weak criticism, when we do not even know what precisely those activities would have been.[68] A year's probation

---

[66] See J. Neusner, op. cit. (n. 64), p. 33ff., on these men. A fairly complete list of Pharisaic scholars in pre-70 Jerusalem is in Jeremias, op. cit. (n.18), pp. 379–80. To it add R. Tarfon, who ministered as a priest in the Temple, though flourished after its fall: see *Jew. Enc.*, s.v. Tarfon.

[67] *RE* 9 (1916), 1936. Followed, e.g. by G. Misch, *A History of Autobiography in Antiquity* (1949–50), vol. 1, p. 325.

[68] On our ignorance of Pharisaic educational institutions, see J. Neusner, *Eliezer ben Hyrcanus: the Tradition and the Man* (1973), p. 295.

was required for those entering the Qumran community, and two years for being allowed to touch the 'drink of the community' (*Community Rule* 6). But there is no reason why two or three months could not be sufficient for some kind of basic course in each discipline. And Josephus may well have devised a way of learning to fit his own requirements, and moved on to the next sect when he was satisfied he had grasped the essence of the last. There is evidently some rhetorical exaggeration in Josephus' language when he talks of 'hard labour' and of having to toughen himself up: once again, it is relevant that Josephus' task in the *Life* is to impress, and, in particular, to prove his moral worth. But, equally, it is again clear that there had to be a basis in truth, and that grossly improbable inventions would only detract from the effect.

What is interesting about Josephus' search for the best philosophy, as he describes it, is that it conforms to a traditional pattern. And now the pattern is one which recurs in the Greek culture of the Roman empire, rather than in Judaism.[69] The search for the best philosophy can have a variety of connotations. It often ends with the acceptance of some sort of special relationship with or route to the supernatural; thus, Justin Martyr, after being profoundly dissatisfied with what he had heard from a Peripatetic, a Pythagorean and a Platonist philosopher, was ripe for the overwhelming experience of Christianity, to which he was converted by an old man (*Dial. with Trypho* 8). Sometimes the search may lead through or to a strange oriental religion.[70] Equally, there may be a more rational exploration of different philosophies and the ways of life they have to offer. An example is that of the great Roman doctor and medical writer, Galen, in the second century A.D.; when he was fourteen, he listened, together with his father, to a Stoic, a Platonist, a Peripatetic and an Epicurean, but thought it a bad idea to fall for any sect immediately.[71] Lucian's entertaining dialogue, *Philosophies for Sale*, representing a market in which all the main types of *bios* ('philosophies of life') are on sale, looks like a satire on precisely this way of describing things—or of going about them. In fact, we

---

[69] For a wide selection of examples, see A. D. Nock, 'Conversion and adolescence', *Essays in Religion and the Ancient World*, ed. Z. Stewart (1972), vol. 1, p. 457 n. Nock, however, does not mention Josephus in this context; cf. *Conversion* (1933), pp. 102ff.; Misch, loc. cit. (n. 67); N. Hyldahl, *Philosophie und Christentum* (1966), pp. 148–54.

[70] Nock emphasises this group.

[71] *On the Diagnosis and Cure of the Soul's Passions* 8.

may be sure that 'shopping around' for the best philosophy was
something of a cliché. Josephus, with his characterisation of the
Jewish sects as rational and definable philosophies, and his detached
and critical approach—'I thought I should be able to choose the
best'—comes closest, among the serious writers, to Galen. This is
understandable, for it would not be to Josephus' purpose to present
Judaism as a strange and mysterious oriental religion. There is little
sense of revelation or enthusiasm in his particular 'conversion'.
That the search becomes a *topos*, a literary formula, by no means
implies that it was not carried out by the individuals who recount
it. Events which actually occur are often perceived and described
in conventional terms. People may act out *topoi*. What is clear is
that Josephus sees this stage of his development in Greek terms.
But when it comes to seeking an explanation for this, and to dis-
cerning the reality of the events which are described in such a way,
we are on far more difficult ground. Perhaps Josephus writes here
as he does because he has formed, by the time he comes to write
the *Life*, what is virtually a habit of talking about the three sects
within Judaism as though they were Greek philosophies. As he
himself says here, he has discussed the subject a number of times;
and mostly (though not exclusively) he has described their differences in an unexpected way, emphasising their disagreements in
the matter of fate versus free will, and explicitly pointing out similarities between Pharisaic and Stoic views, even though it is evident
that these are not the only differences between the sects of which he
is aware (for on one occasion he does point out the crucial fact that
the Sadducees did not accept the Pharisaic oral law).[72] He prefers
to stress those distinctions through which he has a point of contact
with his Greek readers, an opportunity to put a Jewish institution
into Greek garb, so as to make it intelligible to them: for indeed,
differences among the Greek philosophical schools on the question
of the control of the universe were so familiar that even Tacitus
discoursed on them (without troubling to mention the names of the

---

[72] *AJ* 13. 171ff.; 18. 11–22; *BJ* 2. 119–66. *AJ* 13. 297–8. R. Travers Herford, op.
cit. (n. 55), intr., ascribes to Lauterbach (1913) the discovery that the main point
of difference between Pharisees and Sadducees was in their respective attitudes to
the oral law. The distinction in which Josephus is most interested, seems, though
less important, to be a real one: see E. Urbach, *The Sages, their Concepts and Beliefs*
(transl. I. Abrahams, 1975), pp. 255–6.

schools).[73] The point here is that, by the time Josephus is writing
the *Life*, it has become natural for him to think of the sects as
schools. And the kind of choice he sets out is the kind of choice
which has to be made between philosophical schools.

And yet there might also be a deeper significance in the switch
to a Greek framework. After the age of sixteen, Josephus did indeed
move into a wider world, and make a choice. Now, for the first
time, he is not following the straight path. Clearly, in spite of his
talent, he was not content simply to continue with his Pharisaic
education, to progress from the Bible to the type of material which
was later compiled in the Mishnah, then to Talmudic studies: to
aspire to be a sage.[74] 'Usually, if 1,000 men take up the study of
Scripture, 100 of them proceed to the study of Mishnah, 10 to
Talmud, and one of them becomes qualified to decide questions of
law'.[75] Josephus instead looked at new kinds of Judaism, and what
they had to offer. We can understand the need for a serious attempt
to work out a position for himself. The multiplicity of strands and
group in the Judaism of the day (the three main sects were not, of
course, the only ones) would imply that there was a real possibility
of individual choice. They cannot all have had solely hereditary
followings. In its pluralism, the Palestine of this period was remarkable; yet perhaps not dissimilar (though we know less about
them) to other parts of the east under the Romans. Josephus may
have been, during his early manhood, perplexed in a way which
was genuinely comparable to that state of mind reported by Justin,
Lucian and Galen in the next century. It is a key to Josephus to
appreciate that he is the product of an era of great cultural and
social fluidity, both within Judaism and further afield.

It is less understandable that Josephus should have chosen to
spend three whole years in the desert. That seems out of tune with
the Josephus of later years, who shows remarkably little interest in
the mystical (with the exception, perhaps, of his claims about his

[73] Tac. *Ann.* 6. 22. See W. Theiler, 'Tacitus und die antike Schicksalslehre',
Phyllobolia für P. von der Mühll (1946). But G. F. Moore, 'Fate and free will in the
Jewish philosophies according to Josephus', *HThR* 22 (1929), pp. 371–89, exaggerates
in declaring that Josephus seriously misleads his readers; and it is unnecessary to
father the description on to the philosophically inclined Greek, Nicolaus of Damascus. J. Blenkinsopp, op. cit. (n. 23), p. 249, points out that the Greek vocabulary of
fate is found already in the Greek Bible.
[74] Cf. S. Rappaport, *Agada und Exegese bei Flavius Josephus* (1930), intro., xv.
[75] *Midrash Rabbah, Ecclesiastes*, on 7.28 (Soncino Transl., p. 211).

own prophetic powers). It may be that Josephus exaggerated somewhat the duration of his retreat, and the asperity of the conditions
there. An even more disturbing point is that this stay with Bannus
may have brought him into contact not just with a religious community in search of purity, such as the Qumran sect, but with a
group of political activists, which the men of Qumran seem not to
have been, at least until the last stage of the war.[76] This was not
something which Josephus would have been able to mention, in a
work which was rebutting the charge that he had fomented revolt.
The connection between withdrawal into the desert (or, sometimes,
the mountains) of Judaea under the inspiration of some pseudo-
prophet, pseudo-Messiah, or simple leader, and ensuing political
disturbance, is well-established from Josephus' own writings.[77]
There is also evidence, it is true, of the existence of apparently
pacific groups in search of solitude in those parts of the country,
whose detachment from society was not, it seems, translated into
action. But a detail may be indicative: that the actual *name*, Bannus,
of Josephus' mentor is recorded, suggests that the allegiance of his
followers was to him personally, and that they would expect some
immediate change to be brought about by him. The Qumran sect,
by contrast, did not have a *named* teacher or master. Was Bannus
perhaps a figure like Theudas the magician, who (about A.D.45)
had persuaded a great crowd to follow him to the Jordan, where he
claimed that, as a prophet, he would divide the waters; and who
was enough of a threat to prompt Fadus the procurator to send a
detachment of cavalry, and to get him beheaded? While of Theudas
we are not told that he had ascetic tendencies, or aspired to religious
purity, as Bannus did, the withdrawal to Jordan suggests that he
may well have done. Josephus' Bannus is not mentioned in any
other source: we cannot know, but it is a reasonable speculation
that not all who followed him did so for simple religious reasons.

However, if there was any quasi-revolutionary thinking among

---

[76] On purification by water in this sect, *Community Rule* 3; *Damascus Rule* 10. On
their political attitudes, A. Dupont-Sommer, *The Jewish Sect of Qumran and the Essenes*
(English translation, 1954), pp. 148–9. The finding of fragments of Qumran literature
at Masada raises difficult questions about the attitude of the Qumran community
to the revolt. See Y. Yadin, *Masada* (1966), pp. 173–4; S. G. F. Brandon, *Jesus and
the Zealots* (1967), pp. 61–2, n. 4.

[77] *BJ* 2. 261–2; 6. 285ff.; 7. 438; *AJ* 18. 85–7; 20. 97ff., 160, 167ff., 188. Cf. Acts
5.36 and 21.38. M. Hengel, *Die Zeloten* (1961), pp. 235ff. and 259ff. has some
discussion. One obvious advantage of disappearing into the desert was escaping the
tax-collector.

Josephus' desert companions, this was an approach which Josephus would have encountered only to reject it totally.

We next see him among the proponents of diplomacy and compromise, travelling, at the age of twenty-six (therefore in A.D.64) on an embassy to Rome, whose purpose was to negotiate the release of some priests whose arrest he describes as follows: 'During the time when Felix was procurator of Judaea, he imprisoned on a trifling charge certain priests, whom I knew to be excellent men, and he sent them to Rome to give an account to Caesar' (*V* 13).

Although we hear of several embassies from Judaea to Rome in the years leading up to the revolt, we cannot identify Josephus' embassy with any event reported by him in the *War* or in Book 20 of the *Antiquities*. A short time before Josephus' journey, ten leading citizens of Jerusalem, together with the high priest himself, Ishmael ben Phiabi, and the Temple treasurer, went to Rome to defend the action of the Jews in constructing a wall to screen the Temple from the view of Agrippa's newly-extended palace and of the Roman garrison (*AJ* 20.189–96). The two Temple officials, after they had, Josephus tells us, achieved their purpose, were detained as hostages by Poppaea, that wife of the emperor Nero who, according to Tacitus, had every asset except good character: presumably some sort of compromise was struck. While they could still have been in Rome when Josephus arrived, they cannot be the men whom Josephus was to release, for they had gone out under the procurator Festus (?60–2) and not under Felix (52–60?), and they had gone voluntarily, not in chains. Deputations of prominent Jews and Greeks from Caesarea were sent by Felix to Rome as a consequence of riots in the town; or perhaps (according to Josephus' other version) they went voluntarily to accuse Felix after he was succeeded by Festus.[78] Since the Jews lost the argument, and their civic rights, the Jewish delegation may well have been detained. But it would be strange if this delegation consisted of priests. That Josephus does not mention his own embassy outside the *Life* is curious, and we can only conclude that the incident was a routine one; this is confirmation, if confirmation be needed, that such activities took place more often than we are told about them. As in the other cases, arrests of high-ranking Jews were involved: tensions were running

[78] *BJ* 2. 270; *AJ* 20. 182–4 on these events. See Schürer-Vermes-Millar, p. 467, n. 45, and F. Millar, *The Emperor in the Roman World* (1977), pp. 378–9, where Josephus' embassy might be added to Millar's list.

extremely high during the last procuratorships before the revolt. A few years earlier the procurator Cumanus had sent a high priest and other men in chains to explain their quarrel with the Samaritans to the emperor (*AJ* 20.132; *BJ* 2.243). Men like Josephus were engaged in an anxious search for remedies.

However minor Josephus' embassy, it puts him among the foremost men in the city, those to whom he repeatedly refers as 'the powerful men' (*dunatoi*), 'leading men', or, 'distinguished men' (*proechontes*) and whom we might call 'notables' (*gnōrimoi*) (one thinks of the middle-eastern notables of today). This group included a large contingent of high priests and prominent priests, but was not confined to them: the embassy of Ishmael ben Phiabi contained, as we have said, ten leading men. These seem to correspond to the *dekaprōtoi* of whom we hear in other cities of the empire at a slightly later date, with the difference that there they tend to be concerned with finance. In Jerusalem, as in Tiberias, they are ten leading citizens, active as representatives and organisers of the people.[79] But it did not, in Jerusalem, always have to be ten men. Often, an unspecified number of leading figures, perhaps along with the high priest, is said to take part in negotiations with the procurator.[80]

In Judaea, and elsewhere, the Roman government relied upon a body of co-operative local aristocrats. They would mediate between government and populace; they could provide successive governors with information about local conditions; in fact, they could do much of his work for him. Among the Jews, the high priest was the apex of the pyramid, and at this period he was an appointee either of the procurator, or of another Roman official or of the client king.[81]

With these men, Josephus would be establishing his due place. The six years between the end of his education and his embassy must have been occupied with making his mark among them. What would have become of him if the Jewish revolt had not broken out? Would he have hoped for membership of the Sanhedrin, when age

---

[79] Cf. T. Rajak, op. cit. (n. 10), p. 347.

[80] E.g. *BJ* 2. 240 (in connection with the dispute with the Samaritans); 2. 301 (they appear before Florus' tribunal at Jerusalem after he had raided the Temple treasury).

[81] Appointment by a procurator: 18. 34–5, Ishmael ben Phiabi by Valerius Gratus. By the *legatus* of Syria: *AJ* 18. 26, Ananus by Quirinius; *AJ* 18. 95, Jonathan son of Ananus by Vitellius. By the Herods: *AJ* 19. 297, Simon by Agrippa I; 19. 313–6, Jonathan son of Ananus by Agrippa I; 20. 179, another Ishmael ben Phiabi by Agrippa II; 20. 213–4, Jesus son of Gamaliel by Agrippa II.

qualified him to be an 'elder'? Many questions about the character and activities of that body in the first century A.D. remain unanswered. But a few assertions may be made with confidence, and will help us to place Josephus in relation to it. Herod had suppressed the institution, but, under the procurators, it certainly continued to function, though we cannot tell how regularly and how effectively. Its jurisdiction, previously, was parallel with that of the procurators.[82] When the war broke out, the Sanhedrin was the only remaining official authority in the state (*V* 62), but, curiously, Josephus does not mention it in the *War* after the beginning of the revolt. While there is inadequate evidence to support Emil Schürer's contention that the high priest always presided over the Sanhedrin, and it is certainly wrong to invoke Josephus as evidence that this was so, we must still trust the Gospels that high priests and priests were *often* the dominant factor.[83] Biblical support could be found for this practice. And even the Mishnah endorses the importance of that group, when it says that for capital cases the court must consist of priests, Levites, and members of such families as were pure enough to intermarry with them.[84] But leading citizens were to be found as members alongside the high priests.[85] How the individuals were actually selected we do not know, and there is uncertainty about the whole subject. Some scholars have even believed that there existed two or more Sanhedrins; but our different pieces of evidence do not seem irreconcilable: the predominance of high priests at certain times is compatible with the picture emerging from Talmudic literature where various Pharisaic scholars are represented as supreme.[86] And it seems impossible to separate 'religious' from 'political' functions and to assign them to separate

[82] Schürer, *GJV*[4], vol. 2, pp. 260–3.

[83] See, for example, Matth. 26.57ff.; Mark 15.1ff.; Luke 22.66ff.; Acts 5.22ff. The Josephus passage which is taken to point in the same direction, *AJ* 20. 251 only asserts the general leadership of the high priests after the demise of Herod and his son, and is too vague to count as evidence either that the Sanhedrin controlled the state during the period in question, or that the high priests controlled or presided over the Sanhedrin.

[84] *M. Sanh.* 4.2. Whether the Sanhedrin actually retained capital jurisdiction under the procurators is, of course, a hotly disputed issue.

[85] Jeremias, op. cit. (n.18), pp. 224ff.

[86] In spite of the insistence of H. Mantel, *Studies in the History of the Sanhedrin* (1961), that this solution is too accommodating. In contrast, Urbach, loc. cit. (n. 55), pp. 50ff., esp. p. 51, n. 31. An excellent account by W. Bacher in *Hastings Dictionary of the Bible*, s.v. Sanhedrin. For a more extended survey of the evidence, S. Hoenig, *The Great Sanhedrin* (1953).

bodies: the function of a local council in the early empire was to administer the local laws, and in the case of the Jews, this meant religious law. As far as competence in this law goes, some members will have been more suited than others to the task.

At the same time, with the Romans in ultimate control, the attentions of the Jewish ruling class will have been directed outwards, towards the authorities. Issues of importance—such as brigandage or large-scale dissension—went, as we can see, to the procurator, if not the emperor, and the Jews could only exert an indirect influence. That is why small groups of notables figure more often in the pages of Josephus than do council sessions. And that is perhaps why Josephus was already a prominent figure in his country, although not yet a member of the Sanhedrin.

If Josephus had not realised before the importance to a member of the Jewish ruling class of learning to deal with Greeks and Romans, his visit to Rome must have taught him this. Before going, he must already have possessed some of the necessary linguistic and social skills to enable him to fulfil his function there, as will emerge more clearly in the following chapters. At around this time, he will have begun to observe the Roman empire, observations which were to bear fruit in the great survey of the subject peoples and the disposition of the empire put into the mouth of Agrippa II in the *Jewish War* (2.358–87). For Josephus, one of the first products of looking beyond his own country would be the conviction that the fate of Judaea was inextricably bound up with that of Rome.

Many an aspiring young orator in the early Roman empire found himself, at the beginning of his career, participating in one of the various embassies sent out by his city. He might be the companion of older and more experienced me, rhetoricians or scholars, and they might go to the proconsul or legate, to another city, or to the emperor. Plutarch talked of embassies, along with forensic oratory, as a young man's road to fame in an age when there were no more wars in Greece. And we think of the young Plutarch himself, acting as an emissary to the proconsul of Achaea, and subsequently being instructed by his father on how to present his report in the way most tactful to his colleague.[87] To take another, somewhat earlier example, Crinagoras, a poet from Mytilene on the island of Lesbos, was, it is believed, an emissary to Caesar in the 40s B.C., when the

---

[87] On embassies, H. Marrou, *Histoire de l'Education dans l'Antiquité* (1948), p. 294, nn. 21 and 22; C. P. Jones, *Plutarch and Rome* (1971), pp. 20–1, 37.

ambassador was in his twenties.[88] He, like Plutarch, also acted as an ambassador later in life, when he had acquired distinction. The pattern is the same as that which first brings Josephus to Rome.

Yet, whereas these Greeks, and many others like them, will have engaged abroad in exercising those rhetorical skills which had formed the basis of their education, and whereas they, on their travels, could further their cultural and social contacts, hear philosophers or even give lectures, for Josephus, the intellectual milieu was largely new. Cultured Greeks had patrons or friends in Rome. But Josephus and his fellow emissaries were befriended and aided by a member of the lower classes (albeit an emperor's favourite), the actor Aliturus, and by a woman (albeit an empress), Poppaea. And, as we have seen from the occasion on which she detained Ishmael ben Phiabi, Poppaea's support had its limitations, even if Josephus is right in saying that, as a 'God-fearer', she favoured Jews (*V* 16; *AJ* 20, 195). The Herodian house had more respectable contacts in Rome, which, in a previous generation, had included Drusus, the son of the emperor Tiberius.[89] But they do not seem to have offered any help—which would be understandable, in view of the recent quarrel between Agrippa II and the Temple authorities.

With Josephus' journey to Rome, the first phase of his life is concluded. But this account would be incomplete without mention of what happened on the way to the capital, an event which was by no means unimportant to him—for he nearly lost his life—and which, at the same time, returns us opportunely to the problem from which we began, the severe limitations of Josephus' *Life* as a source for his life. The incident was a shipwreck. For all its significance to the author, it is at first sight surprising to find it mentioned at all, let alone as vividly evoked as it is, in so compressed a context. Josephus tells how some 600 people—a strikingly but not impossibly large number of passengers—had to swim through the night and were rescued by a Cyrenaic ship.[90] Now the shipwreck motif was a commonplace. Shipwrecks were, of course, all too frequent in the ancient world. Precisely for that reason, they would interest readers,

---

[88] For Crinagoras: *PIR*[2] 1580, and the literature mentioned there. Cf. G. Bowersock, *Augustus and the Greek World* (1965), pp. 36–7.

[89] On Poppaea: E. M. Smallwood, 'The alleged Jewish tendencies of Poppaea Sabina, *JThS* 10 (1959), pp. 329–35. Earlier, apart from Drusus, there was also Antonia Minor, the mother of Claudius (*AJ* 18.143).

[90] *V* 15; J. Rougé, *Recherches sur l'organisation du commerce en Méditerranée sous l'empire romain* (1969), p. 69.

and in a biography or autobiography, could offer some excitement.
The story of Caesar's shipwreck and capture by pirates in Suetonius'
Life is an obvious example. It is significant that some critics have
treated the story of the voyage and shipwreck of Paul with 275 other
passengers as a conventional motif, and have even tried to suggest,
in spite of its length, its first person form and its abundance of
nautical detail, that it need not be an authentic account.[91]

Josephus' treatment of the shipwreck reveals little about Josephus
himself. But it demonstrates clearly his tendency, in his account of
himself, to pick out traditional themes and happenings. It reminds
us, equally, that material of importance may well have been omitted. So far from claiming that we have a full picture of our author's
background and development, we must admit that we do not even
have a complete outline of it. Nevertheless, by putting flesh on the
bones of his account, we have added to our knowledge.

The Josephus who went to Rome had the intellectual background
of a Jerusalem Pharisee. He will have known Hebrew and the Bible
extremely well, but we should remember that he will not yet have
had much opportunity to handle advanced problems of interpretation. In Rome, he will have been a stranger. However, as we shall
see in the next chapter, he did not entirely lack the technical equipment which would help him find his feet there.

Thus we have already seen the two influences which will continue
to bear on Josephus' career and writings; indeed the Judaism of this
period might be summed up through the same polarity. On the one
hand, the Jews, even in enclosed Judaea, had since Alexander been
part of the Hellenistic world, subject in many respects to the same
conditions as other peoples in the Greek east. On the other, Judaism
with its idiosyncratic political, social and educational institutions,
always offered a self-consciously different way of life (or ways of
life). And so Josephus' youth has emerged as in some ways characteristic of the Greco-Roman world in the first century—his choice
between sects and the embassy; in others, distinctly Jewish—his
kingly and priestly family, his father's much-vaunted justice, the
values stressed in connection with his education, his easy familiarity
with the Bible, Pharisaism and the desert. Setting these two one

[91] See *RE*, 2nd series, 2, 412, s.v. 'Schiffart'. cf. D. Clay, 'Sailing to Lampsacus.
Diogenes of Oenoanda, new fragment 7', *GRBS* 14 (1973), pp. 49–59, on Epicurus'
shipwreck. On Paul, M. Dibelius, *Studies in the Acts of the Apostles* (English translation,
1956), p. 107.

against the other, we see that the Greco-Roman features seem to be outweighed by those of markedly Jewish character. It is arguable that, in spite of surface appearances, this relationship undergoes little change of emphasis in later years.

CHAPTER TWO

The Greek Language in Josephus' Jerusalem

At the time when Josephus set off on his mission to Rome he would have been able to speak Greek, at least after a fashion. For if there were suitable men in Palestine who had the language necessary for communication with Romans—and we shall see that there were—a man who had not would hardly have been selected as ambassador. Josephus' native languages, however, were undoubtedly Aramaic and Hebrew(see Appendix 1). That is clear; but what is far more difficult to grasp is how Josephus stands with regard to the Greek language and Greek culture in the early part of his life. The environment of Jerusalem was the basis for every later development; and the author's exposure to Greek (whatever it amounted to) is relevant to all his writings, if the difficulties and the achievements involved in these are to be fairly judged.

How much Greek, and how much Greek culture, were known in Jewish Palestine are questions which have often been asked—and answered in different ways. Above all, the enigma of the Gospel texts has occasioned their asking, and conditioned the answers given. Usually the evidence from Josephus plays a subsidiary role: to make Josephus the centre of the attention will not only illuminate him, but also give a new perspective to the whole picture.

In the *Life*, Josephus says not a word about Greek studies of any kind. From this silence, however, we may conclude nothing, even if we are eager to believe that there really were none. Such an omission is to be expected; first, because Josephus speaks only of the principal stages in his formal education, and his formal education was Jewish; secondly, because it is his purpose there to stress his Jewish 'credentials', in order to buttress his contention that he had always had the interests of his people at heart (see p. 14). As we have seen, it is a mistake to build arguments upon what is excluded from the *Life*.

However, there are comments of considerable interest in Josephus' other writings, and these are a useful avenue of approach. In his last work, *Against Apion* (written in the nineties), he tells us that he had had help with the presentation of the *Jewish War*, his first work in Greek (written in the seventies): 'Then, when I had leisure in Rome, and my whole argument was prepared, having enlisted some people (*synergoi*) to help with the Greek, I constructed my account of the events.' But the obscurities of this passage are obvious. What was the extent and nature of the help given by the assistants? Did they, perhaps, polish or check an existing composition? Or is it mainly they who are responsible for the form and style of the whole of the *War*? Our first clues lie in the *Antiquities*. By the time of the completion of this large work (which preceded *Against Apion*) Josephus had spent over twenty years in Rome. In the conclusion to the first, he still expresses diffidence about his Greek. He had, he tells us, worked at developing his literary style: 'I took pains to master Greek letters and poetic disciplines, once I had gained acquaintance with the grammar.' He had hinted at the same situation in the preface, talking of his hesitation in translating so great a quantity of material 'into a language whose usage is strange and foreign to us'.[1]

Now protestations of linguistic inadequacy were not unknown in authors writing in Greek. To take just one example, A. Postumius Albinus, Roman consul in 151 B.C., and author of a Greek history of Rome, was rebuked by the elder Cato for making just this kind of assertion. In his introduction, he had written that 'no one ought to hold it against him if anything in these books were put in an unpolished or not quite stylish way'. And Aulus Gellius tells us that he went on thus: 'for I am a man who was born in Latium, and expressing ourselves in Greek is quite foreign to us'; finally, he asked to be excused for any solecisms he might have committed. Cato's retort was merciless: nobody had asked the historian to write, so what was the sense in apologising for what he had written? Yet the truth was rather different: we know from Cicero that Albinus was in fact 'a man of letters, and an eloquent one'; and Polybius says that he had been immersed right from his childhood in Greek

---

[1] The Josephus passages are at *CA* 1. 50; *AJ* 20. 263; 1. 7. The idea that paid writers were responsible for such literary merits as the *Jewish War* possesses was expressed by H. St. J. Thackeray, *Josephus, The Man and the Historian* (1929), pp. 104–6. See also pp. 62–3, with n. 49 and Appendix 2.

education and the Greek language, and furthermore, that he was
one of the men responsible for the spread of Greek culture in Rome.
This exchange took place, of course, many years before Josephus,
at a time when things Greek had been deeply mistrusted at Rome.
But it reveals that such disclaimers had a precedent in the Greek
writing of non-Greeks; and of that Josephus may have been aware,
even if, as is virtually certain, he had not read Albinus. Josephus
may also have recalled that the preface of Dionysius of Halicarnassus' *Roman Antiquities*, a work which in certain superficial respects
was a precursor of the *Jewish Antiquities*, contained an explanation
of how the author had lived in Rome for twenty-two years, learned
the Romans' language (*dialektos*) and made himself familiar with
their literature (*grammatōn*).[2] Josephus had good reason, then, to
overstress rather than conceal his linguistic inadequacies.

Still the apology is framed with care, and its appearance in so
prominent a position as a formal conclusion forbids explaining it
away as a mere pose. Josephus gives an exact indication of how he
studied, so that it is not hard to see what sort of activity was
involved.[3] When he talks of acquiring grammatical skill, which he
associates with an extended exploration of texts, it is clear that he
uses the term 'grammar' in the wide sense, to mean the study of
literature. 'Grammar' had been defined by Dionysius Thrax, a pupil
of the distinguished Alexandrian scholar Aristarchus and the author
of a treatise on the subject, as 'a general familiarity with the diction
of poets and prose writers'; and a broad view of its proper province
remained current, with regard both to Greek and to Latin. Indeed,
Quintilian, an almost exact contemporary of Josephus, grumbles
because, in his day, the sphere of activity of the 'grammaticus' has
grown too much, at the expense of that of the rhetorician. Grammar

___

[2] On Albinus: Gellius, *NA* 11. 8.2; Cicero, *Brut.* 81; Polyb. 39. 12; Dionysius of
Halicarnassus: 1. 7.2.

[3] The translation of the passage does not present any special difficulty; though J.
Sevenster in *Do You know Greek?* (Suppl. 19 to *Novem Testamentum*, 1968), pp. 66–71,
discusses it at length. R. J. H. Shutt, *Studies in Josephus* (1961, p. 76, is over-precise
in insisting that Josephus' sentence structure shows the study of grammar to be
consequent upon the reading, not something separate which preceded it. The reten-
tion in the text of the words 'and of knowledge of poets (much)' found in MSS A
and E, and excluded by Sevenster, is, I think, justified both on grounds of sense—
study of the poets was an important part of 'grammar' (see Suet. *de gramm.* 4, as well
as the sources mentioned in the succeeding notes)—and because we might expect
Josephus to have avoided the cacophonous proximity of two similar-sounding words
which otherwise occurs.

in this sense—knowledge of the important authors and the ability to interpret what they wrote—would have been learnt by well-educated young pagans in the course of their education, as it was by Herod's historian, Nicolaus of Damascus, according to what he tells us. But not by all. Galen writes that in general students of philosophy or of medicine at Rome tended to lack this 'elementary education which the youth of Greece would receive from the start', and therefore were quite unable to distinguish his genuine works from spurious ones by their style.[4] And it was precisely this background which Josephus also had lacked.

It is hard to know what to make of a number of supercilious remarks thrown out also by Galen, and surviving only in Arabic, on the subject of Rufus of Samaria, a Jewish doctor. He, like Josephus, but about a century later and from a non-Jewish zone, moved to Rome, and set about contributing to Greek literature: in this case the contribution was a more modest one than Josephus', a summary of earlier commentaries on Hippocrates which Rufus had in his library. Galen is amazed at Rufus' uncritical endorsement of other men's nonsense: this, says Galen, is what comes of living 'in the land of the Palestinians', for the man had understood not a word of Greek before coming to Rome; and to have been among Greeks and yet knew so little of their language was a disgrace. Galen's snobbish insults are probably an exaggeration: and his last remark, as well as the nature of Rufus' enterprise might suggest to us that, on the contrary, the doctor had always had at last some grasp of the spoken language. This, then, would make his case not so very different from that of Josephus.[5]

The first passage of Galen shows us that students who did pursue the study of Greek could do so to a very advanced and sophisticated level: it was not a question of simple linguistic competence. There is no doubt whatsoever that those who chose medicine or philosophy

---

[4] On Dionysius' statement, *RE* 7. 2 (1912), 1808. And for the broad conception of *grammatice* cf. Cic. *de Orat.* 1. 187; Quint. *Inst.* 1. 4.1–5; Philo, *On Intercourse with the Preliminary Studies*, 148. Cf. M. L. Clarke, *Higher Education in the Ancient World* (1971), pp. 23–8. For Quintilian on grammatice, see *Inst.* 2. 1.4; cf. 1. 8.6. Nicolaus: *FGH* 90. 132.1; Galen: *On His Own Books*, Kuhn 19. p. 9.

[5] Rufus: *Corpus Medicorum Graecorum* 5. 10. 2. 2, pp. 293 and 413. The Arabic passages were translated by F. Pfaff, and his discovery of this Rufus reported in *Hermes* 47 (1932), pp. 356–9. See W. D. Smith, *The Hippocratic Tradition* (1979), p. 164. M. Stern suggests that Rufus may have been a Samaritan, Galen being unclear about the distinction: *Greek and Latin Authors on Jews and Judaism*, vol. 2 (1980), p. 309, n. 7.

instead, none the less had no difficulty in expressing themselves in Greek.[6] The same might be true of Josephus. Furthermore, grammatical studies were not geared to young students alone. Authors might engage in them in order to form their own styles, and, in particular, to become intimately familiar with classical usage. Thus, considerably later, Cassius Dio read 'some of the Greeks . . . so as to be able to Atticize'.[7] Since a writer was conceived of as to a great extent an imitator (see p. 236), this is not surprising. Josephus, as well as compensating for the gap in his education, would have wished to reap the same sort of benefit as Dio later did from his study of authors.

If, then, we assert that there were deficiencies in Josephus' Greek when he came to Rome which would have taken years to remedy, and perhaps could never be fully remedied, the question is by no means one of mastery of the ordinary language, spoken or written. Though Josephus does offer, following on from the passage which we have just discussed, a self-criticism about the way he speaks Greek, it is not such as to cast doubt upon his fluency. What he says is that his pronunciation is not good, and this because knowledge of foreign languages is not highly valued by his people: 'the tradition of my people has prevented my becoming accurate in pronunciation. For they do not approve of those who have acquired the languages of many nations, and deck out what they say in a polished idiom, because they feel this is a capacity within the reach of absolutely any free man, not to mention such slaves as want to have it. They ascribe wisdom only to those who possess a precise knowledge of the laws, and who can explain the Holy Scriptures.' Here, Josephus expatiates on his limitations, in the wider context of Jewish cultural attitudes. The word he uses means, specifically, 'pronunciation', and the most obvious interpretation of his statement is that he spoke the Greek language with some sort of regional accent, which stood out in Rome, and was perhaps looked down on. Limited evidence does exist for this very phenomenon in the Roman empire.[8]

---

[6] Cf. the distinction drawn by Plutarch (*Dem.* 2.3) between understanding the meaning of the Latin which he had to read, and appreciated its stylistic qualities; he taught himself to do the former, but had no time for the latter.

[7] F. Millar, *A Study of Cassius Dio* (1964), p. 41.

[8] Evidence, about both Greek and Latin speaking in F. Millar, 'Local cultures in the Roman Empire: Libyan, Punic and Latin in Roman Africa', *JRS* 57 (1968), pp. 126–7; J. P. V. D. Balsdon, *Romans and Aliens* (1979), pp. 128–36. The claim of B.

Josephus' report of his people's attitude to foreign languages serves to explain why he had never *studied* how to speak or write Greek. What it suggests is that his Greek was such as had come to him naturally from his environment; it had never been treated as an achievement.

It is possible to offer some confirmation of this understanding of Josephus' words. That can be done by surveying what evidence there is (outside Josephus) first for the use of Greek in different contexts in Jerusalem; and secondly for the attitudes to the language and the culture characteristic of the Pharisaic Judaism within which we have placed Josephus. And when this picture has been sketched, it should be possible for us better to understand what it meant to Josephus to devote the prime of his life to writing history in Greek.

The fact that the Greek language was much in evidence in Palestine as a whole has some bearing on our subject: the country was small, and people would travel, so that the sound, at least, of spoken Greek was unlikely to be strange to a Judaean, even though there was no Greek city in Judaea proper. It is true that the evidence which we possess for the language situation in the first century A.D. falls short of proving the point, but every indication suggests that the language had made considerable inroads by then.[9] In the Greek cities and towns which ringed Palestine, Greek was undoubtedly the official tongue, even if some part of the 'Greek' population preferred to use Aramaic or another oriental language.[10] And the Jews who lived, say, in Caesarea or Scythopolis, in such close proximity (even if not amity) with Greeks, must also have managed some Greek.[11] Both archaeological evidence—especially inscriptions of synagogues and of the Beth She'arim necropolis, together with such Dead Sea documents from Wadi Murabbaat as are in Greek[12]—and the Talmudic statements discussed below show that

---

Lifschitz, 'Du nouveau sur l'hellénization des Juifs en Palestine', *Euphrosyne* N.S. 4. (1970), p. 118, that the word *prophora* used by Josephus can mean 'style' rather than 'pronunciation' is inadequately substantiated.

[9] A good survey and assessment of the evidence is Sevenster, op. cit. (n. 2), pp. 97–114.

[10] On this problem, A. H. M. Jones, *The Greek City* (1940), pp. 288–95; V. Tcherikover, *Hellenistic Civilization and the Jews* (English translation, 1959), pp. 114–16; Sevenster, op. cit. (n. 2), p. 98; Schürer-Vermes-Millar-Black, vol. 2, pp. 29–52.

[11] Cf. G. Mussies in *The Jewish People in the First Century* (*Compendia Rerum Iudaicarum ad Novum Testamentum*, section 1, vol. 2, 1976), pp. 1057–60.

[12] For an introduction to this archaeological and documentary evidence, Sevenster, op. cit. (n.3), pp. 145–75.

Greek was commonly written (and so presumably spoken) by Jews
in many parts of Palestine from the *second* century A.D. Inference
has had to fill the gap for the first. But now we have a little help
from the Dead Sea scrolls. The library at Qumran contained non-
Biblical Greek texts; while four Greek loan words have been found
in the vernacular Hebrew of the Copper Scroll discovered there,[13]
suggesting acquaintance with Greek terms on the part of *some* Hebrew users somewhere, even if not of the document's actual authors.

But it is still theoretically possible that a Jew in Jerusalem could
live his life without himself having any need for Greek or use for it:
what happened in other cities need not have affected him much.
Our concern is therefore with the language in the city itself, and
our question is about the likelihood of Josephus hearing Greek
there—and hearing it not only in the street, but in houses which he
might have visited. By the date of Josephus' birth, Greek had had
some sort of presence in Jerusalem for over three hundred years.
Tradition had it that when Ptolemy II Philadelphus of Egypt
wanted to have a translation of the Pentateuch made for his library,
he arranged for the high priest of Jerusalem to commission
seventy-two Jewish sages from Palestine to do the job for him (*Letter
of Aristeas* 32; 46–50; 121). It is impossible to reach a secure judgment on the authenticity of this report; but, if those scholars existed,
some of them, at least, will have come from the country's capital.
The Maccabean crisis of the 170s and 160s B.C. revolved to some
extent around internal contention about the adoption of Greek ways
by the Jerusalem aristocracy, and the conversion of the city into a
Greek *polis*;[14] but the use of the Greek language is not mentioned
as an issue in itself and this may well be because within a limited
sphere it was quite accepted. The Hasmonean period brought with
it a Jewish monarchy which had to conduct diplomacy on the
Hellenistic scene, and therefore to call on the services of those who
could wield at least a functional Greek.[15]

It is less clear whether Jewish works were translated into Greek
or composed in Greek in Jerusalem during the Hellenistic era, and,
if they were, then for what type of readership. The grandson and
translator of the book of Jesus ben Sira (Ecclesiasticus), itself evidently centred on Jerusalem, tells us that he spent time in Egypt (late

[13] See Schürer-Vermes-Millar-Black, vol. 2, p. 78.
[14] V. Tcherikover, op. cit. (n. 10), pp. 161ff.
[15] So D. M. Lewis, review of Sevenster, *JThs.* 20 (1969), p. 584.

in the reign of Ptolemy III Euergetes), and that his translation was intended for use in foreign countries, and thus he excludes himself from consideration here. So too does the author of the fragments of re-written Biblical history which are quoted by Clement of Alexandria and by Eusebius under the name of Eupolemus; for the common identification of this man with the leader of the embassy sent by Judas Maccabaeus to Rome rests on pure conjecture.[16] The author of the Greek II Maccabees, Jason of Cyrene, must have had close contact with Jerusalem to obtain the material necessary for his history, but need not have lived there (II Macc. 1.19–22). Most pertinent is the well-known conclusion to the Greek version of Esther, which proclaims that the translation was made by a certain Ptolemy son of Lysimachus in Jerusalem;[17] however, we do not know whether this includes the free Greek additions to the book. The translator's name sounds Alexandrian. The last is the only one of the productions in question to read like natural Greek, and to have a sufficient degree of polish to allow it to be described as Hellenistic in spirit; and it is not enough to base any conclusions on. For all Martin Hengel's valiant attempts to construct from this material a picture of a Hellenized Jerusalem Judaism,[18] the fact remains that the evidence for the use of the Greek language by the Jews of pre-Herodian Jerusalem is weak; while signs of any sort of pentration of Greek *culture* seem to be almost entirely absent.

In the first century B.C. and the first A.D. there were two obvious sources of Greek speech in the city—the Herodian court, and Diaspora Jews—and these to some extent overlapped. Of the four client kings who had had some responsibility for Judaea, the three important ones—Herod himself, and (almost half a century later) Agrippa I, followed by Agrippa II—all spent time in Jerusalem. Herod had a famous palace there; Agrippa I particularly enjoyed staying there; and Agrippa II's extensions to his palace caused much trouble, as we have seen.[19] The official language of the Herods was Greek: their coins were inscribed in it alone; they sent their sons to be educated in Rome,[20] which was a statement of policy. The fact that family marriages were arranged with prominent

[16] Ben Sira, *Prologue*; Jacoby, *FGH* IIIC. 723 and I Macc. 8.17.
[17] Cf. Lewis, loc. cit. (n. 15).
[18] *Judaism and Hellenism* (English edition, 1974), pp. 58–169.
[19] *BJ* I. 402 etc.; *AJ* 19. 331; p. 39. On the Herodian presence in Jerusalem, cf. E. Bikerman, 'Les Hérodiens', *RB* 47 (1938), p. 196.
[20] *AJ* 16. 6—the sons of Herod; 18. 143—Agrippa I; 19. 360—Agrippa II.

Alexandrian Jews shows that Greek was freely spoken.[21] But the
presence of the king in a city meant also the presence of a large
court circle, as well as his immediate family. It is clear that certain
families had risen into prominence in this circle under the first
Herod, and continued to be prominent throughout the Herodian
period; and some of these were Jewish families of Greek speakers.
An example is that of Alexas, an agent of Herod. His son Helcias
was an associate of Agrippa I, and Helcias' son, Julius Archelaus,
was one of the 'Jews who are also versed in Greek culture' to whom
Josephus sold a copy of the *Jewish War* (*CA* 1.51). In each generation, this family married into the Herodian family.[22] Such men were
not foreigners, and cannot have been entirely isolated from the rest
of the upper classes in Jerusalem. They will inevitably have had
connections with the high priests and members of the Sanhedrin.

Even non-Jewish members of the court circle would be unlikely
to have remained quite apart, and we have two small pieces of
evidence suggesting that they did not. In 66, at the outbreak of
revolt, and when Cestius Gallus was poised to advance on Jerusalem, Agrippa sent two men to parley with the Jews, and these two
are described as being the two of his associates who were best
known to them, by name Borcius and Phoebus. (Unfortunately,
their connection availed them little, for the former was killed and
the latter wounded by the Jewish mob (*BJ* 2.524–6)). Again, Josephus' surrender at Jotapata was negotiated by a tribune, Nicanor,
whom Vespasian specially selected because he was Josephus' friend.
Later, the same man is found accompanying Josephus on those
unpleasant perambulations around the walls of Jerusalem whose
object was to persuade the Jews to surrender, and getting wounded
in the process; by now he is said to be Titus' friend, this being
presumably the product of recent developments (*BJ* 3.346; 5.261).
That Nicanor was a Jew is most improbable; but he can hardly
have known Josephus well in 67 if he was not a local man. He could

---

[21] Thus, of Agrippa II's sisters, Berenice took as her first husband Marcus Julius
Alexander, son of Alexander the Alabarch, and brother of Tiberius Julius Alexander;
and Mariamne had as her second husband Demetrius the Alabarch, evidently a
prominent Alexandrian Jew. See, on these families, M. Stern, 'Herod's policy and
Jewish society at the end of the Second Temple Period', *Tarbiz* 35 (1966), pp. 235ff.
(Hebrew) and M. Stern in *The Jewish People* etc. (see n. 11), pp. 600–12.
[22] Alexas married Herod's daughter Salome (*BJ* 1. 566; *AJ* 17. 9–10). Alexas
Helcias (almost certainly the son of the above) married Cyprus, Herod's grand-
daughter (*AJ* 18. 138). Julius Archelaus married Mariamne, the daughter of Agrippa
I (*AJ* 19. 355; 20. 140).

have been the tribune of a large auxiliary cohort, quite likely one of Agrippa's, or, at any rate, a follower of the client king.

Important Diaspora families, we know, made marriage alliances with the Herods. In other ways, too, Alexandrian Jewry was represented in Jerusalem. At least one Alexandrian clan is known to have settled there, to have provided high priests, and constituted the backbone of the Sadducean party. This was the family of Boethus.[23] It is unlikely that they forgot their Greek. A woman from this family, Martha daughter of Boethus, married Josephus' friend, the high priest, Joshua son of Gamala, and was reduced to penury during the siege.[24]

A phenomenon whose impact was perhaps wider than anything mentioned so far was the existence in Jerusalem of synagogues belonging to Jews from various parts of the *oikoumenē*, some of them necessarily Greek speakers. Such synagogues catered, it would seem, both for a small community of residents, and for pilgrims who would arrive on the 'Three Foot Festivals'.[25] Acts 6: 1ff. describes a dispute about the daily distribution between the 'Hellenists' and the 'Hebrews' set in the nascent Christian community. Stephen was one of those called in to resolve the trouble. This is very valuable evidence that there was a big group of Jews in Jerusalem who distinguished themselves as Greek-speaking—for there can be no doubt that both of the factions among the disciples were made up of born Jews. The 'Hellenists' were perhaps drawn in part from the Synagogue of the Freedmen, of which we hear shortly afterwards; this contained Cyrenians and Alexandrians, as well as people from Cilicia and Asia, and it proceeded to attack Stephen.[26]

---

[23] Stern, art. cit. (n. 5), pp. 246–7. This family's Alexandrian origin is attested in *AJ* 15. 320. Other high priestly clans have been conjectured to be of Alexandrian origin: the house of Phiabi by Stern; and the house of Ananias by S. Safrai, *Pilgrimage at the Time of the Second Temple* (1965; Hebrew), p. 60.

[24] The marriage became a *cause célèbre* because, as a widow, Martha was not strictly permitted to marry a high priest. See Jeremias, *Jerusalem*, p. 156. On the woman, cf. p. 24.

[25] See Safrai, op. cit., *passim*; briefly in J. Juster, *Les Juifs dans l'empire Romain* (1914), vol. 1, p. 357 and n. 2. The *loci classici* on pilgrimage in pre-Talmudic texts are Philo, *Spec. Leg.* 1. 68–9; Josephus, *BJ* 6. 421–2.

[26] For the Hellenists, cf. Acts 9.29 (the only other certain reference). What precisely was the distinction between Hellenists and Hebrews has been long debated: see the summary of C. F. D. Moule, 'Once more who were the Hellenists?', *Expository Times* 70 (1959), pp. 100–2. Of three things there can be little doubt: (a) that the Hellenists had been a group among the Jews, (b) that the Hebrews cannot be defined as men who knew *no* Greek, (c) that the word 'Hebrews' was used in a variety of

There exists an inscription, put up by a man called Theodotus the 'archisynagogus', son of Vettenus the 'archisynagogus', and grandson of an 'archisynagogus', inside a Jerusalem synagogue which he personally had built (along with the adjoining baths and hostelry) and which had been initiated by his 'fathers'. This inscription is entirely in Greek.[27] The appearance of the Roman name Vettenus in the family suggests some connection with Rome—there is no point in speculating upon its nature[28]—and such a connection fits in well with the indication given by the language of the inscription itself that the family was one which spoke Greek sooner than Hebrew or Aramaic. The construction is generally assigned to the first century A.D.

Among the inscribed ossuaries of Jerusalem some, in Greek, belong to Jews from the Greek world. A notable example is the burial of the family of Nicanor of Alexandria, 'who made the gates'. The Greek is followed by a shorter Aramaic inscription recording only the head of the family's name and provenance. The gates referred to are reasonably identified with those which, according to the Talmud, were brought up by Nicanor from Alexandria, and saved from shipwreck by a miracle.[29] This would put Nicanor, the founder of the clan, in the early Herodian period.[30]

---

different senses; sometimes, but not in this case, it meant simply Jews. The most plausible interpretation is that the Hellenists were men whose *primary* language was Greek, while for the Hebrews it was a Semitic tongue. Moule suggests that the Hellenists worshipped in Greek; M. Simon in *Stephen and the Hellenists* (1956), that they followed a Greek style of life. Whether Stephen himself, and his co-arbitrators, were ever Hellenists is uncertain.

[27] *SEG* 8. 170 = *CIJ* 1404. There is a large literature on the inscription and on the synagogue. To the works mentioned by Frey and *SEG*, add useful accounts by M. Schwabe in *The Book of Jerusalem* (vol. 1, 1956; Hebrew), p. 362 and Safrai, op. cit. (n. 23), p. 64.

[28] Vettenus (as well as Vettienus and Vettienius) is known as a *nomen*; see W. Schulze, *Zur Geschichte lateinischer Eigennamen* (1904), p. 101, and, e.g. *CIL* 6. 8052, 28658 and 9. 4157, where we have a whole family of Italian freedmen with this name. Following Reinach, many have held that the father or grandfather of Theodotus must have been a freedman, originally enslaved by Pompey; and the synagogue has even been identified with that of the Libertines in Acts 6; on the office of *archisynagogus*, Schürer, *GJV*[4] 2. 509–12. But, since Josephus talks of the execution by Florus of Jews of equestrian status in Jerusalem (*BJ* 2. 308), we should expect to find Jews in the city, other than freedmen, who had Roman names.

[29] *SEG* 8. 200 = *CIJ* 1256. *M Yoma* 3.10, with a *Baraita* in *TB Yoma* 38a; *Tos. Yom.* 2.4; *TJ Yoma* 3.8. For the literature, see Frey, and add Schwabe, loc. cit. (n. 27). Frey's view that the doors referred to in the inscription are those of the tomb itself is unconvincing.

[30] For a few other certain, or possible inscriptions pertaining to Diaspora Jews, see Sevenster, op. cit. (n. 3), pp. 145–8.

But the natives of Jerusalem too might have their relatives' names scratched in Greek on their ossuaries. Some of these inscriptions would seem to have been executed by masons; many are too crude for that; they often consist of names alone.[31] The proportion of Greek as against Aramaic inscriptions is too high to allow of the supposition that all the Greek ones belong to Jews who were not native to Jerusalem. A calculation based on Frey's admittedly incomplete and out-of-date collection is adequate to provide a rough guide: it shows the number of Greek or bilingual inscriptions to be almost equal to those in Aramaic or Hebrew. More recently discovered inscriptions, mainly from the Kedron Valley, are nearly all Greek or bilingual.[32] Now those who put Greek on their tombs need not be Greek speakers; just as the Latin on English gravestones was not put there by Latin speakers, but adopted because it was associated with worship and study. What the fashion for using Greek suggests is that the language must have played *some* part in the lives of some of the people concerned, even if it was only as a prestige language, not properly understood by everybody. No doubt the surviving burials are those of the relatively prosperous, who could afford to keep family tombs and have durable ossuaries made.[33] We may conclude, then, that, at least in those circles, Greek was not unknown. Whether the picture was exactly the same among more ordinary people, we cannot be certain. But that, fortunately, has less relevance to Josephus.

So far, we have established that Greek was the language of some Jews in Jerusalem, that those Jews played a part in the community and had relationships with other Jews, and that some Jews native to the city made at least a limited use of written Greek. In itself, the presence of Greek speakers need not have brought about a spread of the language in a city: they might, instead, have gradually lost their Greek, or else the situation could have remained static. What ensured the strength and the appeal of Greek was that it was the language of the dominant culture surrounding the Jews, and, above all, that it had already been, long before Rome's advent, the instrument employed by the great power which controlled Judaea.

[31] See N. Avigad, 'The Necropolis', op. cit. (n. 27), p. 331.

[32] Sevenster, p. 146. The figures are 78 to 97. Newer finds: B. Lifschitz, 'Jérusalem sons la domination romaine', *Aufstieg und Niedergang* etc. 8. 2 (1977), pp. 457–8.

[33] Certainly, it was a mark of status to have an impressive family tomb. For example, Joseph of Arimathea, who was a councillor and a well-off man in Jerusalem, laid Jesus in his own new tomb (Matth. 27.57–60; Mark 15.43–7).

Thus, in the Roman period, it was necessary to know Greek to communicate with the procurator. We shall now see that this was an important factor in encouraging knowledge of Greek, to a certain level, among Palestinian Jews.

Here, evidence from the post-70 period is valuable. Although the use of Greek in Palestine increased as this period went on, and although Jerusalem had ceased to be the centre of religious and cultural life, still we shall find that the discussions in Rabbinic sources help us to perceive the complexity of Jewish attitudes to the Greek language and to Greek culture. And it is natural that observations of a later stage in the evolution of a situation should cast light on its earlier stages.

The Greek world around them created a problem for the Rabbis. Utterances quoted in the Mishnah, Tosefta and the two Talmuds show that, on the one hand, the usefulness, or even the necessity, to some people of mastering the language was appreciated, but that, on the other, there was considerable unease, both about the undesirable ends to which easy access to Greeks and Romans might lead, and about the dangerous seductiveness of Greek culture. It was clearly seen that knowledge of Greek had political implications. Tradition had it that there had been bans on the teaching of Greek at times of hostility between Judaea and Rome. One such ban was associated, in the Babylonian Talmud, with the period of the earliest direct contact between the two nations, Pompeius' siege of Jerusalem, and the accompanying civil war of 63 B.C. (*TB Sotah* 59b; *Menahot* 64b; *Baba Kamma* 82b) Another, mentioned already in the Mishnah, was put during either the 'war of Titus' (the first revolt) or that of 'Quietus' (the disturbances under Trajan), depending upon the textual reading.[34] Even if we are inclined to feel that the claims of actual prohibitions are too vague or implausible to gain acceptance, they must at least embody a real recollection of the mood in Palestine at crisis periods—for why, and how, should the story have been fabricated out of nothing? That the coins of both the first revolt and the Hadrianic revolt were in Hebrew shows that to use, or abstain from using, a particular language could be in itself a political statement.

[34] *M Sotah* 9, 14. The Cambridge manuscript, which appears to read 'Quietus' against the others, is generally followed, and is preferable, because the preceding sentence is about the 'War of Vespasian', so that a new war should be in question now. On the supposed bans, see Fischel in *Enc. Jud.* (1972), vol. 7, p. 884ff.

Greek, of course, continued in use. If there were formal bans, they cannot have bitten deep or lasted long. The Talmudic scholars themselves seem to have been puzzled, and asked what the bans can really have been. They produced would-be solutions, which, again, do not appear to have been evolved in total ignorance of the conditions of an earlier age. Thus, the Jerusalem Talmud gives a quotation in the name of a second- to third-century Rabbi,[35] where it is maintained that Greek had been banned only in order to prevent the operations of traitors and informers, in other words only in a limited context: that was why it was still permitted to teach one's daughter Greek—for her it was no more than an ornament. Greek had to be kept away from public life. At the same time, an elucidation in the Tosefta, which recurs in the Babylonian Talmud,[36] tends in the opposite direction and suggests an understanding that it was precisely in governing circles that Greek, in normal circumstances, was indispensable, and justified. Therefore the teaching of Greek was allowed in the household of Rabban Gamaliel, the Patriarch (head of the Sanhedrin and of the Palestinian community), 'because they were associated with the ruling power'.

A different distinction is also attempted in the same passage of the Babylonian Talmud. This is a distinction between the study of the Greek language and that of 'Greek wisdom'. The reasoning behind it seems to be that, since the use of the Greek language was patently never excluded from Palestine, it must have been 'Greek wisdom' which was banned. The proposal does not really get off the ground in its particular context of argument, for it makes nonsense of an implied identity in the previous part of the narrative between the expression 'Greek wisdom' and Greek as a spoken language,[37] and it also comes up against the counter-example of Rabban Gamaliel, in whose house it is explicitly stated that 'Greek wisdom' *was* studied.[38] None the less, it is an interesting analysis, for it points to another significant aspect of the Palestinian situation.

[35] *TJ Peah* 1. 1; *Shabbat* 6. 1; *Sotah* 9. 15. Quotation in the name of R. Johanan (ben Nappaha).

[36] *Tos. Sotah* 15. 8; *TB Sotah* 49b (with a few differences in wording).

[37] Where it is said that 'an old man there, who was learned in Greek wisdom, spoke to them in Greek wisdom'. This can hardly mean that the old man used sophistry on them (he gave them down-to-earth practical advice); nor that he spoke to them as a Hellenizer.

[38] Or taught, in the Palestinian tradition. See E. E. Hallewy, 'Concerning the ban on Greek wisdom', *Tarbiz* 41 (1972), pp. 269–75 (Hebrew). There were said to be 500 pupils, while 500 others studied Torah: but the figures look like a schematization.

While the speaking of Greek, however undesirable or politically hazardous it might sometimes seem, was a fact of life, it was an immersion in Greek ideas which was really challenging. The ultimate possibility of such immersion is what was surely implied by the teaching of Greek: a basic, everyday use of the language would not even have been taught, but simply acquired from the environment. Formal instruction would be aiming at a much higher level of knowledge, and could detach men from Judaism. That is the fear which underlies the widely-quoted question and answer[39] in which the claim of the Torah as against Greek literature is assessed: 'Ben Dama the son of R. Ishmael's sister asked R. Ishmael: "Is a man like me who has mastered the whole Torah allowed to study Greek wisdom?" R. Ishmael applied the verse in Joshua [1; 8] to him . . . "Thou shalt meditate thereon day and night". "Go and find a time when it is neither day nor night and study Greek wisdom".' Here the fundamental incompatibility of two different ways of life and systems of thought is asserted.

The consequences of involvement in 'Greek wisdom' were exemplified, according to one account, in the story of that most famous of apostates, Elisha ben Avuyah. He had been brought up in pre-70 Jerusalem by well-respected parents. Various explanations were given for his apostasy, and one seems to have been that it had been caused by an excessive devotion to Greek culture. He was known as 'Aher'—'the Other, the Different One', and they said of him that 'Greek songs never left his mouth'.[40]

Elisha was exceptional. In the third century, Origen could still say that knowledge of Greek literature was rare among Jews (*Contra Cels.* 2.34). The distinguished work of Saul Lieberman on Greek and on Hellenism in Jewish Palestine[41] is readily susceptible of misinterpretation: it need not, and must not, be taken as demonstrating that pious Jews made a habit of immersing themselves in Greek literary scholarship and logic. In fact, Lieberman himself is very cautious and scrupulous in the inference he draws from Greek words and Greek modes of argument in Rabbinic literature. In his

[39] *Tos. Avodah Zarah* 1. 20 (p. 461, Zuckermandel); *TB Menahot* 99b. See Hallewy, loc. cit. for a discussion of its precise implications.

[40] The point here must be that the songs were Greek, not simply songs. See Soncino transl., n. *ad loc.*, p. 100. Other explanations were offered; in particular, that the apostasy arose out of dabbling in mystical speculation. See *Enc. Jud.*, s.v. Elisha ben Avuya.

[41] *Greek in Jewish Palestine* (1942), and *Hellenism in Jewish Palestine* (1950).

first book he tries to distinguish and name the small minority of exceptional Rabbis who, living in Hellenized towns, had the ability and the breadth of vision to immerse themselves in two cultures at once.[42] In his work on 'Hellenism', he both insists that similarities in methodology between the Rabbis and Greek scholars may be coincidental, and admits that such things may simply seep from one culture to another, and that many phenomena were common to the whole Mediterranean world at any given moment.[43] What is put beyond doubt by the knowledge which some Rabbis demonstrate, as well as by the story of Elisha ben Avuyah, is that Greek authors could be obtained and read in Palestine, by those who so desired. There was social and official pressure to discourage these people, but nothing else stood in their way.

Elisha's Greek formation may not have begun until 70. Are we to read the same attitudes and the same possibilities back into pre-70 Jerusalem? Certainly, the evidence about Josephus has suggested that for him, as for subsequent generations, the Greek language was necessary first and foremost because of its value in fostering good relations between Judaea and Rome. Again, for him there was that same gap between familiarity with the Greek language, which he had, and knowledge of Greek literature, which he lacked until he went to Rome, as the Rabbis ascribed to a later period. The main difference seems to be that it was somewhat harder for a man to acquaint himself with Greek culture, if he so wished, in first-century A.D. Jerusalem than in the more Hellenized cities of Palestine at a slightly later date. Some Greek books must have been available in Josephus' Jerusalem, since, as we have seen, potential readers existed, but there can have been few people, if any, possessed of serious scholarship and capable of imparting deeper knowledge of things Greek. Nicolaus of Damascus travelled much, partly in the service of Herod, and probably spent very little time among the Jews of Jerusalem.[44] It has been conjectured that Herod possessed a large library of Greek books;[45] but there is no

---

[42] Especially, 'The Greek of the Rabbis', pp. 15–29. cf. Lieberman's conclusions in 'How much Greek in Jewish Palestine?', *Studies and Texts, Philip W. Lown Institute of Advanced Judaic Studies*, vol. I (1963) pp. 123–42, that the Rabbis as a group knew just enough of the Greek world to avoid gross misapprehension—rather more than the pagan world knew of the Jewish.

[43] Especially pp. 19, 26f., 37, 99.

[44] For his travels, see *AJ* 12. 126–7; 16. 18–20, 29–58; 16. 299, 333; 17. 54, 219.

[45] So Otto in *RE* Suppl. 2, 105; Schalit, *König Herodes* (1969), p. 413; B. Z. Wacholder, *Nicolaus of Damascus* (1962), appx.

evidence to support this conjecture, and it is patently unreasonable to imagine that Nicolaus would have depended upon the books in his master's library for the allusions and citations with which he decorated his prose.[46] Nicolaus was a man who came to Herod from outside Palestine; this in itself makes a difference; and the suspicion arises that, in general, the Hellenistic culture of the Herodian court was not of a very high level. Agrippa II's secretary, and perhaps historian, was Justus of Tiberias—a man who prided himself upon the quality of his Greek oratory; but the very fact that this expertise was mentioned by Josephus means that such things did not come altogether naturally in his milieu. As for Justus' literary efforts, the evidence does not suggest that they amounted to much.[47]

Whether or not this assessment is correct, there is no reason to believe that Josephus was inclined, in his Jerusalem days, to gravitate towards those restricted circles in which Greek literature might be admired. We should, I think, consider it probable that he had not read any of the Classical Greek authors before he went to Rome. There would have been plenty of time to do this during the second part of his life.

We are now in a better position to understand the role of the assistants mentioned by Josephus as participating in the writing of the *War*. He did not leave Jerusalem equipped to compose the *Jewish War* in Greek. At the same time, as we shall discover, he was not to publish the work until after A.D. 75, when he had been in close proximity to Greeks and Romans for some eight years—in the Roman camp, with Titus in Alexandria, with the Roman army before Jerusalem, and, finally, in Rome itself for half a decade (see p. 195; *CA* 1.48–50). Since, as he tells us, he had begun to take notes with a future history in mind while still a prisoner, he would surely have begun to prepare himself in other ways as well. If he was already a Greek speaker, his task would not have been an intolerably hard one. Moreover, he was to take his time, writing an account of the war in his own language first. It would be rash, therefore, to suppose that he would not be fit, when eventually he came to the Greek *War*, at the very least to collaborate fruitfully with his assistants, and to take the ultimate responsibility for sub-

---

[46] Thus Wacholder reconstructs the library by listing everything which Nicolaus can be shown to have read.

[47] On Justus' oratory, see *V* 40. On his writings, T. Rajak, 'Justus of Tiberias', *CQ* 23 (1973), parts 3, 4 and 5.

stance and style alike. The task of composition required self-education, and some temerity; but was not at all impossible. We would not wish to deprive the assistants of all credit. But, rather than paid employees, they may well have been friends or acquaintances, to whom Josephus sent or showed parts of his work, during the different stages in its composition.[48] This would actually explain rather well why he goes out of his way to make an honourable mention (albeit an anonymous one) of the assistance received. Moreover, that portions of the uncompleted book were circulated by the author is put beyond doubt by two letters which he quotes in his *Life* out of the sixty-two which King Agrippa had sent to him about it (*V* 364–6). In that instance, the recipient seems to have been interested principally in the subject matter; others would have read for style. We think of Cicero, receiving from his friend Atticus a simple account composed by Atticus on the subject of the consulship which meant so much to the orator, sending his own, more worked-out one to a certain L. Cossinius (who then showed it to Atticus), but saying that he would not have dared send this to Atticus himself without doing more work on it; and, finally, asking the famous scholar Posidonius to make a still more elaborate rendering (*Att.* 2.1.1–2). In this way, the final product would have evolved out of many journeys by messengers and much mutual assistance. Nevertheless, one author or another would have taken the final responsibility for form and content, in each case. Or, again, we think of the younger Pliny telling us that it was customary for authors to give readings from their productions before invited audiences in order to gather useful criticisms and be able to insert corrections before the final version was issued, and that he himself went so far as to do the same with his speeches (*Ep.* 7.17).

It is quite safe to take Josephus' works, starting with the first, the *War*,[49] as his own, and to treat him in exactly the same way as we do other ancient writers. It is as well to dispel all fantastic notions of ghost writers at this early stage.

In one sense, it would be true to say that Josephus the writer

---

[48] Cf. G. Schmidt, *de Flavii Josephi elocutione observationes criticae*, vol. 1 (Diss. Göttingen; Leipzig, 1893), p. 26.

[49] As for the *Antiquities*, no assistants are mentioned there. It is, however, in connection with that work, that Thackeray believed he could detect their operations, through an analysis of stylistic irregularities. If this were justified, there would be reason to assign to such writers a significant role in the *War*, too. But see Appendix 2 on the fallacies in these internal arguments.

was a product of Palestinian Hellenism: his settling in Rome and there becoming a Greek writer was the final point on a path which he had begun to tread when he became a pro-Roman politician in Jerusalem. The perpetual, if remote, allure of things Greek for Palestinian Jewry will have been a contributory factor in leading him eventually to Greek literature. And it was because he came from a milieu to which the language was by no means strange that he was able quite quickly to learn to write history in it.

At the same time, there would always be a difference, not so much in basic linguistic ability as in culture, between Josephus and a Greek-educated pagan. The fact that he still found it necessary, towards the end of his life, to define his relationship to the language of his adoption, is in itself revealing of the gap. And he came, as he said, from a people which, in the end, could fully endorse only the contemplation of its own law. Most of those with whom he had associated in Judaea would probably not have approved of his travelling as far as he did along a dangerous path. And he himself, unlike the Jew from Asia Minor whom Aristotle was said to have met, would never wish to become truly 'Greek in his soul'.[50]

---

[50] See *CA* 1.180, taken from Clearchus of Soli = Stern, *Greek and Latin Authors* etc. (see p. 49, n. 5), vol. I (1974), no. 15.

CHAPTER THREE

Josephus' Account of the Breakdown of Consensus

Josephus' embassy to Rome in A.D. 64 was in itself successful; all the more so as he was able to take back to Jerusalem substantial gifts which the empress Poppaea had given him. But his satisfaction, no doubt considerable, was short-lived, for he found his fellow Jews on the verge of revolt against Rome (*V* 17).

Poppaea died and was embalmed during A.D. 65 (Tac. *Ann.* 16.6), so perhaps Josephus' return was not quite as dramatically close as he suggests to the actual incidents, occurring in mid-66 (*BJ* 2.315), which constituted the outbreak of the revolt. But there are few precise indications of time in the summary sections of the *Life*, where he tells of this; and, since Florus seems to have provoked a Jewish outcry by Passover 65 (*BJ* 2.280), what Josephus says can have been in essence true: by the time he arrived, a real break with Rome seemed imminent.

Josephus is eloquent about the avaricious and cruel decisions adopted between 64 and 66 by the Roman procurator Gessius Florus (see pp. 72–5), and what distresses him almost as much as executions and crucifixions is the impact these onslaughts had on the loyalist Jewish élite. Their role became increasingly untenable, and Florus' contempt for their intercession lost them what control they still had over their own people. Josephus, in his narrative, expands on this very theme. For a working relationship between the Jewish ruling class and the Romans was the framework within which Josephus had learnt to operate, and now it was patently in ruins. The extent of the damage will have struck him immediately. And his whole account of the lead-up to the revolt may in fact be seen as a description of the ups and downs of that political relationship.

Admittedly the narratives about the procuratorial period in Palestine, one in the *War* and a second, not dissimilar, in the *Antiquities*, are the products of hindsight; and we shall discover later the contexts in which they were written. But while it is clear that these accounts cannot therefore be taken to reflect accurately Josephus' opinions of the pre-war and war period, they are formed by that experience: prima facie, that would seem to be likely, and our study will show it to be true. For a beginning, we must see what he writes; and on the subject of the origins of the revolt, what is said in the *Antiquities*, even though it is embedded in other material, complements the *War*. The narrative in the former is generally fuller and factually a little different though not contradictory; it suggests that Josephus made a new investigation, but the view that he evolved a second, different interpretation of the procuratorial period is untenable.[1]

Josephus has no doubts about the difference between a good procurator (or prefect, as they were earlier called), and a bad one; and in the sixty years between the removal of Archelaus, Herod's successor in Judaea, and the outbreak of the Jewish revolt, he found a very few examples of ones who were tolerable, a majority who were not, and a deterioration towards the end. Procuratorial rule as such is not criticised and was not unacceptable to him. A satisfactory procurator kept the country in order, maintaining a tight control over Jewish dissidents of all kinds—brigands, violent religious extremists, prophets with a mass following and other such. He left the Temple and the cult strictly alone. He ensured that no offence to the Jewish religion emanated from his staff, or from the local Syrian-Greeks who were the Jews' neighbours and rivals in many places, and who constituted the bulk of the Roman auxiliary troops.[2] But above all he devolved responsibility on the high priests and the 'notables' (see p. 40) of the towns, and did not come into any conflict with them. These opinions, never systematically set out, are built into Josephus' episodic narratives about the procurators. The episodes which constitute those narratives have the marks of being derived from local oral tradition—presumably from

---

[1] On hindsight cf. D. M. Rhoads, *Israel in Revolution* (1976), p. 164. The attempt to trace a 'new apologetic theory' in the later Josephus is made by S. J. D. Cohen, *Josephus in Galilee and Rome* (1979), pp. 154–9; but the claim that Josephus is harder on the procurators in the *Antiquities* founders, as Cohen himself admits, on the case of Albinus. He also overestimates Josephus' benevolence to Felix in the *War* (see the criticism at *BJ* 2. 270), and wrongly claims that *AJ* ignores the respect shown by Cuspius Fadus for Jewish custom (see *AJ* 20. 13ff., on custody of the high priest's vestments: it is just that in *AJ* Josephus knows more about the incident, and knows that the credit was not really due to the procurator but to Claudius).

[2] Schürer-Vermes-Millar, vol. 1, pp. 363–4.

hearsay evidence provided by older colleagues, and in times past, by still older colleagues to them. As for Josephus' own memory, that will not have covered much more than a quarter of the period in question. At the same time, these assumptions about what was expected of a procurator form an integral and unquestioned part of his own approach.

In fact, on the subject of the prefects in Judaea between A.D.6 and 26 when Pilate arrived, Josephus could obtain no information whatsoever; the *War* account does not even contain their names; the *Antiquities* has just names and nothing else, except when high priests were deposed or appointed by Valerius Gratus.

Pontius Pilate was remembered quite distinctly, since there had been four disruptions during his ten years, of which three were known to Josephus. But even here it is interesting that Josephus' information is fragmentary, and the fourth of those conflicts is described only by the contemporary Philo.[3] We could also mention the Crucifixion as a fifth disturbance, virtually unknown to Josephus; for the passage in the *Antiquities* about Jesus could be wholly a Christian interpolation into the text, and, in any case, it has almost nothing to say about the incident itself (*AJ* 18.62–4; cf. p. 131, n. 73). The troubles which occurred under Pilate are seen as having arisen from one simple cause—the prefect's flouting of Jewish religious sentiment; and Josephus does not speculate on Pilate's intentions. On the whole, the historian seems to sympathise with the strong Jewish response to this provocation; yet he is not as indignant about Pilate as about subsequent procurators, who insult not only the Law, but the Jewish ruling group, when the latter presents itself as defender of the Law. In connection with Pilate, the high priests and notables do not come in, and it is ordinary Jews *en masse* who are said to confront him on each occasion. What is more, the first occasion may have caused real offence only to religious extremists. Pilate moved troops to winter quarters in Jerusalem, and they took with them military standards which carried, Josephus says, portrait busts of the emperor. In one version, he maintains that Jewish law altogether forbade image-making, in the other the point is that images were not allowed in the Holy City, and this vagueness surely suggests a lack of conviction on the author's part. Crowds mobbed Pilate in the amphitheatre at Caesarea. He is said

---

[3] Philo, *Legatio* 38. 299–306; P. L. Maier, 'The episode of the golden Roman shields at Jerusalem, *HThR* 42 (1969), pp. 109–21.

to have been impressed by their fervour (a not uncommon motif in so apologetic a writer as Josephus), and he gave in—a satisfactory solution from Josephus' point of view (*BJ* 2.169–74; *AJ* 18.55–9).

The second major clash had a more unhappy outcome. Pilate's employment of Temple funds reserved for sacrifice, in the construction of an aqueduct supplying the Temple, led to the death at the hand of Roman troops both of part of the large and abusive mob which confronted Pilate in the amphitheatre at Caesarea, and of Jewish bystanders (*BJ* 2.175–7; *AJ* 18.62).

The Roman procurators of Judaea had full judicial powers,[4] and their operations within their area of control were as a rule subject only to the rulings of the emperor. But in a crisis the legate of the neighbouring and much larger province of Syria was to intervene.[5] The legates, men of consular standing and of more distinguished and often more Roman origins than the procurators, inclined to a more confident and better rapport with the Jewish upper classes. Vitellius, who got Pilate sent back to give an account of himself to Tiberius, is recorded with approbation by Josephus as having agreed to restore to the Jews the right to look after their own high priests' garments, 'guided by our law' (*AJ* 18.93). If proof be needed that Josephus was impressed, it can be found in the fact that he had already described the changeover once in his *Antiquities*, mentioning on the first occasion (*AJ* 15.404), as he does on the second, how well the governor had been received by the Jews, so that his gesture was in a way a response to (aristocratic) kindness. In relation to the extraordinary emperor Gaius (Caligula), who virtually caused the Jews to revolt already in A.D.40 by insisting on having his statue worshipped in the Temple at Jerusalem, there was one heartening development for the historian Josephus. This was that the legate Petronius conferred repeatedly with the notables and with the people, and had finally decided to disobey Gaius, just before the latter's death fortuitously saved the situation. Philo, who was contemporary with the events and involved in them as an emissary from Alexandrian Jews to Rome, gives a significantly different slant: Petronius is much more torn from the beginning and inclined to prevaricate even before he sends for the high priests and the magistrates. What is more, and quite remarkably, he is himself said to

---

[4] A. H. M. Jones, 'Procurators and prefects in the early principate', *Studies in Roman Government and Law*, (1960), pp. 117–25.

[5] Schürer-Vermes-Millar, vol. 1, p. 360.

be a connoisseur of Judaism, either through an early enthusiasm or through his experience as a governor in Asia and Syria. The influence of the Jewish delegation to the legate also plays a part, but a less decisive one.[6]

The first procurator after the brief interlude of a Herodian client king, Agrippa I, was Cuspius Fadus (A.D.44–*c*.46), sent by Claudius. He is admired by Josephus for ridding the country of bandits, and in the *Antiquities* is registered as more or less satisfactory because he at least showed himself responsive when the high priests objected to his suggestion that the Romans resume control of their vestments. Along with the governor of Syria, he allowed them to send a delegation to Claudius, and a letter favourable to the Jewish case was the result (*BJ* 2.220; *AJ* 20.6–9).

Josephus found reason to be satisfied also with the following two years, the procuratorship of the renegade Alexandrian Jew Tiberius Julius Alexander, during which time there was no interference with local custom, and peace was maintained. This was good, even though he could not personally approve of the man's apostasy (*BJ* 2.220; *AJ* 20.100–104). In reality, the period was evidently an extremely difficult and disturbed one, a time of acute famine (cf. Acts 11.29–30) and of the crucifixion of Jewish rebels. But Josephus does not regard it as crucial in the prelude to revolt, and that not only because—as is evidently the case—he knew little about it, but also, quite clearly, because the procurator retained control, and disciplined the right kind of Jew, without antagonising the wrong ones.

But the era of the next five procurators (48–66) could not, as a whole, be regarded with equanimity. Josephus severely castigates three of them. Of these, Ventidius Cumanus receives a relatively lengthy report in both versions (*BJ* 2.223–46; *AJ* 20.105–36). Perhaps this is due partly to the Herodian client king of the time, Agrippa II (controller of neighbouring areas), who was at one time involved in pressing Claudius to bring Cumanus to trial and was in close touch with Josephus (*AJ* 20.135). But we are still presented with a series of episodes of crisis, just as in the case of Pilate. Cumanus is even less able than Pilate to control the situation, and here again the procuratorship is terminated by the intervention of

---

[6] *BJ* 2. 192–204; *AJ* 18. 261–83; Philo, *Legatio* 209–53, and see especially 210–17; 245, cf. F. Millar, *The Emperor in the Roman World* (1977), p. 377. Josephus does not seem to have read the Philo account, for if he had he would surely have mentioned, at least in the *Antiquities*, the Jewish tendencies of the Roman administrator.

a more capable legate of Syria, Ummidius Quadratus, who refers back to the emperor. This time, however, we have been shown the spectacle of the Jewish leaders anxiously striving to impress their influence on both sides: to make the procurator realise that native hotheads could only be pacified if offences against their religion were seen to be adequately punished, and at the same time to curb Jewish tempers with warnings and argument (*BJ* 2. 233, 237; *AJ* 20.119, 121, 123). There was still, according to Josephus' interpretation, some possibility at this time of compromise succeeding. The first incident, arising from an obscene gesture by a Syrian soldier, resulted in Jews being crushed to death in a stampede; but the second, which sprang from the burning of a scroll of the Law by the military, ended with Cumanus backing down and executing a guilty soldier. Josephus says that the Jews reacted as though their whole country had been consigned to the flames, thus showing that his sympathy for his pious compatriots had its limits. The third incident was the most substantial, and armed conflict between members of two volatile groups, Samaritans and Galilean Jews, and it was here that the high priests and notables urged moderation on the latter, as well as justice on the Romans. That Quadratus executed eighteen militant Jews does not seem to displease Josephus, and he is satisfied that in Rome the Jewish high priests and notables secured a favourable judgment from Claudius. Samaritans were put to death, Cumanus banished, and a Roman soldier (it is not explained who he was) sentenced to the Homeric punishment of being dragged around the walls of Jerusalem, before being killed.

According to Josephus, Cumanus' successor was the notorious freedman Antonius Felix, brother of Claudius' wealthy and hated accountant Pallas. We can hardly supplant this clear sequence with Tacitus' odd report that Cumanus and Felix were procurators side-by-side, in Galilee and Samaria respectively.[7] Brigandage greatly increased under Felix—a phenomenon to which we shall return. But Josephus' report of this administration is not totally negative, and he by no means shares Tacitus' detestation of Felix. There is an interesting suggestion, found in the *Antiquities* alone, that the high priest Jonathan had asked for the freedman to be sent out as procurator, and this implies a surprising level of rapport between Jewish officials and the emperor. But Jonathan overplayed his hand by constantly nagging Felix to improve his performance,

---

[7] Tac. *Ann.* 12. 54. See Schürer-Vermes-Millar, vol. 1, pp. 459–60, n. 15.

and the same *Antiquities* version has it that the Jewish 'knifemen' (*sicarii*) who assassinated the high priest were put up to it by the procurator (*BJ* 2.247–70; *AJ* 20.160–81).

Josephus does not blame Felix for the mushrooming of banditry, political assassination, militant prophets and other inciters of revolt during his procuratorship, and here again he treats in a dispassionate or even approving way the procurator's assault, with a large military detachment, on a charismatic leader and his mass following, all of them probably unarmed.

At Caesarea, a Hellenized foundation of Herod the Great, and now the Roman administrative capital for Judaea, Jews and Greeks fell at about this time into a dispute which was in a few years to prove one of the contributory causes of the great revolt. Felix's way of handling a sensitive issue of this kind, with empire-wide implications,[8] was simply to set his soldiers on to the Jews. It is in the *War* that Josephus makes the highly pertinent observation that those soldiers were themselves largely levied from the local population, and thus were the Jews' traditional enemies. So it was no wonder that not only a number of Jewish deaths, but also extensive plunder and pillage were the result. This was intolerable, but the procurator to some extent redeemed himself by withdrawing the military at the request of Jewish moderates (so the *Antiquities*); no doubt the latter were the same officials who had previously tried and failed to control their own disorderly people by means of various forms of coercion (so the *War*). Following a by now established pattern, representative of both sides in the conflict were sent to Rome (*Antiquities*). And the *Antiquities* account of this procuratorship ends with the disgruntled statement that subsequent Jewish accusations against Felix only failed because of the protection afforded him by his brother Pallas. In general, then, the gulf between respectable Jews and Rome is seen by Josephus to be widening.

The *War* knows nothing about Felix's successor Porcius Festus except that he rounded up many 'brigands'. The *Antiquities* mentions also a military attack on an unnamed salvation-monger, bringing about the deaths of the man and his followers. Festus did allow prominent Jerusalemites to send a delegation of ten men to Nero, in order to register a protest about the Jewish client king Agrippa, who had built an annex to his palace giving him an overview of the

---

[8] Bad relations between Jews and the Hellenized native pagan population were an endemic problem in the Greek cities of the East.

Temple; but this was only after failing to get the Jewish authorities to give way to Agrippa, and to knock down a wall built by them to block the controversial view (*BJ* 2.271; *AJ* 20.185–96). So again the Jewish leaders are shown in trouble, having to go to enormous lengths to make any impact on the situation, all the more so in this case because they are, unusually, at odds with their natural Herodian ally.

Festus was also the procurator who sent Saint Paul to be tried at Rome. This is not alluded to by Josephus, and it may have made little impression on non-Christian contemporaries at the time (Acts 24–6).

The last two procurators are conceived of as men of unparalleled and almost incredible wickedness. This is perhaps natural, since they directly preceded the revolt, and the opinion probably does arise at least in part from analysis *post eventum*. The *War* sketch of Albinus leaves us somewhat at a loss to understand precisely what changes he introduced, let alone why he introduced them. There is a general charge of public rapacity and excessive taxation—but we have little idea what levies are being referred to. None the less, the most substantial allegations, which fit in with those made in the *Antiquities*, are highly germane to our theme. Albinus was too soft on dissidents, releasing many from prison (so as to profit from the ransom money, it is said), and allowing bands of them to roam freely and attack property. A prophet of doom, one Jesus son of Ananias, was also set free by Albinus after scourging and interrogation. The two new developments which are ascribed to this policy are the political kidnapping of members of the high priests' staffs with its strikingly modern overtones—and faction fighting among the notables, with violence inflicted on ordinary priests by the high priests' thugs.[9] In keeping with its general character, the *Antiquities* narrative gives, among other miscellaneous material, additional information on appointments and substitutions of high priests, and breaks off after this section to give a history of the high priesthood (*AJ* 20.224).

This produces a timely break before the culmination of the narrative with a procurator so bad that he made Albinus seem a saint. It is noteworthy that Tacitus too seems to have condemned him (*Hist.* 5.10). Josephus' rhetoric once again makes it difficult for us

---

[9] *BJ* 2. 272–6; *AJ* 20. 197–215. The most brutal was the high priest Ananias; cf. p. 125, n. 57.

to ascertain much of the actual character of Gessius Florus' administration. Again, collusion with brigands is mentioned, and Florus'
rapacity and cruelty are described in a huge overstatement—'he
stripped whole cities and wrecked entire nations'. The reference
here is no doubt mainly to the removal of seventeen talents from
the Temple treasury, according to Florus for administrative purposes, and according to modern suggestions a legitimate way of
recovering arrears of tribute. But his avarice must have seemed
grotesque, for it evoked a splendid satirical response, when some of
the more impertinent Jews passed a collection basket round on his
behalf. We can hardly believe the statement in the *War* that Florus
made a declaration announcing freedom for anyone who wished to
become a brigand; yet that is the perception of Josephus, and no
doubt also of his peers and contemporaries, whose battle against
the rebels was now obviously collapsing for lack of any support with
military muscle behind it. At the end of the *Antiquities*, Josephus
concluded that Florus had forced the Jews to make war on Rome—
and that is his last word on the subject. It must be taken in the
context of the whole nexus of circumstances he has described, not
as an ascription of monolithic causation. It cannot be pressed any
more than can Thucydides' similarly worded and much-debated
assertion that Athens, by instilling fear of her growing power into
Sparta, 'compelled' her adversary to start the Peloponnesian War
(1.23.6). However, it was Florus' failure to control the disorders
among the Jews, and his provocations to those who wished to be
his allies, which brought about a war which in Josephus' view,
could have been avoided up to the last minute.

The sequence of events which was the immediate cause of the
revolt of A.D.66 is presented by Josephus in the *War* in vivid detail
(*BJ* 2.284–555). A rescript arrives from Nero to the disputing parties
at Caesarea which gives control of the city to the Greeks and
provokes a new confrontation between the two communities, centred
on a Greek building constructed beside a synagogue; Florus makes
free with the Temple treasury, backing up this action with military
intimidation: his soldiers run amok in Jerusalem; he rejects an
apology from the Jewish leaders and for some reason scourges and
crucifies Jews, who are Roman citizens, and are described (perhaps
loosely) by Josephus as being of equestrian status; Queen Berenice,
visiting Jerusalem, supplicates Florus barefoot, and the high priests
and leaders of the Jews rend their garments in front of him and in

front of their own extremists; they entreat the latter; two cohorts (either one or two thousand men, we must suppose) rush the crowds in Jerusalem; Jews destroy porticoes adjoining the Antonia fortress where Roman troops were housed when in Jerusalem; the legate of Syria, Cestius Gallus, is invoked by all parties, and a tribune conducts an enquiry on his behalf and shows his respect by praying in the Temple before his departure; when the people demand of the Jewish leaders an embassy to Nero which could denounce Florus (even to be allowed to send an embassy was not an automatic right) Agrippa II makes his famous attempt at pacification, a long speech centred on an exposition of Rome's might and the Jews' weakness; the people momentarily follow his advice, but then throw him out of the city; a youthful priestly group, in spite of desperate appeals from the high priests and leaders, refuses to continue the customary sacrifices made in the Temple on behalf of Rome; the leaders unite with Agrippa to invite Cestius Gallus in to control the crowds. After this, civil war proper commences in Jerusalem. A sequence of further developments completes the precipitous plunge into war against Rome. A Roman garrison is surrounded by rebels, capitulates under agreed terms, but is none the less massacred to a man, with the exception only of the commander, who is allowed to be circumcised instead. Greeks, no doubt emboldened by the prevailing atmosphere of disturbance, set upon Jews in many Greek cities of Syria and in Alexandria; this, in turn, further embitters the Jews in Palestine. Cestius Gallus brings the twelfth legion and additional troops down from Antioch. However, in spite of easy success in leading his men from camp on Mount Scopus up to the upper city and into position for an assault on the Temple, an abrupt and still inexplicable withdrawal leads to defeat at Beth-horon, a steep defile in the Judaean hills known as the scene of many great military reversals, and especially Judas Maccabaeus' victory against Seron. A supply problem, and the prospect of winter, may be the explanation.

Cestius then left Judaea. His volte-face had, in Josephus' eyes, been crucial: 'had he . . . continued for a short while with the siege, he would have captured the city on the spot.'[10]

---

[10] *BJ* 2. 539. Cf. the implication of 2. 334, that Cestius could have gone into Jerusalem at an earlier stage in the proceedings, and maintained order. On military aspects of the withdrawal, B. Bar-Kochva, 'Seron and Cestius Gallus at Beith Horon', *PEQ* 107 (1976), pp. 13–21; M. Gichon, 'Cestius Gallus' campaign in Judaea', *PEQ* 1981, pp. 361–2.

Certainly, the rebellion was now understood to be on. Some notables had already departed but now many distinguished Jews left the city, 'as though a sinking ship'; and the remaining pro-Romans were brought by force or persuasion to assist the revolt which they could not prevent. In the circumstances, much persuasion is hardly likely to have been necessary. Josephus was one of this group, who were soon to purchase for themselves a brief extension of their discredited authority, and (in some cases a less brief one) of their lives, by putting their experience, and perhaps also their resources, at the disposal of the rebels. Before long he was to become commander of Galilee in revolt, that post of which his controversial tenure was to provide him with a long-lived notoriety.[11]

This crowded narrative of Florus' procuratorship presents the immediate antecedents of the Jewish revolt in the same way as the episodes of Potidaea and Epidamnus did for Thucydides. As far as this level of explanation goes, Josephus' documentation of these final stages cannot be faulted.

As a historian, he is in fact in an unusually privileged position, for his knowledge of the crisis is to a great extent that of an eye-witness, or else, where he was not physically present, derived from the evidence of eye-witnesses. One such could have been Queen Berenice, who probably lived with Titus in Rome during much of the period when Josephus was writing the *Jewish War*, and he could hardly have missed her, since he was in contact both with her brother Agrippa II, who supplied him with information on other matters, and with the imperial court.[12] Eye-witness evidence carries its own problems, but as the ancients—and Josephus—were well aware, its advantages are undeniable.[13] Josephus knows what went on; and, as an explanation of a certain kind, his narrative speaks

---

[11] See also (from a different angle) pp. 128–30.

[12] It is reasonable to accept the implication of the epitome of Dio that Berenice was in Rome as Titus' mistress until her first dismissal before Vespasian's death in A.D.79: J. Crook, 'Titus and Berenice', *AJPh* 72 (1951), pp. 62–75. For Agrippa supplying Josephus with information, see *V* 362–6. *BJ* 2. 335 shows that Agrippa himself returned from Alexandria only quite late in the proceedings.

[13] Josephus' statements are at *BJ* 1. 1, 3, 18; *V* 358, 361; *CA* 1. 46. Among his predecessors, see especially Polybius 3. 4. 13; 12. 25 and 27; 20. 12. 8. Coming after Josephus, Lucian, *How to Write History*, 29 and 47. Discussion in G. Avenarius, *Lukians Schrift zur Geschichtsschreibung* (1954), pp. 73–7, and G. Nenci, 'Il motivo dell' autopsia nella storiografia greca'; *Studi Classici e Orientali* 3 (1953), pp. 14–46. Cf. also Luke 1.2.

clearly enough for itself. His own occasional comments are to the
effect that different behaviour on the part of any one of a number
of individuals could have nipped the trouble in the bud at any
stage.

   The inadequacy of most of the later procurators had been, for
Josephus, highly unfortunate, and yet something which the Jews
should have overlooked. Their viciousness is admitted in Agrippa's
long pacifying speech to the people, which, as we shall see, expresses
in large measure Josephus' sentiments. But Agrippa tells them that
this should not be allowed to push subjects into revolt, because
procurators come and go; and he explicitly makes the point that
the emperors are not behind the procurators' misdemeanours: the
ruler at Rome should not, it is argued, be held accountable, because
he cannot always keep in touch with the extremities of so far-flung
an empire. In keeping with this exhortation, Josephus, writing *in
propria persona*, finds fault with no emperor except Gaius. Even Nero,
of whose general deficiencies he is not unaware, is dissociated from
what was done by Florus; and, while it is true that, in the *Antiquities*,
his rescript against the Jews of Caesarea is said to have led to war,
the claim that his Greek secretary, who had been bribed, persuaded
him to issue it, serves as a kind of exoneration.[14] As long as the
emperor was not implicated, there was always a possibility of redress. In the course of the narratives we have surveyed, the occasions of this kind of intervention from above have indeed been
stressed by Josephus, who, after all, was himself a member of one
of the embassies sent to Rome in pursuit of it. In holding that the
emperor could normally keep the lid on a seething situation (even
if he could do nothing to improve it), Josephus was perhaps right;
for it was just at the time when Nero, shaken by a major conspiracy
in A.D.65, finally lost touch with Roman affairs and was, indeed,
disporting himself in Greece, that the revolt in Judaea broke out.[15]

   Our agreement with Josephus can extend even beyond this. While
it is clear to the outsider, operating at a great chronological and
geographical remove, that there are many deeper factors which
made an eruption in Judaea probable (see Chapter 4), the close

---

[14] Nero's evils: *BJ* 2. 250–1; *AJ* 20. 153ff. The rescript and the Greek secretary:
AJ 20. 183–4, Cohen, op. cit. (n. 1), p. 158, is misleading in saying that Nero is
condemned for favouring the Greeks who had bribed him.
[15] For parallel outbreaks, ancient and modern, see S. L. Dyson, 'Native revolts in
the Roman Empire', *Historia* 20 (1971), p. 273.

vantage point from which Josephus looks, even if sometimes blinding, can be an excellent place from which to pick out features of the landscape which might have ceased to be obvious today. It is largely because of Josephus that the miscreant procurators have become for us such familiar figures, as well as the conciliatory high priests with their entreaties. Almost without thinking, we tend to follow him in this basic point of interpretation; yet usually he is denied the credit for shaping an influential and valuable analysis. If we do give the matter some thought, whether or not we go along with Josephus in exonerating emperors or belabouring fanatics, we are impelled to accept his view that the inadequacy of the administration on the spot, whose character he knew so well and reacted to so strongly,[16] had a central role in precipitating trouble. It may with justification be said that, given the disposition of the Jewish militants, this turned a probability into reality. At the same time, one of the limitations of Josephus manifests itself in his being readier to offer open criticism of Roman procuratorial offences than of the faults of his own class, the Jewish notables. Here there is a need for correction; but the corrective, as we have seen and shall continue to see, also emerges from within Josephus' writings.

[16] See P. Gay, *Style in History* (1974), p. 198: 'I am not prepared to deny—how could I?—that the historian's mental set or secret emotions often cause partial blindness or involuntary distortions, but I would argue that they can also provide a historian with a clear view of past actions that other historians have been too ill-prepared to understand, too indifferent even to see . . . Passion, notorious as the historian's most crippling liability, may become his most valuable asset.'

CHAPTER FOUR

Josephus' Interpretation of the Jewish Revolt

Beyond the sequence of events which triggers off the outbreak of a war, ancient and modern interpreters alike have naturally conceived of underlying causes, even if these were of less pressing concern to the ancients than they are to us.[1] But since it was Josephus' view that co-existence between Judaea and Rome would have been quite feasible, he might be particularly disinclined to look beyond specific incidents to anything more fundamental. And that, on the whole is the case. His interpretation of the war, as far as he has one, is that a rift between Jews and Romans had been opened by bad governors and was widened by various criminal or reckless types among the Jews themselves, for their own ends, or out of their own madness. Leaders of various revolutionary factions misled the people, and took up arms. The inactivity of the established leadership made this possible; and a spirit of divisiveness and internal hostility to which the population was at this time prone, was the soil in which the revolutionaries flourished. An explanation of a limited kind thus emerges through the recital of events. But the social and political implications of this explanation have tended to be overlooked by Josephus' readers; and here I shall try to give them a more adequate emphasis.

Beneath this level, there is another. While the revolt may not have demanded extensive interpretation, what for a religious Jew most certainly did was the destruction of the Temple, for the second time in Jewish history. This cataclysmic happening reverberates through the *Jewish War*. It was necessary to make religious sense of it: Josephus' theory is Hellenized in its presentation, but is essentially Jewish, concerned with God's purpose for the world and his arrangements for the destiny of nations, and centred on a scheme

[1] A. D. Momigliano, 'Some observations on causes of war in ancient historiography', *Studies in Historiography* (1966), pp. 112–26.

of sin and punishment. On this aspect, scholarly attention has been lavished, for Josephus' works have traditionally been a hunting-ground for theologians. Yet his thinking even here has remained somewhat elusive, and will only be really intelligible when removed from isolation. For what is striking and even bold in Josephus is the very fact that he had introduced a distinctive Jewish interpretation into a political history which is fully Greek in form, juxtaposing the two approaches. In a way this foreshadows the idea behind his later work the *Antiquities*, which also, in its external features, follows a Greek tradition of historiography, while working out a Jewish idea of God and His Providence.

The various strands of Josephus' interpretation of the revolt fall into place, and make sense, when the simple point is understood that his opinions are, as is quite natural, the product of his position within Palestinian society, and that they are those of a partisan on one of the two sides in a violent civil conflict. The influence of Rome will, by contrast, seem peripheral. The interpretation created by Josephus cannot have been fully formed until after the revolt; obviously, it is only after 70 that he will have had to try to understand the fall of the Temple. But most of it is intimately related to what went before. Since it is on Josephus that we depend for our knowledge of the events themselves, we shall attend to what he says about them first, and only afterwards offer a modern assessment of what happened, and what part he played in it.

Josephus is the kind of author who likes to make his opinions explicit at frequent intervals. Indeed, he might be criticised for doing so to excess, weakening them with overemphasis. He is a highly emotive writer, as he more than once tells himself; and early on he justifies his adoption of a personal approach, admitting that it is foreign to the conventions of history, but protesting that he needs to express himself: 'the actions of both sides, I shall faithfully recount; but I shall add my own interpretations of the events to the narratives, allowing room for my personal feelings, and bewailing my country's tragedy.'[2] Note the insistence here that strong emotion does not disturb his capacity (also often expressed) to tell the truth and nothing but the truth. Such are the sentiments in his preface;

---

[2] *BJ* 1. 9. Cf. *V* 19, where he pulls back from lamentation, saying that the rules of historiography require a return to the narrative. H. Lindner, *Die Geschichtsauffassung des Flavius Josephus im Bellum Judaicum* (1972), pp. 132–41, fits Josephus' statement into the context of Old Testament lamentation. See also *V* 566.

and although there are conventional elements about the way Josephus presents himself there, the quoted sentence is, without doubt, among those which are individual enough to be taken seriously. For while prefaces in Greek historiography followed, up to a point, a set pattern in form and content, still most Greek historians were expected, within the given framework, to make important statements about the book they were presenting.[3] All Josephus' works, apart, as we would expect, from the *Life*, carry interesting and indeed striking prefaces which are not to be lightly dismissed.

Above all, it is the speeches ascribed to protagonists in the history which allow an ancient author to comment personally on events. Even so austere a writer as Thucydides, whatever his professed intentions were, used speeches not so much to report, or even to try to reconstruct what was actually said on specific occasions, as to present analyses of different political positions, and to generalise about human affairs.[4] In principle, what Josephus does is no different—the speeches are a vehicle for his thoughts.[5] However, his thoughts are of quite a different type and quality: emotion and prejudice are obviously involved; and what is most striking of all is that the overwhelming bulk of the speech material is an expression of a single cluster of sentiments, springing from a single essential position. Josephus stands out among surviving ancient historians in that he ascribes as many as three orations (of which two are major ones) to himself:[6] that alone is telling. It is also revealing that of the eight principal orations in the *Jewish War*, apart from the two of Josephus, three belong to his political allies—the high priests, Joshua and Ananus, and the king Agrippa II, and two more to the Roman, Titus: all these characters could consistently be made mouthpieces of some part of the author's views. Just one pair of imposing speeches is ascribed to the famous rebel leader of Masada, Eleazar ben Yaïr, and even he, as we shall see, is at moments

[3] Useful remarks on both Greek and Latin prefaces in T. Janson, *Latin Prose Prefaces* (1964), pp. 64–7. Examples in the first part of D. Earl's 'Prologue form in ancient historiography', in *Aufstieg und Niedergang der Römischen Welt* (ed. H. Temporini and W. Haase), 1.2 (1972), pp. 842–56.

[4] On speeches, G. Avenarius, *Lukians Schrift zur Geschichtsschreibung* (1956), pp. 149ff.; F. W. Walbank, *Speeches in Greek Historians* (Third J. L. Myres Memorial Lecture); T. P. Wiseman, *Clio's Cosmetics* (1979), pp. 28–30; and, for Thucydides, P. A. Stadter (ed.), *The Speeches in Thucydides* (1963).

[5] Stressed by H. Lindner, op. cit. (n. 2), p. 18ff., though with much over-simplification of the rôle of speeches in Thucydides etc.

[6] The most obvious parallel is Xenophon: see esp. *Anabasis*, book 3.

Josephus' mouthpiece.[7] In letting him speak, Josephus probably follows what was a tradition among ancient writers, Tacitus being a noteworthy exponent, of putting stirring and even anti-Roman words into the mouths of defeated enemies.[8] Ironically, this has become the best known section of the whole *Jewish War*, a paradox which Josephus, whose speeches are full of somewhat laboured paradoxes and ironies, might himself have been capable of enjoying.

This is not to say that the speeches are not fitted to the context in which they are placed. The notion that they had to be appropriate was prominent in later Greek thinking about the orations in historians.[9] In Josephus, each has a practical purpose within the historical situation, and most of each one could conceivably have been uttered at the time in a form not very remote from the one given even if, as a matter of fact, it probably was not. But, without being implausible, Josephus manages to be remarkably repetitive across the various speeches. And so it turns out that many, even if not all, of the texts which will expose Josephus' personal attitudes to us are in speeches.

Nowhere is Josephus more emotive, or more repetitive, than in what he writes about the rebels. It would be impossible to miss the point that he ascribes primary responsibility for the revolt to them. In the final book of the *Jewish War*, before he reaches the fall of the fortress of Masada, which is the work's climax, having explained the descent of the *sicarii* who held the fortress, Josephus digresses to expatiate upon the evil deeds done by each of the rebel leaders and rebel groups. 'Somehow', he writes, 'that period became productive of every kind of evil among the Jews, so that no crime was left undone.' (*BJ* 7.259) Josephus catalogues those crimes, and concludes that whatever the evil-doers eventually suffered cannot have equalled the suffering they inflicted. The accusations, although attached to individuals, are wide-ranging and unspecific, not to say wild: we hear of lawlessness, cruelty, slander, conspiracy, unjust executions, offences to friendship and kinship, brutality and every sort of barbarity; even contravention of the Jewish dietary laws. The Greek tradition of invective has, in part, given the assault its

---

[7] See p. 83. Cf. the discussion of this speech in the second part of P. Vidal-Naquet's 'Flavius Josèphe et Masada', *Revue Historique* 260 (1978), pp. 3–21.

[8] See H. Fuchs, *Der geistige Widerstand gegen Rom in der antiken Welt* (1938), pp. 15ff.; R. Syme, *Tacitus* (1958), pp. 528–9.

[9] See Quintilian on Livy (1.1.101); cf. Avenarius, loc. cit. (n. 4); P. Scheller, *De hellenistica historiae conscribendae arte* (1911), pp. 51–2.

form. But of Josephus' loathing for the rebel factions there can be no doubt.

Another feature of the preface to the *War* is the promise that one of the book's major themes will be a description of 'the brutality of the tyrants towards their compatriots', to be set against the clemency of the Romans (*BJ* 1.27). It is mainly from the fourth book on that this motif is unfolded. Indeed, from this point the emotional pitch of Josephus' narrative is much higher, and more extreme reactions come out. The explanation is not hard to find. The Galilee had been subjugated, and the bands of revolutionaries had moved into Jerusalem and had begun to take over the city. Josephus seems to have undergone a deep and understandable revulsion at the reign of terror for which they were responsible (*BJ* 4.135ff.; see pp. 132ff.).

Much of what he writes afterwards is dominated by this feeling of outrage; and, as Josephus details the atrocities perpetrated by Jews upon their fellows, his castigations become more frequent and more strident. He deplores the murder of the high priest Ananus, according to him a great man and the moderates' last hope,[10] and that of his own friend, Joshua son of Gamala, the slaughter of 12,000 well-born young men, and the merciless attacks made on many others of the 'powerful' in the city (*BJ* 4.357). These monstrosities must have been prominent in bringing him to the view, more often repeated than any other general judgment in the *Jewish War*, that the rebels harmed the city far more than ever the Romans did (*BJ* 2.10; 3.297; 4.397, 558; 5.28, 362; 6.122–4). This is a striking claim and, even if it is somewhat exaggerated when the Roman cruelties are considered (e.g. 3.303–5, 329, 336–9; 5.450.1), we may grant it a measure of truth. We should not insist on explaining it away as mere flattery of Rome on the part of a grateful renegade.

Josephus uses the speeches of Book 4 (162–92, 239–69) for even stronger denunciations of the rebels than those made *in propria persona*. To Ananus the high priest, soon to be killed, they are murderers, tyrants, evil-doers whose audacity is unlimited; to Joshua son of Gamala, they are the scum and dregs of the whole country, men at the extremity of madness, sinners. Since the sentiment of these speeches is in accord with what Josephus himself says elsewhere, they can be taken to represent his feelings. But the

---

[10] On an apparent contradiction with his usual view of Ananus, see p. 151, n. 17.

speeches do also fit their context, and such a response is directly connected with what happened in Jerusalem at that time.

In Book 6 (99–112), Josephus himself speaks to the people, and especially to their leader, John of Gischala, from the walls of Jerusalem, and here he reserves his deepest disgust for the most recent and, in his eyes, most horrific development, the defilement of the Holy Places. He is, after all, a priest. This had already been tied to the by now familiar, and no longer surprising, contrast with Roman behaviour, in another of the author's own orations (cast at this point in indirect speech) (5.362–74). What is more remarkable is that even the Masada leader Eleazar ben Yaïr, in his grand and sometimes stirring declamation, is made a mouthpiece of such unlikely opinions and rather unconvincingly admits of himself and his followers that they had been 'teachers of crime to the others' (7.330). That is certainly Josephus, as we have begun to know him, expressing his own conviction.

At the heart of all these denunciations lie three main points: the rebels were cruel and violent; they were sinful; and (paradoxically for lovers of liberty) they divided the population and tyrannised over the masses, enforcing compliance with their orders. This last charge is the most crucial to the argument of the *Jewish War* as a whole. Its implications, that most Jews had not genuinely wanted to revolt, could again be dismissed as Josephus trying to ingratiate himself with the Romans; but, again, it does in fact arise quite naturally out of what Josephus himself saw. And in a later chapter we shall find that the Romans cannot be held responsible for Josephus' arguments.

Josephus' analysis is not an over-simple one. It certainly would not be fair to say that he throughout represents this relatively small contingent of fanatics as the only supporters of the revolt, even if he does hold them responsible for its prolongation (e.g. at *BJ* 5.53). While he tends to show 'the people' in general as out of sympathy with the extremists in the later stages of the war, this is not true earlier. There he readily admits that the crowd was at times behind the war-party, and that, when a great battle took place between the two groups for control of Jerusalem, the war-mongers, in the lower city, outnumbered the protagonists of peace in the upper. He sometimes envisages the population, then, as containing a middle element which could be swayed either way. It was the excesses of the revolutionaries and the persuasion of 'moderates' like Ananus which gradually won this group over to the cause of peace (*BJ* 2.320, 422ff.; 4.158ff.).

In a crisis any centre group tends to be merged with one of the two extremes, or to be destroyed, just as occurred during the civil war in Corcyra, according to Thucydides' classic description (3.82.8). And between the extremes there can, as Thucydides knew, be no meeting. So in the Palestine of the Second Temple period there was no compromise possible between the 'Sons of Light' and the 'Sons of Darkness'. In Josephus' view the simple reason for this was that the zealots (in the wide sense of the term) moved further and further beyond the pale.

Sometimes, Josephus refers to the rebels as 'brigands' (*lēstai*), and in a few places in his writings we find the term *archilēstai*, brigand chiefs. There is a common belief about his use of these terms, which is largely mistaken: the words are not, for him, mere terms of abuse, which he hurls at them whenever he feels like it. He writes more accurately than that. It is only in the *Life*, a polemic, that we see *lēstai* in regular employment as the standard name for the rebels.[11] In the earlier part of the *War*, this word is confined to groups of men who seem (whatever their underlying purpose) to have behaved as true brigands, perpetrating acts of robbery and violence in the countryside: those, that is, who roamed the country under the last procurators,[12] and those, known also as *sicarii*, who seized Masada at the beginning of the war, and who brought assistance to the rebels in the Temple when they confronted the peace party in the upper city (*BJ* 2.425, 433). In the defamatory character sketch of one of the rebel leaders, John of Gischala, with whom Josephus had a great deal of trouble in the Galilee, and whom quite simply, he detests, the label *lēstēs* appears among a variety of slurs (*BJ* 2.587); it is not unfair to call this occurrence a special case. In the other instances, the activities involved are activities accurately described by the chosen word. But what is implausible, even so, is that such groups should really have consisted of simple criminal robbers, who had no motive for what they did other than theft for itself. And, if this is so, Josephus, even though correct on a technical level, shows very clearly by his silence that he has no patience for any of the claims of such people, and can imagine no exoneration

[11] Cf. H. Kreissig, *Die sozialen Zusammenhänge des jüdäischen Krieges* (1970), p. 137. References collected by D. M. Rhoads, *Israel in Revolution* (1976), appendix.

[12] *BJ* 2. 235, 253 (a man active for over 50 years), 264–5.

for their actions. Brigandage was, of course, the enemy of the settled and propertied throughout the ancient world; even Rome could not always keep it at bay in the empire. Greek and Roman writers were, for the most part, settled and propertied people, and so it is hard to estimate, from the writings left to us, the social component which this criminal behaviour undoubtedly contained.[13] The significant point here is that Josephus, for all that he fought briefly with the Jewish rebels, had no more sense of identification with the Jewish oppressed and dispossessed than the upper classes elsewhere seem to have had with theirs.

Bandits are an extreme case. What, in general, Josephus scarcely recognises (which an impartial commentator would have to) is that most of the rebels had grievances of a different order from those of his own class, and that some of them at least were driven by a vision—perhaps indistinct, and occasionally Messianic, but for all that not devoid of practical content—of a better society (see p. 139). Josephus shows an intolerance and a lack of understanding of the essence of the whole resistance movement characteristic of men's approach to their political opponents.

There is a distinction which asks to be drawn between Josephus' record of the activities—as it were, the external history—of the different rebel groups, which even if not always as full as we would like, is consistent and seldom imprecise; and his treatment of their internal character, which is more seriously deficient. Josephus has ways of describing the rebels, or some of them, which indicate his own attitude quite plainly; but it is not done in such a way as to conceal the emergence and identities of separate sub-groups, and his distortion should not be exaggerated. That we cannot, from Josephus' evidence, trace with certainty a *continuous* pre-war history of any number of years for any rebel 'party' is largely because the groupings were too fluid and unorganized for there to be any such

---

[13] On brigandage as a form of primitive protest, see E. J. Hobsbawm, *Bandits* (1969); features strikingly similar to those observed by Hobsbawm among relatively recent bandits are to be found in the brigandage of the Roman empire, on which the best brief account is M. Hengel, *Die Zeloten* (1961), pp. 24–35. R. McMullen, *Enemies of the Roman Order* (1967), ch. 6 and appendix B, minimises the social element: see review by O. Murray *JRS* 59 (1969), p. 264. There seems to be no justification for connecting Josephus' use of the term 'brigands' with the Roman legal distinction between robbers and public enemies (e.g. *Dig.* 49. 15. 4). The Jewish war was a full-scale war, producing a triumph for Vespasian and Titus. On Galilean bandits, cf. pp. 132 and 144.

history to trace;[14] only partly can we lay the blame at the door of Josephus' distaste for doctrine. He does not let us down as much as modern scholars, with their fondness for speculation, would have us think.

The words most frequently used by Josephus in talking of the rebels in general are ones drawn from the Greek political vocabulary, 'fomentors of civil strife', 'revolutionaries' and, for the leaders, 'tyrants'.[15] Their pejorative sense would be taken for granted by a Greek reader. They imply the standpoint of a political opponent— an opponent, it would seem, within the Jewish state, for it is there that the rebels are, in the first instance, creating innovation and revolution, rather than in the Roman empire as a whole. But I do not want to make too much of this vocabulary, for it is quite probable that Josephus deployed those words and not others partly because they were the ones which happened to spring readily to mind and looked appropriate to a Greek history. They can hardly have had close Aramaic equivalents: in what terms he would have spoken of the rebels in Jerusalem during the revolt itself we cannot know.

The term 'Zealots' may suggest itself; but this actually has a limited reference, and although, today, writers tend to use it for convenience as a general label (this has not been altogether avoided here), it is as a rule applied by Josephus with some care and precision to particular groupings, above all when it comes to the last stages of the revolt. It appears once in speaking (apparently in a non-technical way) of the enthusiastic personal following of an ambitious but short-lived leader, Menahem; and next it describes people anxious to proceed with the war after Josephus has taken control in the Galilee; but the name soon settles firmly with a distinct group, under John of Gischala, which occupies the city, lets in the Idumaeans, and holds the Temple against Ananus the high priest and his men, who are in possession of the lower city (*BJ* 2.444, 651; 4.161–2, 224ff., 514, 538–44, 556ff.). Subsequently, Elea-

[14] M. Hengel, op. cit., perhaps makes them too rigid. Morton Smith, 'Zealots and Sicarii, their origins and relations', *HThR* 44 (1971), pp. 10–15, offers a partial corrective. M. Borg, 'The currency of the term "Zealot" ', *JThSt* 22 (1971), pp. 504–12, points in the right direction, with the specific argument that the name 'Zealot' for a resistance party was not in use before A.D. 66.

[15] See e.g. *BJ* 2. 274, 330, 407, 410, 422, 425, 442, 652; cf. Hengel p. 43 and n. 8. These terms are overlooked by S. Applebaum, 'The Zealots: the case for revaluation', *JRS* 61 (1971), pp. 163–6.

zar ben Simon, who had been one of the original leaders of the group, separates his followers from this party, and he appears then to have taken the party name with him, so that it is consistently attached to his following. This faction seems to be largely drawn from the lower échelons of the priesthood.[16]

It is when we start enquiring why and whence 'Zealots' that Josephus leaves us in the lurch. There are enough fragmentary indications, however, even in Josephus himself, to convince us that there was more in their ideology and religious convictions than we are in a position to know. Modern scholars have had to resort to more than the usual amount of reconstruction, starting from their own awareness of the Biblical prototype for zealotry, Phineas, and going on to follow up contemporary possibilities. Of the name 'Zealots', Josephus only remarks, in the midst of his vehement retrospective attack, that its holders purported to be so called because of their zeal for the good: 'men who by their acts justified their name; for they took to themselves every wicked deed; they did not even fail to emulate such earlier ones as were recorded in the tradition from olden days. And yet they adopted a name from those who had been zealous for virtue, either in ironical jest at the expense of those they injured since their characters were brutal, or else really believing the greatest of evils to be good.' [17]

The most detailed—and interesting—discussion which Josephus offers on the subject of the revolutionaries' inspiration occurs in connection with the opposition in Judaea to the census of A.D.6, at which point he seems to put the beginning of the dissident movement. In the *Jewish War*, the account is very brief: Judas, a Galilean, attacked his countrymen for being willing to pay tribute to Rome, thus implicitly accepting human masters, whereas before their Lord had been God; he founded a Fourth Philosophy, distinct from the other three Jewish 'philosophies'—which are now explained. Judas is described as a man from Gamala in Gaulanitis; and a companion is named—Saddok, a Pharisee. In the *Antiquities*, Josephus adds a few details about the beliefs of the group: they hated the census

---

[16] *BJ* 5. 1ff, 250, 358, 528; 6. 92, 148. See M. Stern, in *World History of the Jewish People* (1977) vol. 8, p. 297. For Stern, Eleazar is the leader of the true Zealots from the very beginning, and John an independent operator.

[17] *BJ* 7. 268–70; cf. 4. 161. There is no explicit association in any second Temple text with the 'zeal' of Phineas in Numbers (25.11–13), or of the Maccabees (I Macc.). The Hebrew equivalent 'Kannaim' is used in Rabbinic literature, in one context, of the rebels during the siege: Applebaum, loc. cit. (n. 15).

because it was a symbol of slavery, their passion was for liberty, their contempt for death, and apart from these principles, they accepted the tenets of ordinary Pharisaism.[18] But the value of such information is much reduced by the fact that we never again hear explicitly of this impressive Fourth Philosophy, and that we are not told what was the relationship between the doctrines of the rebels of A.D.6, and any of those of 66 (see Chapter 5). It is observed, first of all, that there is a succession of dissidents springing from one family and culminating, in 66, in actions separate from those of the Zealots. Then in the second Masada speech of Eleazar ben Yaïr, Josephus indicates that the defenders of the fortress were fired by the determination to accept no master but God—the same conviction as he had ascribed to the Fourth Philosophy. And the suicide of the defeated at Masada, justified by Eleazar, exemplifies that contempt for death said to characterise them (*BJ* 7.323, 341ff.).

The occupants of that stronghold are called *sicarii* (knife-men) by Josephus. And so too are the people who, when the revolt in Palestine was over, fled to Egypt and to Cyrene, and fomented disturbances in both those places. Those at Alexandria are praised for the endurance and courage with which they withstood torture so as not to have to 'call Caesar master'; their self-appointed task was to persuade other Jews to regard God alone as their Lord, the Romans as their equals. Again, then, we have the approach of the Fourth Philosophy, and telling indications that we are dealing with the spiritual heirs of its founders. In this way it is possible to put the pieces together. But our tentative identifications have to remain unconfirmed.

The notorious rebel leader Simon bar Giora, although he had early on joined those in Masada, seems never to be regarded as one of the *sicarii*; but whether this was simply because he soon left again, and established his own following in the hills, or because of a difference in ideology, we cannot tell.[19]

What is more, the expression 'Fourth Philosophy', is, we may suspect, Josephus' private coinage, for it brings the ideas of the new group into relation with the three principal sects, which he likes to

---

[18] *BJ* 2. 118; *AJ* 18. 23. There is not the serious inconsistency between the *Antiquities* and *War* versions which W. R. Farmer claims to detect: *Maccabees, Zealots and Josephus* ([2]1958).

[19] *BJ* 4. 503–8. On all this see Hengel, op. cit. (n. 13), chs 2–4 and Stern, op. cit. (n. 16), pp. 271–83.

describe as philosophies. It is improbable that the members of those sects saw their own groupings in such terms, and so there is no reason to think that the members of the fourth one did. And it is doubtful whether what they had to offer was a new brand of Judaism, intended to contrast with the other three:[20] all this looks suspiciously like Josephus' own schematisation, made for the benefit of his Greek readers. Thus we are left in the dark as to how the enemies of Rome aligned themselves within the Jewish religion.

The speeches which Josephus put into the mouth of Eleazar ben Yaïr do show that the author could at least acknowledge the rebels' courage, but they cannot go far towards indicating what was distinctive about their attitudes. Their main subject, discussion of the virtues of suicide, is designed directly to parallel Josephus' own Jotapata speech, in which he had argued the exact contrary (*BJ* 7.341–8; 3.362–82). Those two speeches, though not juxtaposed, form a set, and recall the famous pairs of speeches of Greek and Roman historians, for example the arguments about the death penalty in the senatorial debate at the end of Sallust's *Catiline*. The *Roman Antiquities* of Dionysius of Halicarnassus, in some respects a model for Josephus, contains many paired speeches. In Josephus' work, the pairing is an adornment; in so far as it can be said to serve a specific function, this would seem to be to show that Josephus' own behaviour had been at least as respectable and justifiable as that of the heroes. (Here personal apologetic clearly *is* involved.) Apart from this, the Masada oratory is used, as we have seen, as a vehicle for Josephus' own thought.

No one else wrote a Greek history like Josephus; but his mentality is not in all respects unusual. The subsequent elision in the later Rabbinic literature of the apocalyptic strains of thought which existed within Judaism is in a way comparable to the attitude of Josephus. It is tempting to call him here something like 'proto-rabbinic'. At the same time, non-rational popular ideologies did not on the whole fall readily within the scope of Graeco-Roman historiography.[21] Beyond this, there is the fact that, these ideas had dangerous political implications built into them. So Josephus had every reason to eschew mention of that other world of thought and vision.

[20] See p. 36, and cf. Hengel, pp. 79–86.
[21] Cf. A. D. Momigliano, 'Popular religious beliefs and late Roman historians', in *Essays in Ancient and Modern Historiography* (1977), esp. pp. 140–5.

There is a type of leader described by him as a false prophet, a magician, a deceiver; often such figures are said to go hand in hand with the 'brigands'. The term 'false prophet' is, interestingly, one which gained currency in Hellenistic Judaism, though not employed in the Hebrew Bible. The popular mentors known to Josephus were no doubt in fact purveyors of some kind of ethical or Messianic teaching, without themselves being pseudo-Messiahs. But for Josephus they too are quite simply components of that motley criminal collection which first fomented, and then fanned the flames of misguided revolt. They are distinct, however, from the rebel leaders who are never themselves spoken of as prophets.[22]

A number of minor characters of this type make their appearance in his pages, but once again, Josephus deals the major blow to the enemy in a retrospective digression (*BJ* 6.285ff.), a device which is indeed proving to be characteristic of his technique. The prophets of the period are summed up at a most crucial moment in the *War* narrative. It so happened that, when the Temple fell, there were destroyed with it some 6,000 ordinary people (if Josephus' figure is to be relied upon), among them women and children, who had taken refuge in it because a 'false prophet' had told them that their God would make manifest 'the proofs of salvation'. The event was striking enough for Josephus to be impelled to comment that at this period many prophets offered false hope to the people, and were readily believed; this, he sensibly points out, usually happens in times of adversity. Moreover, according to him, the 'tyrants' made cynical use of these individuals to try and stop desertion from the rebel ranks. In this way Josephus' portrayal of the revolutionaries separates the religious element from the political, attempting thus to devalue both.

But for himself he by no means makes this separation. What is unexpected, and may be said to devalue the author's own diagnosis, is that his contempt for contemporary prophecies of imminent change is highly selective. Predictions of doom and of the end of Jerusalem were to be applauded; and still in the same digression, he goes on to tell of portents and omens, to him highly meaningful,

---

[22] When John of Gischala is described as a *goēs*, magician, the word is being used in an extended sense, to mean merely 'trickster': see *BJ* 4. 85. Josephus' separation is overlooked by J. Blenkinsopp, 'Prophecy and priesthood in Josephus', *JJS* 25 (1974), pp. 239–62; but see Hengel, op. cit., pp. 235–9. For 'pseudo-prophets', see the material in J. Reiling, 'The use of "pseudoprophētēs" in the Septuagint, Philo and Josephus', *NT* 13 (1971), pp. 147–56.

which foreshadowed the fall of the Temple, but were either ignored or misinterpreted. These are a strange collection: a star, a comet, a sacrificial cow giving birth, a spontaneous opening of the gates, a chariot fight in the sky, and a mysterious voice in the inner court had all been witnessed shortly before the destruction; and already four years before the war, a peasant called Jesus had taken to prophesying doom day after day, and night after night, but loudest at festivals. The prophecies went on for seven years in spite of repeated procuratorial floggings, until this eccentric and brave individual was killed accidentally by a stone from a Roman catapult. And so, concludes Josephus, we see that God does care for man, and offers him a road which, once taken, leads straight to salvation.

It is remarkable that Josephus recounts this peculiar and minor episode at some length, following it with two further oracles. In view of this, it would be quite wrong to say that he is totally unwilling to recognise the claims of popular superstition, the less respectable side of religion. On the other hand, what he does in effect is to subordinate his interpretation of such things to his political purpose within Judaism. Only prophets who are on the right side are acceptable. Indeed the story only appears at this point as a contrast to what had been said about false prophets exploited by the Zealots. It is as though Josephus will not allow the enemy to occupy even an inch of ground—even when the ground is (for him) as slippery as this territory. This sometimes seems cynical, something which could never be said of his approach to the central truths of the Jewish religion—the Deity itself and the Torah in its historical and legal aspects.

We can sum up by saying that throughout Josephus treats the rebels, in all their guises, simply as political adversaries. A person is not inclined to consider the merits of the other side when he is engaged in a bitter civil struggle nor, for that matter, when he has been through one.

There can be no more telling confirmation that Josephus actually saw his own situation in such a light than the prominence of the concept of *stasis*, civil dissension, as an interpretative tool in his work on the Jewish war. In seeking to understand the fall of the Holy City and the Temple, he offers one general explanation repeatedly: they were destroyed by *stasis*. Under this heading and within this explanation we find a number of different strands. First, there can be two different levels at which the *stasis* operates as a causative factor. Secondly, it is not always the same parties who play the leading roles. Sometimes fratricide is the principal sin which, on the theological level, brings punishment in its wake. This moral motif, even if by no means alien to Greek or Roman thought, makes Josephus stand out sharply among Greek and Roman historians because of the consistency and intensity with which it is pursued, and because it is conceived as part of a continuous process through history, in which this is but one of many exemplifications of the same pattern. Before elaborating on it, however, we may profitably ask what Josephus actually meant by *stasis* in cases where it is a political phenomenon. In the preface to the *Jewish War*, he writes that in his book he will be showing, among other things, how civil war destroyed Jerusalem, and how (as Titus could attest) the Jewish 'tyrants' forced the unwilling Romans to lay hands on the Temple— 'that civil war destroyed it (my country) and that the Jewish tyrants drew the unwilling hands of the Romans, and the conflagration on to the Temple, Titus Caesar who sacked it, can himself bear witness'. He does not appear to mean simply that, on the supernatural level, the conduct of the rebels necessitated the Romans' becoming the agents of God's punishment. Something more down to earth is also suggested: the Zealots' fanaticism, the desperate struggle they carried on in their own most sacred edifice, and their obstinate refusal to submit, left the Romans with no practical alternative but to storm, and thus destroy the Temple. Here it is unclear in exactly what sense the Zealots' activities are held to be *stasis*. Presumably the point is that fighting Rome entailed rebellion against their own leaders. But it is certain that, as well as a theological connection between the internal Jewish situation and the disaster, some sort of political connection is in question.

This key concept of *stasis* is used a number of times where Josephus' meaning is clearer. More than once, it is applied—very reasonably—to the warfare between the different groups of revolutionaries which emerged in Jerusalem after the murder of the high priest Ananus and before Vespasian advanced on the city (see p. 135). At *Antiquities* 18. 8, commenting on the beginnings of the revolutionary movement, and looking forward, he talks of the future rivalries of different parties which would emerge, when 'civil wars, the murder of citizens and internecine slaughter' would be the result of their desperate feuds. He offers, also, a close analysis of the reasons why the leader John of Gischala separated himself from the

rest of the Zealots. He is conscious of the immediate tragic consequence of the division, talking of *stasis* as the third scourge, after
war and 'tyranny', to afflict the people. He follows the history of
this *stasis*, telling how it was put aside in the face of the Roman
siege-engines, when the Jews made their first sally, but soon erupted
again: 'not even when the Romans were encamped before the walls
did the civil war inside calm down.' Nevertheless, we soon discover
that the three factions did subsequently, and more permanently
re-unite (*BJ* 4.397; 5.255, 278). Thus Josephus' previous rather
fanciful statement that it was the *stasis* which captured the city and
the Romans the *stasis* is not quite borne out.

When Josephus refers to the rebels in general as *stasiastai*; dissidents, as he often does, he is using the word with another application, and apparently means to indicate by it that they were engaged
in a struggle against the rest of the population, which wanted peace.
The term *neōterizontes*—innovators or revolutionaries, on occasion
put beside it, confirms that he has in mind their opposition to the
established internal order. The word *stasis*, too, can have this sense
for him, and it is one which is particularly interesting to us. An
important example occurs where he points out that, after the conquest of Galilee, *stasis* broke out first in the countryside, and then
in Jerusalem, between the peace and the war parties (*BJ* 4.128–34).
In a passage influenced by Thucydides, he describes how the Jews
turned on each other whenever they had momentary relief from the
Roman attack. The *stasis* is described, in rhetorical yet not unreal
terms, as dividing friend from friend, relative from relative, and, in
particular, young (and rash) from old (and prudent). The difference
between the two parties, then, is simply their attitude to the war.
Josephus' dramatic account of the agonised personal separation
caused by the war and his concentration on the young-old distinction,[23] a theme he probably also derives from Thucydides, prevents
him from considering any general social differences between the two
sides. But there can be no doubt that these existed in this case, as
we shall discover they did elsewhere, and that Josephus took it for
granted that this was so.

The one occasion when Josephus uses *stasis* to describe an overt
economic struggle between classes occurs in a passage from the
Antiquities (20.179ff.; see p. 125). He points to the high-priesthood

[23] See Thuc. 2. 8, 20.2, 21.2, and (stressing Alcibiades' youthfulness) 5. 43.2, 6.
17, 18.6.

of Ishmael ben Phiabi (during Felix's procuratorship) as a land-mark, because during it open hostility broke out between the high priests, on the one hand, and on the other the ordinary priests and the leaders of the people. Each faction had its own thugs, and when the high priests sent their slaves to seize the tithes from the threshing floors, some ordinary priests starved to death.

No one would claim that, in the *War*, Josephus relates *stasis* particularly to the conflict between rich and poor, yet the fact that such conflicts do play an important part in the work and, further-more, that many Greek writers took it for granted that the main division in a city was between the rich and the poor, may make us suspect that he had a conception of this sort of dissension in mind when he insisted on the important role that *stasis* played in destroy-ing the Jews.[24] And, conversely, though he does not use the word, it is indisputably *stasis* that he is speaking of when, in the excursus on the rebels, he writes of the early *sicarii* treating all pro-Romans as enemies, and goes on to describe a distinct social conflict, in which the pro-Roman possessing class had its property removed and its houses burnt.[25] Again without the use of the actual word *stasis*, a little later in the same tirade, Josephus speaks of the period as one of division in the population, during which 'those who had power oppressed the masses, and the masses were eager to destroy those in power; the former wanted for themselves tyrannical control, the latter, violence, and the seizure of rich men's property'. And so, reluctant as we may be to build too extensively on Josephus' rather erratic use of the concept *stasis*, this survey of its major appearances has, at the very least, entitled us to say that, in the author's view, the Jewish revolt was as much a civil war (or wars) as a struggle against any external enemy.

Josephus dislikes the destruction of property. Yet, however par-tisan he is, it is not this aspect of *stasis* which most shocks him, at any rate if we are to judge by what he says. His most vehement condemnations have a religious tinge. It is the wickedness of shed-ding blood, and, above all, of polluting God's Temple, which is stressed: and indeed the precise character of the divisions involved is in this context irrelevant. The schema of incorrigible sin, followed by the withdrawal of God's favour, and then punishment, is that of

---

[24] On this dichotomy, see pp. 118ff.
[25] *BJ* 7. 254–5; cf. P. A. Brunt, 'Josephus on social conflicts in Judaea' *Klio* 59, 1 (1977), p. 15.

the prophets of the First Temple and post-First Temple period.[26]
When Josephus talks of the Romans as God's agents through whom
He will punish his people, he draws explicit comparisons with the
Assyrians of old.[27] And when, in a plea to the besieged Jews from
the walls of Jerusalem, he argues that it is their own impiety which
is now reducing them to slavery, he does this by marshalling a
succession of different instances of civil dissension, starting from the
war of 63 B.C. between the two Hasmoneans, Hyrcanus and Aristobulus. What mainly stands out there is the way in which *stasis* is
made to fulfil just the same role as sins of a different kind. For he
goes on to give an impressive list of other evils: 'for you did not
disdain secret sins, I mean theft, treachery and adultery; while you
vie with each other in raping and murdering; and carve out new
and outlandish paths of evil; and the Temple has become the re-
ceptacle of all this.' The tradition of the prophets is here unmistakeable, and, especially when pollution of the sanctuary is the
climactic offence, the cries of Ezekiel against the vile abominations
practiced there in earlier days are clearly evoked.

Ancient tradition is explicitly mentioned on two occasions when
Josephus talks of the fulfilment in the present war of famous old
prophecies that the city would be taken and the Temple fall only
after Jerusalem was divided against itself (*BJ* 4.388ff.; 6.109ff.).
Here, as elsewhere when Josephus cites ancient prophecies, there
is little point in trying to decide which particular Biblical or
extra-Biblical passage he has in mind. In this case one thinks, for
example, of the statement, no doubt of earlier origin, recorded in a
Biblical commentary some centuries afterwards, 'Rabbi said:
"Great is peace, for even if Israel practise idolatry but maintain
peace amongst themselves, the Holy One, blessed be He, says, as
it were, 'I have no dominion over them' . . . But when their hearts
are divided, what is written? 'Their heart is divided; now shall they
bear their guilt.' " ' (Hos. 10.2).[28] For the purposes of this utterance,
stasis is not just a sin, but the ultimate sin.

Josephus' condemnation of the civil strife which, he believed, had
been engendered by the rebels, could thus be intensified by its

[26] See e.g. Jer. 4–6; 21. 11ff.; 26; Ezek. 12–18; Hosea 4–13; Micah 3. On the
theme's prominence in II Macc., V. Nikiprowetsky, 'La mort d'Eléazar fils de
Jaïre', *Hommages à André Dupont-Sommer* (1971), p. 471, n. 2.
[27] *BJ* 5. 404ff. For Josephus' Biblical references, see p. 32.
[28] *Genesis Rabbah* 38, 6. The 'Rabbi' referred to is Judah ha-Nasi, of the late second
century A.D..

assimilation to other acts of disobedience to the Law manifested by
a generation as wicked, for him, as the one destroyed at Sodom (*BJ*
5. 566). His political analysis is built into a deeper structure.

God had said: 'if you spurn my judgements, and do not obey all
my commandments, but break my covenant, then be sure this is
what I will do: I will break upon you sudden terror, wasting disease,
recurrent fever, and plagues that dim the sight and cause the ap-
petite to fail. You shall sow your seed to no purpose, for your
enemies shall eat the crop. I will set my face against you, and you
shall be routed by your enemies. Those that hate you shall hound
you until you run where there is no pursuit.' After other terrible
curses had come a redoubled warning: 'if, in spite of this, you do
not listen to me and still defy me, I will defy you in anger, and I
myself will punish you seven times for your sins. Instead of meat,
you shall eat your sons and daughters . . . I will make your cities
desolate and destroy your sanctuaries; the soothing odour of your
offerings I will not accept. I will destroy your land, and the enemies
who occupy it shall be appalled. I will scatter you among the
heathen, and I will pursue you with the naked sword; your land
shall be desolate and your cities heaps of rubble.' [29] Much of what
had been threatened was now, for the second time in Jerusalem's
history, actuality. The details seemed to correspond closely—it was
even said that during the siege of Jerusalem a mother had eaten
her child (*BJ* 6.201–13). The first response of a mind imbued with
the Old Testament—perhaps of any religious mind—would be to
seek out the sin which had occasioned the catastrophe. Whether the
emphasis is laid on Adam's original sin (as in some of the apocalypses) or on recent offences, on the group or on the individual, the
theme is common to all literature written under the impact of the
destruction of 70. Josephus gives us its fullest exposition. And Josephus, who was not the man to dwell—at any rate in what he
wrote—on his own misdeeds, handled the issue by stressing the
guilt of one sector alone of his compatriots.

It may be that the author of the contemporary Baruch Apocalypse
was adopting the same selective approach, in his own veiled manner, when he depicted the high priests, after the Temple had gone,
throwing its keys back up to heaven, and confessing that they had
not been good custodians. In this powerful image, the author of this

---

[29] Lev. 26. 15–33; cf. Deut. 28. Recalled in the Maccabean period by Daniel 9.
11–14.

apocalypse (writing in the name of the scribe of Jeremiah who was carried off to Babylon after the first destruction) seems to provide an interpretation which is the mirror image of Josephus' one, casting the high priestly group in the role in which Josephus casts the rebels. And indeed II Baruch has been credited with an anti-priestly sectarian bias. But much more often Baruch speaks about the people in its entirety, just as does another, even more impressive piece of apocalyptic writing, the book known as IV Ezra. The authors of the apocalypses wrote in a vein which was rigidly excluded from Josephus' history, but their speculations on profound mysteries, while perhaps addressed to a restricted following, are set in a framework of traditional Jewish piety not very different from Josephus' own.[30]

Punishment for sin could, of course, be averted through repentance; or else repentance and atonement might follow punishment and lead in the end to a reconciliation between God and man, in accordance with the Covenant. Such a scheme underlies another, non-apocalyptic text ascribed to Baruch, this one included among the Apocryphal books of the Greek Septuagint. It is thought to belong to our period. In it, the people's offence—disobedience to the Law—and their punishment are spelled out in the manner which has already become familiar; indeed, the detail confirms that the inspiration is the same. 'Nowhere under heaven have such deeds been done as were done in Jerusalem, thus fulfilling what was foretold in the law of Moses, that we should eat the flesh of our children, one his own son and another his own daughter. The Lord made our nation subject to all the kingdoms around us, our land a waste, our name a byword to all the nations among whom He has scattered our people.' Collective suffering as payment for national sin was a traditional preoccupation, and still alive in the first century. In general, punishment was a theme which appealed to Jews of this period: from Biblical, and perhaps also from Greek roots,

---

[30] On these themes, see M. Simon, *Verus Israel* (²1964), pp. 19–24. Keys of the Temple: II Baruch, 10, 18. The image recurs in Rabbinic literature, see Simon, loc. cit. II Baruch survives in Syriac, IV Ezra principally in Latin. See the translations and commentaries in R. H. Charles, *Apocrypha and Pseudepigrapha of the Old Testament* (1913). For II Baruch, see also P. Bogaert's edition (*Sources Chrétiennes*, 1969). For a definition of apocalyptic, J. Barr, 'Jewish apocalyptic in recent scholarly study', *Bull. John Ryl. Lib.* 58 (1975–6), pp. 9–35. The only surviving complete MS of Baruch, the Ambrosian, contains, interestingly, also *BJ* 6 (on the fall of Jerusalem), under the title V Macc. (see Bogaert, pp. 34–6, 161–2).

was drawn a macabre fascination with the dreadful forms of death by disease endured by those who had offended against the Deity, especially persecutors of the chosen race. Philo, in a treatise, surveys the curses called down on the heads of sinners: cannibalism is included, and there are also detailed descriptions of disease. Evil individuals, both pagan and ostensibly Jewish, meet terrible ends, usually involving consumption of the flesh by worms, in II Maccabees, Philo, Josephus and Acts: Antiochus IV, Herod the Great, Herod Agrippa, Avillius Flaccus the Prefect of Egypt, Apion, Catullus the Governor of Libya (whose death concludes the *Jewish War*). The Christian Lactantius was to take up this theme, as applied to persecutors.[31] So there was no difficulty in grasping the meaning of punishment. Atonement was more difficult to conceive of, especially after 70. For it has been suggested that the destruction of the Temple produced a crisis in Judaism for the very reason that, once the opportunity to expiate sin through sacrifice had gone, it was difficult to know how to atone. Apocalyptic literature, it has been said, cut the knot by looking forward to an imminent new era in which the world and the human condition would be transformed.[32] This problem may also explain a curious feature of the *Jewish War* of Josephus: there is much talk of sin and punishment, a good deal less of repentance and reconciliation. Yet there is no doubt that Josephus subscribes to the usual schema, and, in a strongly-worded invocation to Jerusalem, inserted at the point where faction fighting has taken over the Temple itself, and famine is about to set in, Josephus insists that even then the city could have been saved, had she propitiated the God who was destroying her. The author's own long speech from the ramparts puts the matter beyond doubt: 'the Deity is easily reconciled to those who confess and repent.' (5.19, 415) Both long term and recent sins must be covered by this, since Josephus believed that the Jews had committed both kinds.[33]

[31] Bar. 2, 3–6; Philo, *de praem. et poen.*, esp. 143–6; II Macc. 9; *BJ* 1. 656–7; *AJ* 17. 168–79; Acts 12.23; Philo, *Flacc.* 91; *CA* 2. 143–4; *BJ* 7. 451–3. Some of these Hellenistic Jewish instances are cited by W. Nestle, 'Legenden vom Tod der Gottesverächter', *Archiv für Religionswissenschaft* 32–3 (1935–6), pp. 246–9, who argues that the motif has Greek origins. Useful information in D. J. Ladouceur, 'The death of Herod the Great', *CPh* 76 (1981), pp. 25–34.

[32] J. Neusner, 'Judaism in a time of crisis: four responses to the destruction of the Second Temple', *Judaism* 21 (1972), pp. 313–27 = *Early Rabbinic Judaism* (1975), pp. 34–49.

[33] Old sins: *BJ* 5. 398; newer ones: *BJ* 5. 404ff, 413; 7. 34, 264.

Most often, the subject of sin leads Josephus in a different, surprising direction, to a comparison between Jewish offences and Roman innocence, Jewish cruelty and Roman compassion, Jewish sacrilege and the Romans' concern to try and save the city and the Temple. This is an important motif in the history, contrasting strikingly with the angry complaints of the Apocalypses of Baruch and Ezra, where the injustice of the triumphant oppressor intensifies the anguish of the defeated in the face of God's rejection (II Bar. 11; IV Ezra 5). But it would seem that the role of the Roman-virtue theme in Josephus is rhetorical rather than theological; given no independent standing, it is regularly brought in as a reference point to demonstrate the depth of Jewish wrongdoing. It also provides a link with an even more central doctrine, that of the divinely planned transference of power to the Roman side. God, or the Deity, or Fate, or Destiny, or Providence, or Chance had decided that the Romans should be victorious,[34] just as, in the visions of Daniel (7–11) and of IV Ezra (10–13), He had arranged for mighty kingdoms to succeed one another, rising and falling in turn. Vespasian was the chosen agent; and Titus was under special divine protection (*BJ* 3.6, 404; 4.622; 5.2, 60; 6.314). In the furtherance of this objective, specific Roman successes and Jewish disasters had been arranged, and the Jews rendered blind.[35] The destruction of Jerusalem, with the Temple, was but a part of this pattern (*BJ* 4.104; 6.267).

In some of the many instances where this doctrine is expounded, the Deity is described as having been roused to anger, and punishing the Jews because they have wronged Him. In others, the process appears to be one of inexorable fate, and there is no suggestion that anything could have been changed. The latter view is strictly incompatible with the sin-punishment cycle (as well as with Josephus' political interpretation of the revolt). If nothing can avert what has been decreed, it should not matter how nations and individuals behave. But the reconciliation is one which has somehow to be made, if God is seen as omnipotent and omniscient, while man is made responsible for his actions; and both these premises are hard to avoid in the Jewish religion. And so, in one form or another, reconciliations were made. A compromise position was attributed by Josephus to the Pharisees (*BJ* 2.162–3; *AJ* 13.172; 18.13).

[34] See Lindner, op. cit. (n. 5), pp. 42–8.
[35] Successes: *BJ* 3. 293; 6. 411–12; disasters: 4. 297–8, 573; 5. 39; 343, 572; 6. 371, 399; 7. 33.

Statements ascribed to the first Rabbis (the Tannaim) suggest an
implicit awareness of the need for resolution, presumably inherited
from the Pharisees; while the later Rabbis had the makings of more
complex solutions.[36] From our perspective here, it is particularly
striking that Josephus rests, in his own narrative, on the same
assumptions as he ascribes to the Pharisees in his excursuses: 'they
hold that to act rightly or otherwise rests mainly with men, but that
in each action, Fate co-operates.' We have found here another,
overlooked, confirmation that Josephus was, from early on, a
Pharisee.

Among Greek thinkers, the Stoics also strove to reconcile fate
with free-will in a far more sophisticated and technical way.[37] Josephus is able to draw on Stoic terminology, by now to some extent
common currency, and he owes to that source both the term *heimarmenē* (what is fated), and the description of God's Providence as
pronoia (forethinking). Both terms, in fact, had already been adapted
to Jewish theology by Philo, who had even written a work, surviving
in fragments, entitled 'on Providence'.[38] In Josephus, there is no
evidence of serious immersion in Stoic philosophy; he seeks merely
to express his own beliefs in terms intelligible in Greek. Often
enough, indeed, *heimarmenē* is used by him not as the name of an
abstract force, but as a way of talking about God's arrangements.[39]
This was a convenient ambiguity, and precisely the one later cen-
sured (in the equivalent Latin terms) by Augustine: 'without any
doubt, it is by divine providence that human kingdoms are set up.
If anyone ascribes them to "fate" because he uses that term for the

[36] *M Avot* 3.16 (ascribed to Rabbi Akiba) is the best-known statement; though E.
Urbach, *The Sages, their Concepts and Beliefs* (Eng. transl., 1975), p. 257, takes it in
quite a different sense. See Urbach's ch. 11 for an interpretation of the evolving
Rabbinic debate, pp. 268, 284 for a positive evaluation of Josephus' remarks on the
Pharisees. Contrast G. F. Moore, 'Fate and free will in the Jewish philosophies
according to Josephus', *HThR* 22 (1929), pp. 371–89, who tries to argue that they
are a Stoic distortion of Pharisaism. H. W. Attridge comes close to my point in *The
Interpretation of Biblical History in the Antiquitates Judaicae of Flavius Josephus* (1976), pp.
154–5, n. 2.
[37] A clear account in J. Rist, *Stoic Philosophy* (1969), ch. 7.
[38] For the claim that Philo believed in 'relative free will', see D. Winston, 'Freedom
and determinism in Philo of Alexandria', *Studia Philonica* 3 (1974–5), pp. 47–70.
[39] The pagan and Jewish senses in Josephus are well distinguished in the entry of
the unfinished Thackeray-Marcus Lexicon (1955). Cf. also G. Stählin, 'Das Schick-
sal im Neuen Testament und bei Josephus', *Josephus-Studien: Festschrift für Otto Michel*
(1974), pp. 319–43. Attridge, op. cit. (n. 36), pp. 154–5, interestingly observes that,
in *Antiquities*, *pronoia* takes over, while the impersonal terminology disappears.

will or power of God, let him maintain his conviction, but correct his language ... For when men hear this word, ordinary usage leads them to think of nothing but the influence of the position of the stars.' (*Civ. Dei* 5.1).

It was fortunate for Josephus that Greek readers were used to contemplating the involvement of a monotheistic deity in the process of history: such forms of expression go right back to Herodotus.[40] Furthermore, that Josephus wanted his doctrine to have universal appeal, rather than a narrowly Jewish one, emerges unmistakeably from the curious way in which the Roman generals themselves are often made to express it—and in the more monotheistic of its versions. (*BJ* III, 144; 484; 494; IV, 366; 370; 626; VI, 38–41; 411).

When it comes to the concept *tyche*—Providence or Chance—which he uses in connection with the growth of Roman power, Josephus is surely exploiting, and probably consciously, the schema of that other observer of Roman power, Polybius, for whom *tyche* is the most prominent tool for explaining Rome's rise (even though most of his history is concerned with an account of rational factors), and who, perhaps surprisingly, is prone to see this force as a power punishing wrong-doing. For him too, what is more, 'God' is a viable alternative term. More conscious than Josephus of method and coherence, he explains: 'in the case of things of which it is difficult or impossible for mortal men to grasp the causes ... one may justifiably refer them in one's difficulty to God or Tyche.' [41] However, Polybius goes on to delimit very narrowly the area in which such explanations might be required, and all the instances offered are those of natural phenomena: 'but as for matters of which the origin and cause are discoverable, I do not think that we should ascribe them to the deity.' In short, the similarity is only apparent, and Josephus handles the theme of supernatural judgment with an emphasis which could never have allowed him to say that it was just a second-string explanation. In contrast with Polybius, who applies such explanations to various contexts, for Josephus the other factor in the question is usually the same—the people of Israel, in the time-honoured Jewish manner.

[40] See J. L. Myres, *Herodotus* (1953), p. 521f.; H. Lloyd-Jones, *The Justice of Zeus* (1971), p. 64; G. Lachenaud, *Mythologies, religion et philosophie de l'histoire dans Hérodote* (1973), pp. 193–209.
[41] Polybius 36. 17; and further references and discussion in F. W. Walbank, *Historical Commentary on Polybius*, vol. 1 (1957), pp. 16–26.

There is an element of contrivance, one is inclined to say of literary artifice, in the ready way in which Josephus wields this type of explanation, with its undifferentiated affinities to diverse traditions. He seems undisturbed by the implied inconsistency, sometimes asserting that the rise and fall of great powers is a sort of cyclical process which lies in the nature of things, often, as we have said, stressing the notion of punishment for Jewish sins.

In a writer so concerned with easy surface effect as Josephus it makes little sense to insist at every point on the question of what he really thought. Perhaps it is because he was originally a stranger to Graeco-Roman historiography that he could become over-concerned with following, at different times, one convention or another, rather than seeking some sort of resolution between form and content. But it should not be forgotten that the Greek historiography of his day was in general undistinguished; and, even if Polybius was sometimes a model for Josephus, most of those whom he rivalled and imitated were writers now lost, but certainly of far lower quality.[42]

Nor, after our survey, would it be fair to conclude that coherent lines of thinking do not exist in the *Jewish War*; some of the inconsistency about causation and determinism can be justified by the fact that there are, after all, no easy answers available in that area. There was a certain courage in Josephus' very attempt to reconcile the Jewish view of God's role in history with a Greek tradition in which the logic of political events played a more prominent part. When, later, Christian historians were confronted with the same problem, they evaded it, and moved away from the established forms of pagan historiography. Though Josephus was influential in some respects, they did not copy him in this.[43]

Some of the problems which Josephus grappled with were to have a long history. But for the immediate purpose of understanding Josephus in his own time, we may well conclude that it is the unconscious assumptions underlying his writing which have proved most useful. Consciousness of himself as a Jew is not absent, but

---

[42] For Josephus' awareness of contemporary trends in historiography, see *BJ* 1. 6–9, 13–16.

[43] A. D. Momigliano, 'Pagan and Christian historiography in the fourth century A.D.', in Momigliano (ed.), *The Conflict between Paganism and Christianity in the Fourth Century* (1963), pp. 79–94 = *Essays* etc. (see n. 21), pp. 107–19. Momigliano alludes to Josephus, but does not discuss the basic point of difference. See also R. P. Milburn, *Early Christian Interpretations of History* (1954, ch. 4).

most of all, and even in some of his theological utterances, he speaks from his specific vantage point as one of an erstwhile governing class among the Jews, always ready to come to an understanding with the government of Rome, and remote from its own populace in spite of a still partly-potent religious bond. It is natural that he should ascribe to the misdemeanours of that populace most of the blame for the destruction of Jerusalem. The theology of the *Jewish War* is turned in a political direction. Furthermore, inasmuch as Josephus' political class (with its strong Diaspora connections) sought some integration into the world of Greek culture (see Chapter 2), and an accommodation with Rome (see Chapter 3), it was not unfitting that Josephus should record its demise in a historical work of Graeco-Roman type, in which traditional Jewish themes were not unimportant, but were viewed through a Hellenizing glass.

CHAPTER FIVE

The Structure of the Jewish Revolt

The earliest accounts of an episode as turbulent as the first Jewish revolt are likely to derive from individuals who have an axe to grind. The historian of the succeeding generation might feel that he writes 'sine ira et studio', but he will depend upon coloured contemporary accounts. Very often, there will be no version which even approaches neutrality. And, if Josephus' writing does display a singularly high degree of involvement, that is in keeping with the acuteness and violence of the conflict he depicts, and of his importance in it. There is nothing that is in principle extraordinary about the historical record of the Jewish revolt. Yet it is customary now to pour scorn upon this author as utterly partisan, and near despair has, in recent times, been repeatedly expressed about the possibility of learning anything of what happened from what he tells us.

Perhaps this is due in part to the fact that a great deal is expected of him. He provides virtually our only evidence on the subject of the revolt. The relevant parts of Tacitus' *Histories* are largely lost; all that survives are a few allusions in Book 2, and, from Book 5, a digressive preamble on Jewish origins, followed by four chapters which take us down to the start of Titus' siege. There are some remarks of the biographer Suetonius, related to the fortunes in Judaea of the Flavians Vespasian and Titus; and another four sections in the epitome (summary) of the third-century historian Cassius Dio, almost entirely about the siege of Jerusalem. Although each of these writers has details which conflict with Josephus, and seems thus to be at least partly independent of him, these details are not, on the whole, such as to inspire any great confidence, and there is no real challenge here to our author. Apart from this, there are the coins issued by the rebels, valuable but tantalising, and some anecdotes in Talmudic literature, notoriously hard to interpret. Archaeology has substantially confirmed Josephus' topogra-

phy in a number of cases—notably, of course, Masada—and
revealed a few traces of Roman activity; but it cannot be expected
to do more.[1] Josephus' near-monopoly of the historical field makes
for some difficulties. But we should not let it obscure the fact that,
in various ways, Josephus serves us well.

His subjectivity has, in some respects, a positive advantage for
us, arising, as it does, from the part he played in the conflict itself.
First, being so close, he is bound to see certain things very clearly.
And second, if the work contains strong prejudices, those prejudices
are themselves informative and interesting: as well as being a narrative, and a commentary on the events, Josephus' book is itself a
continuation of them, through the medium of literature. His vigorous interpretation has in it echoes of the ideology of the revolutionary era; and through it we come to know something of how
one group of participants reacted to the course of events.[2] Their
deepest resentment was turned against those rebellious compatriots,
whose sedition against Rome and whose sin against God destroyed
Jerusalem.

Yet we need to be sure that we are not dealing with one man's
highly personal, perhaps eccentric opinions, especially since the
man is one who had found himself, at times, in singular positions.
He might have erected a sophisticated edifice to justify himself by
condemning others, to dissociate himself from the revolt, by depicting it as the work of disreputable elements in Jewish society.
Through luck, or God's agency (Josephus himself said he was not
sure which) (*BJ* 3.391), he managed to survive the war, and to
conclude it in extraordinarily favourable circumstances. The way
these things turned out is a well-known story: at the end of a six-

---

[1] Tac., *Hist.* 2. 4; 5. 1–13; Suet., *Vesp.* 4. 5–6; 5.6; 6.3; 8.1; *Tit.* 4.3; 5.2; Dio, *Ep.*
35. 4–7, and 9.2. Tacitus diverges on the numbers of besieged in Jerusalem; however,
his account is the only one which *could*, in spite of this and two other small differences
derive wholly from Josephus; on the differences: M. Stern, *Greek and Roman Authors
on the Jews and Judaism*, vol. 2 (1980), p. 3. Archaeology: Y. Yadin, *Masada: Herod's
Fortress and the Zealots' Last Stand* (1966); and, with possible evidence of Roman
post-war road-building, B. H. Isaac and I. Roll, 'A milestone of A.D. 69 from Judaea',
JRS 46 (1976), pp. 15–19. Suetonius has the procurator Florus dying a violent death
(not so Tacitus), and Vespasian wounded in the knee rather than the foot, as in
Josephus. Dio says that Babylonian Jews did participate, that Roman soldiers deserted to the Jews (not impossible) and that Titus, too, was wounded. For the coins,
see pp. 139–40 and 142, and for Talmudic material, pp. 132–3 and 135–6.

[2] See especially pp. 85ff. For an analogous relation between author and subject,
cf. C. Hill on Clarendon, 'Lord Clarendon and the Puritan Revolution', *Puritanism
and Revolution* (1958), pp. 199ff.

month command in the Galilee, there is the fall of Jotapata, the
fortress to whose defence he had come; there follows Josephus'·
attempt to surrender, forcibly prevented by his companions, his
opposition to their suicide, and the eventual abandonment of the
suicide pact he had to make with them. He gives himself up to the
Romans, and prophesies Vespasian's imminent rise to the purple;
the success of this prophecy changes him from prisoner to court
favourite, companion of the conquerors at the siege of Jerusalem,
and their protége when they and he are installed at Rome (see p.
185ff.). Josephus is, then, a man who assisted his former enemy and
was paid for it. His views could well have been determined by his
situation in court circles in the imperial capital, where, after the
failure of the revolt, he wrote his historical works. His uniqueness
may, it might be suggested, disqualify him from being a witness to
much beyond his own psychology.

But was Josephus in all important ways unique? It is indubitable
that he pictures himself, during the first part of the war, as a man
with associates and allies: sometimes he is at odds with some of
them, but he is still not an isolated figure. There are prominent
Jews who are portrayed as sharing the moderate outlook which
Josephus ascribes to himself, notably Ananus the high priest and
Joshua son of Gamala, Josephus' family friend—both of whom,
unlike Josephus, perished because of their convictions, or their lesser
resourcefulness (see p. 82). This portrayal is fully integrated into a
detailed and intelligible narrative of Jewish politics during the war.
If we find that the portrayal makes sense—in terms, naturally, of
our own conception of the logic of human behaviour and political
events, we must acknowledge that it is not a tissue of lies: such a
web it would be beyond the wit of a writer of normal capacities to
weave; and it is probably only the fact that Josephus was seen as
a traitor which has made it at all possible to envisage him as the
author of so great a lie. In fact, our situation is not entirely an
unhappy one, and we are not thrown back on the grim choice,
either of reproducing Josephus' story as it stands, with varying
degrees of credulity, or of dismissing it in its entirety.[3] From the

[3] As suggested most recently by S. J. D. Cohen, *Josephus in Rome and Galilee* (1979),
p. 181, even though he, in the end, manages to extract much information from
Josephus. More extreme (and in criticism of Cohen): H. R. Moehring, *JJS* 31, 2
(1980), pp. 140-2. Most extreme, Y. Baer, 'Jerusalem in the times of the Great
Revolt', *Zion* 36 (1971), pp. 127-90, and 37 (1972), p. 120 (Hebrew, with English
summary). On the traitor-liar connection, P. Fornaro, *Flavio Giuseppe, Tacito e l'impero*
(1980), p. 7.

narrative provided by the historian, which, if nothing else, is full and circumstantial, and from his analysis, treated itself as a pertinent fact, a full and realistic picture emerges. We may seem to enter into a circular argument, with Josephus as the basis of a reconstruction, which is then used to support or explain Josephus. But there is no logical fallacy, if what is offered is not a strict argument which is to stand as a proof, but, rather, a proposal for putting together the pieces in a multi-dimensional puzzle.

Josephus' revolt had, we found, three salient themes. First, there were the origins of the uprising, traced through narrative to Roman maladroitness, the rebels' intemperance, and the resulting inability of the Jewish ruling class to fulfil its mediating role. Although this decline in the élite's political effectiveness, proceeding in fits and starts, was blamed by Josephus on the inflexibility of the parties on either side, rather than on the mediators, he did at any rate acknowledge the weakness of the latter. Secondly, while the *Jewish War* is formally centred on Roman-Jewish relations, and does contain much about the Roman campaign, what stands out as most alive is the author's concern with internal questions. More than this, the later discussion on the war, found in his 'autobiography', is almost entirely about the interaction of various Jewish factions, the Romans having dropped out of view. Thirdly, there is the division of the Jewish population into two groups, suggested by the favoured concept of *stasis*, and also explicitly demonstrated.[4]

Of course, Josephus was not the man to undervalue his own nation's uprising against Roman might; indeed, for a man of his opinions, he was unexpectedly enthusiastic about, for example, the heroes of Masada (see pp. 219–21). But the dynamic element, the interpretative key to the *Jewish War*, is the civil conflict between zealots (in the broad sense) and the rest of the population. He depicts what amounts to two distinct phenomena: the beginning of the revolt leads to a civil war, and during three and half years, from autumn 66 to spring 70,[5] the two wars occur side by side, with sometimes the one taking precedence, sometimes the other. Furthermore, there are in essence two sides to the conflict; this is not controverted by the activities of a would-be centre group (which included Josephus himself) in the early stages. As it proceeds, the civil war changes shape, producing, as revolutions will, unremitting

---

[4] These themes are displayed in Chapter 4.

[5] For the dates, *BJ* 2. 528 and 555; 5. 277 and 302 (unification of the factions, and destruction by the Romans of Jerusalem's first wall).

faction warfare among its makers and their followers: this dominates Jerusalem in spring 70, and Josephus calls it the tripartite war (*BJ* 5.2). But these developments still do not obscure for Josephus the fact that there was a measure of fundamental common interest existing among the revolutionaries.

The collapse of the Jewish ruling class (and this is what Josephus' first theme amounts to, even if his partisan viewpoint prevents him from identifying it quite thus) makes the link between rebellion and civil war. Failure to deliver the goods which they were expected to deliver disastrously weakened whatever hold they still had over their people. Next, the outbreak of anti-Roman action directed minds to violence and hands to weapons; these could then readily be turned against the more ubiquitous, and therefore often more hated, compatriot enemy (cf. *BJ* 7.255).

This is the explanation to which we are led by Josephus. It is possible to evaluate it, first by considering the fortunes of the Jewish élite within Palestinian society in a slightly wider social perspective; and secondly by close analysis of the beginning of the civil war and the events which, soon, though not immediately, spelled the elimination of the ruling class.

Closer definition is perhaps necessary. The élite of which we have talked is one which had itself been subject to considerable variation in its character and connections over the period of more than two hundred years which had elapsed since the Maccabean revolt. We have already suggested that its composition in Josephus' day was largely the outcome of Herodian patronage, and of the Herods' hostility to their Hasmonean predecessors. But its roots reach, in part, even further back, as was attested by the claims Josephus saw fit to make on his own behalf when he boasted of his Hasmonean ancestry.[6] Furthermore, despite changing personnel, the structure of control in Judaean (if not Galilean) society had been fairly constant since at least the later years of Hasmonean rule, that is from around 100 B.C. There existed a loose and not entirely closed grouping, with prominent members of high priestly families and some other wealthy priests at its heart, and large landowners, as well as court officials, associated with them: they propped up, and at the same time benefited from, the monarchy.[7]

---

[6] P. 21. On Josephus' ancestry, p. 15.

[7] See M. Stern, in *The Jewish People in the First Century, Compendia Rerum Iudaicarum* etc. I, vol. 2 (1976), p. 566.

Equally, it is to the Hasmonean period that we must look for the beginnings of new groupings, which had the effect of rendering the élite unacceptable to various types of people, even at a time when its social and political role was still in the ascendant. And there was a marked emergence of alternative holders of prestige in Jewish society, who came to command greater allegiance than those who were formally and materially in control. No more than a sketch can be offered here.

We have seen, in connection with Josephus' choice of sect, something of the fragmentation and pluralism of first century Judaism.[8] Self-contained groupings of varying size possessed their own figures of authority and perhaps also a separate hierarchical structure, an enclosed style of life involving some measure of deliberate withdrawal from others, and a private interpretation of the Jewish religion, especially of its sacred text, the Torah. Today we know most about the Qumran sect, which called itself *yahad*, a community. It is distinguished by its rejection of Temple and high priesthood, for which were substituted its own priests and an imaginary Temple; by its adoption of a sectarian calendar and an original eschatology. It was not just a small monastic group, but in effect a complete alternative society, since both men and women were included, and only some members were celibate. Its library contained a mixture of special sectarian works with the Biblical, apocryphal and pseudepigraphic texts which were in general circulation.[9] Again, the teaching of Jesus Christ was firmly based in Judaism, yet he evolved a distinctive expression of its ethics, and rejected the political and spiritual authority of the old order among the Jews. 'He entered the temple, and the chief priests and elders of the nation came to him with the question: "By what authority are you acting like this? Who gave you this authority?" Jesus replied, "I have a question to ask you too; answer it, and I will tell you by what authority I act. The baptism of John: was it from God, or from men?" ' (Matth. 21.23–

---

[8] P. 37 Cf. R. A. Kraft, 'The multiform Jewish heritage of early Christianity', *Studies for Morton Smith etc.*, ed. J. Neusner, vol. 3 (1975), pp. 188–99; P. Vidal-Naquet, *Flavius Josèphe ou du bon usage de la trahison* (1977), pp. 72ff., 106ff., with a strange attempt to explain the subsequent splits among the rebels during the revolt, in terms of this diversity in Judaism.

[9] On marriage and celibacy in the community, Schürer-Vermes-Millar-Black, vol. 2, pp. 570 (esp. n. 55), 578. For the library, the published documents are listed by provenance and type together with bibliography, by J. A. Fitzmeyer, *The Dead Sea Scrolls: Major Publications and Tools for Study* (1975).

7; Mark 11.27–33; Luke 20.1–8). Again, it is worth remembering that the principal sects (*haireseis*) described by Josephus offered their own courses of training or initiation, and that a young man as well connected as he thought it of value to put himself through all of them. Different systems of education give rise to different systems of values.

In early Rabbinic sources, we find mentions, relating to this period, of the *havurah* or association of friends. It appears that all Jews are theoretically fit to be members if they swear to fulfil certain obligations and become dedicated to ritual purity, especially in the matters of consumption of food and correct tithing. Whatever concrete form such associations took (and sometimes it may have meant no more than an undertaking to pursue certain kinds of domestic conduct), at least in their own minds, the associates or friends (*haverim*) were separate from the rest of the community, who were *amei ha-aretz* (people of the country); and at times it seems that families were split by these contrasts. That much is clear, even for this early date. When it comes to detail, there are complicated discriminations and rulings concerning the behaviour of members to be found in the Mishnah and its parallel text the Tosefta, but it is more than likely that they have little relation to the pre-70 era; and it is equally difficult to accept the idea that there were different stages of initiation into the fellowship, an idea sometimes used to resolve contradictions in the texts.[10] These doubts do not matter here. The *havurah* was probably a Pharisaic institution, though some would dispute even this.[11] Either way, a noteworthy point is that the Pharisees were separated off in a comparable way, and indeed derived their very name, *perushim*, from their separateness. This name has to mean 'men set apart', and, as has been sensibly observed, whether the separation was taken to be from their fellow

---

[10] See J. Neusner, 'The Fellowship (Haburah) in the Second Jewish Common-wealth', *HThR* 53 (1960), pp. 125–42; on the contradictions, p. 131 and n. 46. For the *havurah* in general, cf. Neusner, *The Idea of Purity in Ancient Judaism* (1973), pp. 64–71; A. Oppenheimer, *The 'Am Ha-aretz* (1977), ch. 4. On the texts, see also S. Lieberman, 'The discipline in the so-called Dead Sea Manual of Discipline', *JBL* 71 (1952), pp. 199–206 = *Texts and Studies* (1974), pp. 200–7. The term *hbr* for a member of a religious association was also used in very different contexts, e.g. among pagans at Hatra: J. Teixidor, *The Pagan God* (1977), p. 6, n. 8.

[11] E. Rivkin, *The Hidden Revolution* (1978), esp. pp. 162ff.

men, or from uncleanness, the effect of detaching them socially was the same.[12]

The roots of this pluralism go back a good distance, and an early impetus was probably provided by the Hasmonean (Maccabean) dynasty, a Jewish ruling house of revolutionary origins which soon became established, Hellenized, and unpopular, and whose members made the grave mistake of calling themselves high priests.[13] The Wicked Priest, envisaged by the Qumran sectaries as the arch opponent of their founding Teacher of Righteousness, was almost certainly a Hasmonean ruler, and was probably to be identified with one of the earliest, Jonathan, high priest in 153–152 B.C.[14] The Pharisees have by some been traced right back to the *hasidim* (just men, saints) of the Maccabean wars.[15] If this is too speculative, it is at any rate evident that a Pharisaic party was crystallized through opposition to John Hyrcanus (135–104 B.C.), principally, it seems for his occupation of the high priesthood.[16] It is interesting that Hyrcanus, as though to strengthen his own appeal, claimed prophetic powers for himself.[17] Under Alexander Jannaeus (103–76 B.C.) a major civil war arose, and Josephus ascribes its origins to arguments between the king and the Pharisees' leader, Simon ben

[12] See Schürer-Vermes-Millar-Black, vol. 2, p. 396. The Gospels suggest that the individuals known as 'scribes' had more or less merged with the Pharisees by this date; and so J. Jeremias, *Jerusalem in the Time of Jesus* (1969), pp. 233–45. But some think they were still distinguishable by their concern for study of the Law, e.g. E. Bickerman, in *The Jews, their History, Culture and Religion*, ed. L. Finkelstein (1949), p. 49, calling them an 'intelligentsia'; J. Neusner, *Early Rabbinic Judaism*, (1975).

[13] However, their origins are explained in entirely ideological terms by Morton Smith, 'The Dead Sea sect in relation to ancient Judaism', *NTS* 7 (1961), pp. 347–60, arguing that schism was the natural result of allowing overriding authority to law. For a recent political explanation L. I. Levine, 'The political struggle between Pharisees and Sadducees in the Hasmonean Period', in A. Oppenheimer, U. Rappaport, M. Stern (eds.), *Jerusalem in the Second Temple Period: Abraham Schalit Memorial Volume* (Jerusalem, 1980; Hebrew, with English summaries), pp. 61–83.

[14] See G. Vermes, *The Dead Sea Scrolls: Qumran in Perspective* (1977), pp. 142–56 (with bibliography).

[15] E. Rivkin, op. cit. (n. 11).

[16] *AJ* 13. 288–98. Rabbinic tradition is uncertain whether it was John Hyrcanus or Alexander Jannaeus who first fell out with the Pharisees, and G. Allon therefore rejected the Josephus version relied on (tentatively) in this reconstruction: see 'The attitude of the Pharisees to the Roman government and the House of Herod', *Scripta Hierosolymitana* 7 (1961), pp. 53–78 = *The Jews, Judaism and the Classical World: Studies in Jewish History in the Times of the Second Temple and Talmud* (transl. I. Abrahams; 1976), pp. 18–47.

[17] *AJ* 13. 282–3; *BJ* 1. 68–9. Rabbinic passages have him receiving information from a divine voice in the Temple.

Shetah. By now the Pharisaic following was apparently considerable;[18] but on the religious plane, their sectarian and separate characteristics evidently lasted. Alexander's widow, Queen Salome Alexandra, had to make peace with them. But then, during the long reign of Herod (35–34 B.C.), a new pattern was established: Herod devalued the high priesthood in a different way, not by occupying it himself, but by making and cancelling appointments to it. For this and other reasons, the Pharisees as a body rejected the king, for all the careful respect that he tried to show them.[19] The palace, in its turn, gave circulation to a story that a prophetic Essene had foreseen the kingship of Herod as a boy, and this claim of Essene endorsement suggests to a suspicious mind that there might have been trouble with them too (*AJ* 15.373–9). And in the end, the violent disturbances released by Herod's death, in many ways the precursor of the great revolt, saw the beginning of the activity of Judas son of Ezekias, who was in all probability the same man as the Judas who founded the rebel tendency known as the 'fourth philosophy' (see p. 115).

If we seek now to explain Jewish pluralism, instead of merely tracing a line of development (or some points along such a line), then we may see it as a phenomenon arising out of cultural and political pressure; first there was the compelling and at first challengingly different Greek culture which surrounded the Jews; then came the Roman imperial conquest, and its by-product, a client monarchy. 'Composite societies' are likely to develop out of such situations, both because of the appeal or imposition of outside ideas and new institutions, and because they tend to bring with them an admixture of new population of diverse origin. Such societies are structurally pluralistic, and contain a number of value systems. New values may take time to evolve, but in due course challenges to the old holders of political power will readily be thrown up, because the latter's power is not upheld by sufficiently widespread respect and approval.[20]

---

[18] To judge by the numbers they could continue to mobilise against Alexander: Josephus has 5,000 Jews killed in a six-year war, *AJ* 13. 376.

[19] *AJ* 15. 368–70; 17. 42–51; Allon, op. cit. (n. 16).

[20] Anthropologists have concentrated on simpler societies affected by more sophisticated ones; we might not wish to call the pre-Hellenistic Middle East, and especially Palestine, primitive, but the model seems applicable in some respects. See A. R. Radcliffe-Brown, *Structure and Function in Primitive Society* (1952), p. 202ff. On the indispensability of prestige to a regime of 'notables', see P. Veyne, *Le Pain et le Cirque* (1976), pp. 110–15.

Charismatic leaders, in Max Weber's sense, which still seems useful and which makes a valuable contrast between charisma on the one hand and traditional or 'bureaucratic', rule-determined forms of authority on the other,[21] thrive in such transitional, unsettled situations;[22] they flourished all the more in Jewish Palestine, where the religious appeal which characteristically validates such authority was readily available. There is ample evidence of their presence during this period. What we find are leaders, from outside the established élite, with a distinct teaching to communicate and an obvious need to discredit those in control so as to gain acceptance for themselves. It is undeniable that the activities of Jesus fit this description in some respects. At Qumran, the shadowy Teacher of Righteousness had been seen to offer, in a comparable way, a renovation of the doctrine of the unregenerate old Israel; and the persecution suffered by him and his elect at the hands of the Wicked Priest forms a pivot of the sectarian interpretation of, for example, the book of Habakkuk.[23] Through the documents, his image remained vivid for succeeding generations in the sect. At the same time, it must be said that the communal organisation revealed by the scrolls scarcely leaves room for a pre-eminent inspirational figure who might have followed in the Teacher's footsteps, unless perhaps it be the sect's high priest: devotion to the Teacher's memory was presumably the mainspring of loyalty. What is clear, however, in the case of both Christ and Qumran, is that the message is enhanced through its setting in a consciously-contrived atmosphere of eschatological expectation.[24] In each case, furthermore, communication of the teaching is, to a significant extent, achieved in a distinctively Jewish style, through Biblical exegesis or citation or allusion; but while the Teacher is the true interpreter of the Law of Moses, Christ, in contrast, largely rejects it.

A striking feature of such charismatic leaders as these two is that

[21] *Economy and Society* (ed. G. Roth and C. Wittich; 1968), pp. 241–54; 1111–57. Weber's conception is still useful, in spite of the difficulties associated with it, on which see, notably, P. Worsley, *The Trumpet Shall Sound* ([2]1968), introduction. The incoherence of such Weberian notions as 'institutionalised charisma' does not concern us here.

[22] See N. Cohn, 'Medieval Millenarism: its bearing on the comparative study of millenarian movements', in S. L. Thrupp (ed.), *Millenial Dreams in Action: Comparative Studies in Society and History*, suppl. 2 (1962), pp. 32–43.

[23] *Commentary on Habakkuk*. For an English version, see G. Vermes, *The Dead Sea Scrolls in English* ([2]1965), pp. 235–42.

[24] For the parallel between Jesus and the Teacher of Righteousness, see G. Vermes, 'Jewish studies and New Testament interpretation', *JJS* 31. 1 (1980), p. 11.

their impact is confined to a very limited circle, and seems scarcely to have extended beyond it. Were it not for the Dead Sea discoveries, we should know nothing of the Teacher of Righteousness; if we depended on Josephus, we should know next to nothing of Jesus Christ.[25] What is of supreme importance to some, is considered scarcely worthy of notice by others.

If the Qumran sectaries looked back to only one great teacher, for the Pharisees there were many—provided, that is, we are right in assuming that the 'sages' of Rabbinic literature were Pharisaic teachers (see p. 29 n. 55). While it may well be true that, until the emergence of Rabbinic Judaism (after A.D.70), no one was so brazen as to claim accurate knowledge of utterances made by the earliest authorities,[26] still the whole process would not have been possible unless there had been a habit of ascribing dicta to specific individuals. The best known tractate of the Mishnah is *Avot*, the Fathers, and the first four chapters collect together moral precepts made between about 200 B.C. and A.D.200 (or shortly before), ostensibly by named persons, who appear to be addressing the circles of their disciples. For a period, stretching from around the mid-second century B.C., the teachers are grouped as five pairs, and, as emerges from other sources, the members of each take opposing sides in controversies: such a dual structure would seem appropriate for a phase in which the basic ingredients of the oral law are being evolved through argument. Although these figures are presented as heads of the Sanhedrin,[27] their moral authority certainly preceded whatever formal powers they acquired. It was a moral authority which grew posthumously and enhanced the claims of teachers lower down the line. What is more, in early Rabbinic Judaism, if not before,[28] Moses himself has become the alleged ultimate source of any teaching that is thought worthy of transmission, thus providing an unimpeachable endorsement of later claims. E. Urbach, who mapped out the thought-world of the sages, described them as men with the same status as the prophets of ancient Israel, who, like them, required no official position for the performance of their distinctive activity. The point emerges nicely from stories like the

[25] Cf. Vidal-Naquet, op. cit. (n. 8), p. 74.

[26] J. Neusner, *The Rabbinic Traditions about the Pharisees before 70*, 1–3 (1971), especially 1, pp. 143–179.

[27] According to Mishnah, *Hagigah* 2.2.

[28] Neusner, loc. cit. (n. 26); op. cit. (n. 12), pp. 84–5; Neusner, *From Politics to Piety* (²1979), ch. 6, explains in simple terms his scholarly reasons for ascribing the claim to late, Yavnean origins.

one told of Hillel, the greatest of the first crop of teachers: 'it happened once that when the sages entered the house of Guryo in Jericho, they heard a Heavenly Voice say, "there is a man here who is worthy of the holy spirit, but his generation is not worthy of it," and they all looked at Hillel.'[29]

For Urbach, wisdom rather than charisma was the leading attribute of the sages, but this was merely because he was using the term 'charisma' in a more restricted sense than that employed here. Historians of religion have been quite considerably concerned of late with 'charisma' in the narrow sense, with such individuals as are thought to have direct contact with the divine—miracle-workers, exorcisers, healers. First-century A.D. Judaism also contains remarkable examples of this distinctive phenomenon; and vivid pictures have recently been painted of two strange individuals who were evidently popular enough to leave at least some mark on a Rabbinic tradition generally hostile to their kind. One was Honi the Circle Maker, so intimate with God that he could produce rain by blackmailing Him, refusing to move until he got what he wanted; the other was Hanina ben Dosa, who remained unscathed when a snake bit him as he was lost in prayer.[30]

The anti-Roman movement which Josephus calls the Fourth Philosophy began, according to him, as a branch of Pharisaism, and its development is understood by him in terms of the fortunes of successive leaders. There is almost a parallel here to the line of high priests on the one hand, and to the succession of Pharisaic teachers on the other; but here the succession is within one family group. Judas of Gamala (or Gaulanitis), the founder, is probably the same man as the one Josephus calls Judas son of the bandit Hezekiah (Ezekias). The father was killed, with his followers, by the young Herod, and must already have had considerable appeal, because the Sanhedrin used the murder as a pretext for trying Herod.[31] We are told that Judas, in his turn, inspired much

---

[29] E. E. Urbach, *The Sages: their Concepts and Beliefs* (transl. I. Abrahams; 1975), pp. 564–76. On Hillel: *Tos. Sotah* 13.3; *TP Sot.* 9.13. 24a; *TB Sot.* 48b. Cf. Neusner, op. cit. (n. 28), p. 13.

[30] References and discussion of sources in Vermes, *Jesus the Jew* (1973), pp. 65–78.

[31] *AJ* 14. 158ff.; *BJ* 2. 56, 118; *AJ* 17. 271–2; 18. 2–10, 23; M. Hengel, *Die Zeloten* (1961), pp. 336–40; M. Stern, 'Sicarii and Zealots', in *World History of the Jewish People*, vol. 8, *Society and Religion in the Second Temple Period* (1977), pp. 266–71. The chronological objections of E. M. Smallwood, *The Jews under Roman Rule* (1976), p. 153 n. 40, are not fatal to the identification, especially since there is no evidence that Judas of Gamala was killed in A.D. 6.

devotion, especially among the young. His sons, James and Simon, were judged and crucified under the procurator Tiberius Julius Alexander and the emperor Claudius (*AJ* 20.102). An even better-known son was Menahem, leader of the *sicarii* until his murder in autumn 66. He is described interestingly as a *sophistes* (teacher of the law?), and was arrogant enough to appear at the Temple for ritual purposes in regal array, accompanied by an armed bodyguard of devoted followers.[32]

There is no question of ascribing the actual outbreak of revolt against Rome in a simple way to the activities of influential individuals. The connection between the flourishing of uninstitutionalised leaders in the Second Temple period and the events of 66 is, in the first instance, indirect. I have suggested that it lies in habituating the people to disregard or challenge its leaders. Then, when revolt slides into revolution, the role of powerful outsiders will be discernible; and it is perhaps no accident that one of them is Menahem son of Judas.[33]

The war started in two urban centres, Jerusalem and Caesarea, and, in the usual manner of wars, it came about as though by chance, out of collisions which were in themselves nothing unusual. Josephus himself remarked on this (*BJ* 2.285). A negative reply from the emperor to the appeal for support sent by the Jews of Caesarea provoked new trouble between Jews and Greeks there, and an arrest by Florus of local Jewish notables (cf. pp. 73ff.). Then a sympathetic reaction at Jerusalem was rendered explosive by what must have been a quite separate, but appallingly ill-timed action on Florus' part—the collection of seventeen talents from the Temple treasury to meet some imperial requirement, with a full military backing designed to beat down the opposing masses. Florus' fury at an attempted intercession by the Jewish leaders, and at their failure to co-operate in picking out trouble-makers for trial before his tribunal, might have united the Jewish population. Instead, as the confrontation continued, the gap between the Jewish groups grew, stretched by their contrasting responses to the procurator: the people resolute and embittered after the troops' stampede through

---

[32] *BJ* 2. 433–40, 444–8. At 444, his supporters are called *zēlōtai*, enthusiasts; the word is being used here in a non-technical sense, and there is clearly no reference to the Zealot 'party'.

[33] Vidal-Naquet calls such leaders 'rois chauds' (ordinary rulers being 'rois froids'): op. cit. (n. 8), pp. 87–95.

the upper city had left a number of dead, the leaders channelling their increasing desperation into abject appeals. A trivial, but crucial focus of disagreement was whether or not to salute the second wave of Roman troops; it had apparently become known that Florus had ordered them to advance from Caesarea without returning any salute offered. The Jewish salutes were duly delivered, and so was the Roman insult, an act of omission. This was the moment for the agitators to incite opposition to Florus, and for the Roman troops to attack again, backed up by pursuing cavalry. Yet, when Florus withdrew from Jerusalem, distressed that the porticoes between his military headquarters and the Temple had been wrecked, the Jewish leaders saw fit to promise that they would maintain order. The only form of action they would consider, and that only under pressure from the now frantic populace, was verbal criticism of Florus, made behind his back: first in a letter to the governor of Syria (another was written by Queen Berenice), then in an encounter with the governor's representative. But when the people wanted a letter to be sent also to the emperor himself, Florus drew the line, and insisted on restraint in a pacific and pacifying oration.

So runs Josephus' sharply drawn story; and in it we see a population too disparate both in its modes of political behaviour and in its assumptions ever to maintain a consistent common front against Roman provocation. Rather, the differences already in existence were profoundly aggravated during those unpleasant days. Admittedly, Josephus does say that the proposed embassy to Nero was to serve, for the people, the purpose of clearing them of any suspicion of revolt through their denunciation of Florus; but in this ascription of motive (which is not an event) we may legitimately doubt him. That their anger was greatly aroused is quite clear. Next, King Agrippa's tearful expostulations, that the people were putting themselves into a war with Rome by being so imprudent, served only to infuriate them further; all the more as it was followed by a dutiful and demonstrative collection of tribute arrears. The angry expulsion of Agrippa from the city was countered by his sending the officials and notables to present themselves to Florus, now at Caesarea, as the instruments by which the procurator might collect the tribute still due from the countryside. There was apparently no objection.

The act which in fact constituted a declaration of war on Rome was the refusal to offer any longer the customary sacrifices made in the Temple twice a day on behalf of the emperor. This refusal was strongly resisted by high priests, notables and priestly experts.[34] Even if, as Josephus suggests, the argument on this issue remained more or less orderly, it led straight away to the predictable confrontation between the two parties of Jews. The rebels established themselves in the lower city and Temple, their opponents held the upper. It was in the course of this confrontation that the house of Ananias, the palaces of Agrippa and Berenice, and the archives which contained the money-lenders' bonds, were deliberately burned; as Josephus has it, the indigent were turning upon those who were more prosperous (*BJ* 2.426–7).

Roman pressure opened up the rift, but could not have created it out of nothing. Indeed for Josephus it is an established feature of Jewish society. He takes it for granted that the chief priests and other important elements will behave one way, the less reputable elements another. The distinction evidently corresponds to what we call the upper classes—those whose property, as he says, makes them keen on peace—as against the lower. Close analysis has no shortage of hazards, both due to lack of evidence and because of the difficulty of determining what categories are appropriate. There are those who argue that distinctions of status were more significant in the classical world than differences of class.[35] But even they concede that, at least in an attenuated sense, description in terms of upper and lower classes is unavoidable. How, beyond that, we might apply to that era a concept derived from Marx (and itself not free of ambiguities) remains a troublesome problem—and an interesting one.[36] What is at any rate clear, and for the present sufficient, is that the bitter internal quarrels of classical Greece and of Roman Palestine were often enough not between the more and the less important citizens, but, as both Aristotle and Josephus in

[34] *BJ* 2. 409; cf. 2. 197; *CA* 2. 77; Philo, *Leg.* 157. According to Josephus, though not Philo (who is likely to be wrong) the Jews had met the expense of the sacrifices themselves. For a demonstration that such sacrifices were in keeping with Jewish (Pharisaic-Rabbinic) tradition, see C. Roth, 'The debate on the loyal sacrifices, A.D. 66', *HThR* 53 (1960), pp. 93–7.

[35] M. I. Finley, *The Ancient Economy* (1973), ch. 2. See also S. C. Humphreys, *Anthropology and the Greeks* (1978), pp. 73–5.

[36] For different ways of making the application, see J-P. Vernant, *Myth and Society in Ancient Greece* (transl. J. Lloyd, 1980), ch. 1; G.E.M. de Ste. Croix, 'Karl Marx and the history of Classical antiquity', *Arethusa* 8 (1975), pp. 7–42; E. M. and N. Wood, *Class Ideology and Ancient Political Theory* (1978), pp. 41–64 (cruder and less successful). R. A. Padgug, 'Classes and society in ancient Greece', *Arethusa* 8 (1975), esp. pp. 97–100, confusingly adopts the term 'estate' to mean a class that is not fully formed.

their very different ways were quite well aware (not to mention other writers), they were between the rich and the poor, the propertied and the non-propertied.[37]

We have already offered an impressionistic account of the wealthy sector of Jerusalem society (see pp. 22–6). Even about such people there is much that we would like to know and probably never will: there is no answer to fundamental questions, such as how large a rich man's large estate really was: the poor man's perception, which is essentially what we have in the parables of the Gospels, tends to be vague. Again, we do not know whether the big landowner was most often a townsman, and an absentee landlord, or whether he might equally well be found living on one of his estates.[38] Quantitative studies based on several fragmentary surviving land registers from various parts of the empire, spread over some four hundred years, suggest that everywhere substantial accumulations of landed property were in the hands of the wealthy: not only is there a high degree of differentiation between the largest and the smallest landholdings in any one list, but also the single largest estate constitutes in each case a strikingly high percentage of the total. Although more smallholdings appear to survive in the east than in the west, the difference is probably marginal.[39] Here, at least, scholars have bypassed the subjective and limited awareness of literary sources; but it is highly dubious whether any such light might be shed on the wealthy landowners of first-century Palestine.

For the others, people who left little mark on the record, the difficulties are still greater. We cannot say anything about the status of the typical peasant, whether he was often independent, or tended to be a tenant, a hired labourer who had to wait in the market place for some work to come his way, or even, as seems to have been common in the eastern Roman provinces, some kind of debt bondsman, like the wretched debtor in Matthew's parable, whom we find about to be sold together with his wife and children.[40] We cannot

[37] de Ste. Croix, op. cit. (n. 36), pp. 23–5; R. MacMullen, *Roman Social Relations* (1974), ch. 4; Vernant, op. cit. (n. 36), pp. 12–13.

[38] A phenomenon stressed by MacMullen, op. cit. (n. 37), pp. 5, 15, 20–1, 23, etc.

[39] R. P. Duncan-Jones, 'Some configurations of landholding in the Roman Empire', in M. I. Finley (ed.), *Studies in Roman Property* (1976), pp. 7–33.

[40] See Matthew 18.23–35 for the bondsman-to-be. On debt bondsmen in general see W. E. Heitland, *Agricola* (1921), pp. 209ff.; MacMullen, op. cit. (n. 37), pp. 31, 51–2; P. Garnsey, 'Non-slave labour in the Roman world', in *Cambridge Philological Society*, suppl. vol. 6, ed. Garnsey (1980), p. 36, and n. 11. For wage labourers, see the parable of the vineyard, Matthew 20.1–16. H. Kriessig, following Klausner, and

assess the effects of tithing and taxation on the individual's subsist-
ence. We do not know how poor the poor really were. Archaeology
might help. But the investigation of settlement patterns in the region
has scarcely begun; and, in any case, it does not contain the whole
answer. For, while interesting archaeological evidence does now
exist for the presence in Judaea, Samaria and western Galilee of
large, fortified farms and of aggregated villages, sometimes associated with monumental tomb complexes, and this may tell us something about those who held the land, it yields no conclusions about
the status of the agricultural labour attached to the cluster.[41] Again,
especially because the revolt against Roman domination was urban
in origin, the relation of the rural poor to the towns needs to be
understood. As for the towns, it is worth noting that during the
revolt Josephus observed in other places the same social split as he
recorded for Jerusalem. On the other hand, in some ways Jerusalem
(which has to be our main concern) was a special case; for its cult
had been the common possession of Judaea since the days of David,
and a particularly well-developed road system took peasants there
at festivals and at other times too. Here town and country must
have had an unusually intimate involvement.[42]

Whatever the uncertainties, there can be no doubt that without
some sort of tentative economic commentary we are at sea. We have
interpreted change in Jewish society in terms of plurality of ideology,
and transformations of status. Yet the economic character of Josephus' dichotomy is often quite plain. If it is true that we are talking
about what has come to be described (following Karl Polanyi) as
an economy 'embedded in society', then perhaps the two approaches

---

against Dalman, holds that, in Palestine, small free farmers were first in importance,
followed by tenant farmers; but, except for the Gospels, the evidence used is mostly
for the post-70 period: see *Die sozialen Zusammenhänge des judäischen Krieges* (1970),
pp. 19ff.; an earlier, shorter version of this monograph is 'Die landwirtschaftliche
Situation in Palästina vor dem judäischen Krieg', *Acta Antiqua* 17 (1969), pp. 223–
54. The various types of leaseholders appearing in Mishnah, Tosefta and the Bar
Kokhba documents (all post 70), seem to belong to the well-to-do sector of society:
for the terminology, see Applebaum, op. cit. (n. 7), pp. 659–60. Cf. also, for Galilee,
S. Freyne, *Galilee from Alexander the Great to Hadrian, 323 B.C.E. to 135 C.E: a study of
Second Temple Judaism* (1980), pp. 165–6.

[41] Applebaum, op. cit. (n. 7), pp. 641–6; and 'Judaea as a Roman Province', in
Aufstieg und Niedergang der Römischen Welt (ed. H. Temporini and W. Haase), 2, 7
(1977), pp. 365–6.

[42] Social split in Tiberias: *V* 32; Gadara: *BJ* 4. 414. Access to Jerusalem: M.
Har-El, 'Jerusalem and Judaea: roads and fortifications', *Biblical Archaeologist* 44, 1
(1981), pp. 8–19.

may be in considerably less tension than they would be in discussing more recent history.[43] Economic resentment was not consistently perceived as such, but in religious or social terms. If the established political élite clings to political power (within the overall framework of Roman rule) while its authority and prestige are diminishing, and increases its offensiveness by increasing its assets and oppressing the poor, then both processes converge to lead towards revolution.

What would seem indispensable in interpreting the conflict between poor and rich is some information on the direction of economic change in the preceding period. Were the rich all the time getting richer, and the poor poorer? Or, as often happens, could the pre-revolutionary period have been one of generally rising prosperity, and therefore increasing expectation among the lower classes, followed by anger when that expectation was unfulfilled? The question is partly one of the long-term impact and distortions of the local situation which are produced when a region becomes involved in the Roman empire, either as a province (like Judaea and Galilee from 63 B.C.), or else as a client kingdom (like Judaea between 37 B.C. and A.D.6 and Galilee even longer). The change in legal status in itself signifies little, but an influx of new personnel and a network of new external connections are likely concomitants. A client king, if he is vigorous and ambitious, may well do more to alter a region's social and economic life than direct rule.[44]

There are some signs, if nothing more, that the second of the two is the more correct interpretation. The growth of Jerusalem, with its partly parasitic temple and palace, is a notable feature of the first centuries before and after Christ. So too is the development of towns, and even cities, throughout the region, fostered both by the client kings, and also, to a lesser extent, by the procuratorial administration. Herod had more scope for his activities as city benefactor in non-Jewish territory than in Jewish; but in or around the latter, quite apart from his large-scale enterprises at Jerusalem, there was the construction of the harbour and city of Caesarea, the foundation of Phasaelis in the Jordan valley above Jericho, and of Sebaste, a military settlement in Samaria. Herod Philip, one of his successors, turned the village of Bethsaida, on the North side of the Sea of

---

[43] See especially Humphreys, op. cit. (n. 35), p. 31ff.

[44] For an interesting attempt to minimise the change, see C. R. Whittaker, 'Rural labour in three Roman provinces', in *Cambridge Philological Society*, suppl. vol. 6, ed. Garnsey, pp. 73–99.

Galilee, into Julias, and established a new foundation, Caesarea Panias, at one of the sources of the Jordan. The first principally Jewish city was the Tiberias of another successor, Herod Antipas. It has been claimed that the density of cities in western Palestine under the Roman empire was remarkably high in comparison with other provinces.[45] Building programmes and public display, whether funded principally by the local rich or through the royal treasury, must have been parasitic also on the labour or the productivity of the surrounding countryside. Ancient cities were, in a sense, consumer cities. Yet, at the same time, by creating markets, and stimulating consumption, they could prove ultimately advantageous to an agricultural hinterland which, as was the way in the ancient world, catered almost exclusively for local demand.[46] Josephus attests the fertility and populousness of first-century Palestine, saying that the towns were densely distributed, and (perhaps exaggerating) that the smallest village had over fifteen thousand inhabitants. He also has indications of the quality of life in some of the 204 Galilean settlements.[47] Jerusalem and the Temple may have siphoned off the produce of the countryside, but they were also an unusual kind of asset, bringing in coin in the shape of the two-drachma Temple tax contributed annually by Jews everywhere, as well as tithes, other gifts and a regular influx of pilgrims.[48]

It remains an open question whether the long reign of Herod, certainly crucial to the evolution of Roman Palestine, made only modest, or very crippling demands on the purses of ordinary people; and limited evidence is available in support of either view.[49] If those

[45] M. Broshi, 'The population of western Palestine in the Roman-Byzantine period', *BASOR* 236 (1979), pp. 3–10. On the administrative significance of the new units within Judaea-Samaria, A. H. M. Jones, 'The urbanisation of Palestine', *JRS* 21 (1931), pp. 78–85.

[46] Cf. K. Hopkins, 'Economic growth and towns in Classical antiquity', in P. Abrams and E. A. Wrigley (eds), *Towns in Societies* (1978), pp. 35–77. In contrast, the economic insignificance of ostentatious building programmes is suggested by N. J. Pounds, 'The urbanization of the Classical world', *Association of American Geographers, Annals* 59 (1969), pp. 135–57.

[47] *BJ* 3. 42–55; *V* 235; *BJ* 2. 504—houses built in Tyrian style at Chabulon.

[48] There is ample evidence that the money was actually paid; the question of how the tithing regulations were treated in practice is more obscure; see Jeremias, op. cit. (n. 12), pp. 134–38.

[49] Moderate demands: A. H. M. Jones, *The Herods of Judaea* (1938), pp. 86–8, pointing out that Herod twice made remissions in land tax, and that his sales tax would probably have hit chiefly the upper classes. Crippling demands: J. Klausner, in *World History of the Jewish People*, vol. 7, *The Herodian Period* (1961), ch. 5; Applebaum, op. cit. (n. 7), p. 665.

who revolted after his death demanded a reduction in taxation and obligations, this shows that the imposition was resented, not that it was intolerable. Complaints against Herod after the suppression of the revolt included the rhetorical claim, emanating, it seems, from the well-born, that Herod had impoverished the country and decimated their ranks—but the resentful feelings of such persons are a different problem (*BJ* 2.4).

In this period Judaea and Galilee seem to have imported a wide range of manufactured goods, especially eastern luxuries, and to have exported a select number of specific items—olive oil, dates, and such balsam as reached the open market.[50] The quantities involved were mostly small, and talk of a commercial sector is misplaced.[51] None the less, it must be admitted that the new harbour of Caesarea facilitated operations: not so long before, the Jews had lost control even of its much less adequate predecessor, the port of Joppa.[52] In this respect, Herodian activity was advantageous.

In the decades following, there is no reason to postulate a drawn-out economic crisis leading up to the great revolt. Banditry was widespread, but this has many contributory causes: weak government, dislocation of populations, rapid change in a society and its values, urbanisation; bad harvests simply serve to step up its level somewhat. Banditry was also to be found in areas which played no part in the revolt, notably in Trachonitis where it was so permanent that the brigands kept food, water and cattle in underground hideouts and in caves.[53] Furthermore, because Josephus sees the intimate connection between bandits and the insurgents of the revolt, he tends to highlight earlier brigandage in anticipation; and this is a twist of explanation around which we do not have to follow him. An attractive suggestion has been made that land hunger was

[50] S. Zeitlin, *Rise and Fall of the Judaean State*, vol. 2 (1967), pp. 266–80, has a useful account of agricultural and manufactured exports, but makes too much of them. A generous estimate also in Applebaum, op. cit. (n. 7), pp. 667–80.

[51] Finley, op. cit. (n. 35), ch. 5. Still, the great variety of items involved should not be forgotten; so Hopkins, op. cit. (n. 46).

[52] Removed from the Jews by Pompey, recaptured by Herod.

[53] Preconditions of banditry: E. J. Hobsbawm, *Primitive Rebels* (1959), pp. 23–6 etc; *Bandits*[2] (1981), pp. 22–9. A connection between unsown crops, lack of harvest, unpaid tribute and a consequent resort to banditry is put by Josephus into the mouths of the Jews who protest to the Roman governor about the statue of himself which the emperor Caligula had put in the Temple: that they had left their fields thus proves the depth of their feeling: *AJ* 18. 274. Trachonitis: *AJ* 15. 346–8 (I owe these references to an unpublished paper by B. Isaac).

becoming acute among the Jewish inhabitants at this time, and that it came to a head in A.D. 66. Pompey's removal of coastal and Jordan territories from Jewish control, and the absorption of land into royal territory, and of farmsteads and whole villages into large estates are held to blame, while disputes over territory both before and during the war are deemed a struggle for marginal land.[54] However, this theory presupposes that there had been a substantial independent Jewish peasantry in the preceding years, since for tenants a change in the ultimate owner of the land is likely to make little difference. What is more, even free farmers need not have been expropriated just because of a nominal transfer of control.

Thus, far from steady impoverishment, especially of rural areas, there is reason to postulate some general increase in economic activity and prosperity, which at first benefitted all sectors of society. But such benefit was bound to be unequally distributed, so that towards the end of our period, when rising expectations at the lower levels of society had outstripped any possibility of realisation, and some short-term economic crises had brought about real difficulty, conflict understandably became acute. That there was poverty in Palestine before the reigns of Claudius and Nero is patent. But to explain the social revolution described by Josephus, we do not need to show that destitution was more marked or permanent there than elsewhere. The poor, in Josephus, are all those who are not rich; and the difference must have been apparent indeed, even without the poor being always desperate.

The purpose of this argument is to give depth to the picture, but not by any means to slur over the fact that there did emerge some sort of real economic trouble in Palestine in the two decades before the revolt. Shortly before Florus became procurator, work on the last outbuildings of Herod's Temple was finally at an end, and more than 18,000 men were laid off (*AJ* 20.219ff.). Even if we discount Josephus' figure (which, like most of those in his work, is likely to be wrong), his attestation of the event is valuable. So too is the added information that 'the people' urged Agrippa II, whom Claudius had put in charge of the Temple, to offer new employment by raising the height of the porticoes, and that Agrippa was responsive. Earlier in Claudius' reign, a serious famine had struck the region, on a scale unknown since the great famine of 25 B.C. to

[54] For the argument, see Applebaum, op. cit. (n. 7), pp. 660, 691; and op. cit. (n. 41), pp. 360–1, 378–85.

which Herod had responded with impressive ministrations. This time, relief was despatched from abroad.[55] The Claudian famine is probably to be dated to A.D.47–9; but within twenty years there seems to have occurred yet another serious one. For a curious allusion in the Moses narrative of Josephus' *Antiquities* to a famine which came shortly before 'this war', and fell under the priesthood of Ishmael, is used by the author to demonstrate the piety of the high priests: it was the Passover, and so they did not touch a crumb of the dough which was brought to the Temple. Ishmael ben Phiabi is known to have been high priest around A.D.60, under Nero, and so it is probably in confusion with the other famine that Josephus alludes to Claudius here.[56] In any case, whatever we decide about its date, we cannot fail to notice that the famine made a very strong impression on Josephus, and more specifically that he sees fit, so much later, to try to exonerate the high priests from charges of greed in connection with it. And this is hardly surprising, since, as we read elsewhere in Josephus, Ishmael ben Phiabi's high priesthood was the first of two occasions when humble country priests allegedly perished from starvation because members of the high priesthood forcibly seized their tithes from the threshing floors.[57]

Most difficult of all to assess, but perhaps also most significant, are hints of an empire-wide crisis engendered by Nero's wild expenditure and neglect of administrative duties. The city of Rome may have been the first victim of a bad emperor (Tac. *Hist.* 4.74.2), but was by no means the only one, and according to our literary sources the provinces were affected on this occasion.[58]

In Egypt, papyri reveal intense difficulties and irregularities around this time in the collection of taxes: depopulation of villages

---

[55] *AJ* 20. 51 and 101; Acts 11.28–30. Herod's famine: *AJ* 15. 299–316.

[56] *AJ* 3. 320–2. Equally, there would be room in the list of high priests for another Ishmael to be inserted, and this remains a theoretical possibility. K. S. Gapp is still useful, in 'The universal famine under Claudius', *HThR* 28 (1935), p. 261, n. 11.

[57] *AJ* 20. 181; cf. 206–7, where exactly the same behaviour, with the same results, is ascribed to Ananias in the sixties A.D. Whether the high priests were claiming the priests' share of the first tithe, or rather the second tithe, which was supposed to be taken to Jerusalem, or whether perhaps they were insisting that, contrary to the law as formulated subsequently, all the tithes ought to go to there, we cannot be sure. There is some evidence that the latter was occurring during the period; in any case the claim of the Temple treasury or of the high priests to appropriate the proceeds would seem illegitimate, and it is interesting that Josephus does not try to justify it. On the relevant *halakhah* (law), see A. Oppenheimer, in *Enc. Jud.* 15, 1027, s.v. *Terumot and Ma'aserot*; Oppenheimer, *The 'Am Ha-aretz* (1977), ch. 2, esp. pp. 35–42.

[58] B. H. Warmington, *Nero: Legend and Reality* (1969), pp. 68–70.

in the face of exorbitant demands, the reluctance of collectors to do their work. Taxation had probably not become heavier, but the provincials' ability to pay had declined, and the administrators' shortfall was more pressing.[59]

As for the Jews of Palestine, their reality does seem to have corresponded to the reports of Josephus. There is every reason to believe that they were becoming two nations, with a gulf between them created partly by the poverty of the poor, even more by the ill-gotten gains of the rich. Once the two sides were in confrontation with one another, there came about an internal war, which turns out to conform in a startling way to the pattern and course of development of other revolutions, closer to us in time and incomparably better known to historians. The connection with an external war is in this case particularly close, with the revolutionaries from beginning to end involved in both kinds of activity; but there were still marked lulls in the Roman campaign, which allowed the civil dissension to mature.[60] No one would expect there to be a uniform course followed by all so-called revolutions; indeed, definition, classification and comparison are all matters for intense debate.[61] But a modern reader of Josephus can hardly fail to remark that the events he describes fit into the type. And that they accord particularly well with the scheme proposed in one of the more successful and enduring of modern studies of the revolutionary cycle, that of Crane Brinton, has not escaped scholarly observation.[62] Before the outbreak there are social tensions, an inefficient government, a financial crisis. The first steps are not clear to the revolutionaries

---

[59] H. I. Bell, 'The economic crisis in Egypt under Nero', *JRS* 28 (1938), pp. 1–8; Bell in *CAH* 10 (1952), pp. 314–15; S. L. Wallace, *Taxation in Roman Egypt* (1938), pp. 346ff. However, MacMullen, op. cit. (n. 37), pp. 36ff., prefers to believe that things were always much the same, and consistently bad. It is hard to assign a date to the dreadful story in Philo, *Spec. Leg.* 3, 159–62 of tortures applied by a tax-collector to defaulters, and suicides undertaken to avoid these.

[60] See p. 138. On connections between external war and revolution, W. Laqueur, 'Revolution', in *International Encyclopedia of the Social Sciences*, vol. 14, p. 501.

[61] The debate is discussed by N. Stone, *The Causes of the English Revolution 1529–1642* (1972), ch. 1.

[62] C. Brinton, *The Anatomy of Revolution* (1938). The characteristic sequence of events is analysed differently by L. P. Edwards, *The Natural History of Revolutions* (1927) and G. S. Pettee, *The Process of Revolution* (1938). The application to the Jewish revolt, is in C. Roth, 'The Jewish Revolt against Rome', *Commentary* 27 (1959), pp. 513–22; and is discussed, but rejected, by U. Rappaport, 'Remarks on the causes of the Great Revolt', *'Kathedra' for the Study of the Land of Israel and its Inhabitants* 8 (1978), pp. 42–6 (Hebrew).

themselves, but a 'dramatic, crystallising scene', following a government attempt to collect money from people who do not want to pay, sets the action in progress. Those who do not like the revolution tend to see the first moves as a series of plots by an unprincipled and scheming minority, but others take them as a spontaneous mass uprising. The revolution is carried by a cross-section of classes initially, and its leaders are moderates of good family. But 'the revolution, like Saturn, devours its children':[63] intransigent groups of radicals and extremists insist that the moderates are betraying the cause, and oust them in due course. Thus in France the Girondins may be interpreted as moderates forced into actions which were to them disagreeably extreme. The control of the government is itself a source of weakness to these moderates. The crisis stage is the capture of power by the extremists, when there is seizure of property, heated debate and street fighting. The ordinary man is likely to drop out, but the few become devoted to certain leaders, practical men but possessed by prophetic fire. Revolutionary courts and tribunals lead into a reign of terror, but this period, which is characterised also by extreme forms of religious enthusiasm, is usually brief. A struggle for power between the radical leaders follows.

In the case of the Jewish revolt, we can recognise that the Roman administration initially plays part of the role of the old regime. Otherwise, as we shall see, there is little that is not illuminated by this exemplar. The historical logic of Josephus' story will go a good way towards establishing his credibility, at least with regard to the principal actions and events. For while it would be patently improper to say of history, as E. M. Forster did of poetry, that 'it is true if it hangs together', there is a more limited assertion which may be made: if we find no internal grounds for impugning the historian's story, then, in the absence of evidence from outside, it must have a prima facie claim on our belief. And although a comparison with the pattern of other revolutions is not a proof of anything (still less a source of supply for missing facts), it does help us to assess the story put before us by Josephus. A nineteenth-century French historian might be expected to have a good instinct for such events, and, in 1867 Dérenbourg expressed our point admirably, when he wrote: 'cette succession dans l'avènement des

---

[63] Quoted by Brinton from Vergniaud, a French moderate.

partis doit être vraie parce qu'elle est aussi conforme à la nature des choses et à la loi qui préside à toutes les insurrections, qui, n'étant pas étouffées à leur naissance, grandissent et se transforment en révolutions.'[64]

The involvement of 'moderates' like Josephus in the early stages of the revolt comes as no surprise. While the position of Agrippa and his followers has emerged as unequivocally pro-Roman (even if his sister was a little less decisive), the constraints and tensions to which other elements in the Jewish élite were subject are a rather different matter. All are said to resist the ending of the Roman sacrifices in the Temple, for Josephus says that at this point notables, high priests and leading Pharisees alike were vigorous advocates of peace. This is quite believable.[65] Yet, as pious Jews, they were evidently disturbed by Florus' conduct, and as guardians of the Temple had a duty to protect it. They were ultimately more involved—and more implicated—than the royal entourage, most of whom detached themselves and took refuge in Herod's palace after that of Agrippa was burned (*BJ* 2.431).

The rest of the élite also now began to fragment, and the first notables and priests sought to make their escape. Some fell victim to the insurgents' murderous fury, as did the high priest Ananias: he was not the serving high priest, but a person of enormous wealth, and his high-handed behaviour had become the symbol of arrogance in the high priesthood, for he was the man who had sent his servants to seize tithes from the threshing floors.[66] Desertions, from both sections, continued apace. The courtiers could, of course, find protection in Agrippa's kingdom and, through him, expect to gain Roman favour. But there were others who remained, such as Ananus, Josephus, Simon son of Gamaliel and Joshua son of Gamala: indecision, hope, and that residual sense of affinity with their co-

---

[64] Cf. M. I. Finley, 'Generalizations in Ancient History', in *The Use and Abuse of History* (1975), ch. 3; Forster cited by P. Gay, *Style in History* (1974), p. 191. And see J. Dérenbourg, *Essai sur l'histoire et la géographie de la Palestine* (1867), p. 264.

[65] Roth, loc. cit. (n. 34). The Pharisees may have been split. But it is certainly clear that Johanan ben Zakkai, the foremost spiritual leader after the destruction, played no part in the revolt, and negotiated his own escape with the Romans; and he is also said to have prophesied Vespasian's rise in a manner curiously reminiscent of that of Josephus: see further p. 188ff. Simon ben Gamaliel was the representative, in this generation, of the illustrious house of Hillel, and apparently leader of the Sanhedrin; later on, he is shown by Josephus, along with the high priests Ananus and Joshua, trying to halt the activities of the Zealots who had occupied the Temple.

[66] *BJ* 2. 429, 441. For the threshing floors, see p. 125 n. 57.

religionists must have played a part in this; and also, we may presume, some patriotic emotion will have been fostered by the disturbing news of continued Greek attacks on Jews in cities outside and inside Palestine.[67] These men were thus, by inclination, something approaching political moderates.[68] But there was no middle position for them to occupy: in a situation of *stasis*, when the middle ground falls away, the seeker after compromise can do no more than move from one side to the other, as the circumstances appear to warrant. So the first choice of these moderates was the cause of peace, in which they really believed. Even now, when Cestius the Roman legate moved in from Syria with a substantial force, a group which included Ananus sent him a message in which they offered to open the gates. To their dismay, they were ignored and had to take shelter in their homes to escape reprisals from the rebels. Thus it was initially their decision to stay on, and then, finally, fear, that pushed them briefly to the other extreme, that of rebellion. Cestius' abrupt withdrawal of his army from the Jerusalem area (see p. 74) was the principal external agent in the situation, for this was the 'dramatic crystallising scene' (to use Brinton's expression) which set both revolt and revolution in motion.

A scheme of social classification usually has its exceptions; and upper class idealists are not a rarity. They are often found among the young, and one figure who seems to fall into this category is Eleazar, son of the murdered high priest Ananias. This Eleazar first proposed the cessation of the sacrifices, and was a staunch supporter of the ordinary priests against the high priests. He was responsible for leading the war party in its early attacks on the peace party in the upper city, for the assassination of the rebel leader Menahem, and for the perfidious murder of the Roman garrison under Metilius.[69] But he does no damage to Josephus' generalisation.

[67] The conflict was endemic, but the tension with Rome, and among the Jews themselves exacerbated it, and was, in turn, affected by it: U. Rappaport, 'The relations between Jews and non-Jews and the Great War against Rome', *Tarbiz* 17 (1978), pp. 1–14 (Hebrew, with short English summary).

[68] Their views are presented as moderate: that the Greek word 'metrios' (closest in sense to our 'moderate') is not applied to them by the author is inadequate as proof that they were not of this persuasion, as claimed by Cohen, op. cit. (n. 3), p. 186, n. 9. On the moderates, cf. D. M. Rhoads, *Israel in Revolution* (1976), pp. 150–8.

[69] *BJ* 2. 409–10, 450ff. On the massacre, see p. 74. Eleazar is a key figure in E. M. Smallwood's attempt to find a significant part of the high priesthood which was by conviction anti-Roman: 'High Priests and politics in Roman Palestine', *JThS* 13 (1962), pp. 14ff.

Josephus does not tell us in so many words how it was that a part of the Jewish 'establishment', which included not only himself but even members of high priestly families, managed to be accepted as leaders of revolt. Yet there is no problem in understanding this twist of events.[70] These individuals had at least not deserted. From the rebels' point of view they possessed one valuable asset, their political experience.[71] Their wealth, too, may not have come amiss, although resources seem not to have been short, for Josephus points out that the public treasury and a part of the Roman spoils were in the hands of the Zealot Eleazar ben Simon. He also says that the Zealot, in spite of this, was denied 'office', and this indicates that leaders who could command wide enough respect were harder to find than funds. It is understandable that, even when an élite is to a large extent discredited, some of its members should retain appeal as leaders, especially in a frightening crisis. The 'moderates' were prepared to play this last card. It certainly does not follow from the appearance of high priestly leaders of revolt that Josephus had previously exaggerated the differences in the population.

Probably four, but certainly three of the ten newly appointed organisers are of high priestly family (*BJ* 2.562–8). Another was Josephus. We know nothing of the social background of the other five. There is one who may possibly have been a full-blooded revolutionary, Niger the Peraean, who had already made his mark in an encounter with Cestius outside Jerusalem; on the other hand, we notice that he later fell victim to the Zealots when they massacred the Jewish nobility (*BJ* 2.520; 4.359–63). Ananus, the elderly high priest, was one of the two overall commanders, and in charge of the defence of the city. The other was Joseph ben Gorion; and it was almost certainly his son, named Gorion, and described as being of high rank and birth and superior attainment, who was soon also to be killed by the Zealots. Some, however, have preferred to see Joseph, somewhat anachronistically, as a 'city bourgeois'.[72]

How wholeheartedly or how efficiently the reluctant revolutionaries went about their business, it is hard to tell. In his encomium on Ananus, Josephus writes: 'peace was his real goal. He knew that Roman power was irresistible, but, when driven to provide for a state of war, he tried to ensure that, if they would not come to

---

[70] Though Cohen has one: op. cit. (n. 3), pp. 187–8.
[71] Cf. Roth, op. cit. (n. 62), p. 517.
[72] The idea of J. Dérenbourg, op. cit. (n. 64), p. 270.

terms, the Jews should at least give a good account of themselves.' This is a convincing accolade, and the position, if genuinely held, could be a respectable one. On the other hand, we might detect a certain defensiveness in Josephus' praise, and be inclined to suppose that Ananus' record, like Josephus' own, had its shady areas.[73] There is blow-by-blow documentation only for the historian's own command, in the Galilee, and even there the interpretation is not without its problems. Comparable sentiments to those of Ananus are uttered by the next in seniority among the high priests, Joshua son of Gamala, but these are written into a speech where Joshua is rebutting a charge of treachery, so they are certainly not above suspicion. At the same time, there is one surprising touch here, which perhaps vouches for a degree of authenticity: oblivious of his own conduct at Jotapata, writing in seemingly unconscious self-criticism, Josephus makes Joshua say that once committed to the fight, he would choose a noble death before Roman captivity (*BJ* 4.249–50).

Whatever the case, the fragile alliance did not hold. The period of 'dual sovereignty in the early stages of a revolution is bound to be unstable, especially when the moderates do not really believe in the big words they have to use'. (Brinton). The end of the revolt in the Galilee, in mid-67, brought into Jerusalem a man who had by now turned himself into a powerful rebel leader, John of Gischala. Here came independent gangs and individuals from the countryside who had no interest in compromise (*BJ* 4.135ff.). What had happened there had in any case probably destroyed any confidence they may have had in the official leadership. Furthermore, the issue of war or peace was now again wide open; to surrender before Judaea was occupied would have been an obvious move, and in the

---

[73] *BJ* 4. 320. I discount the conflicting verdict on Ananus appearing at *AJ* 20. 199–203, where he is said to be bold and heartless, and held responsible for engineering the death of James, brother of Jesus, through the Sanhedrin. The case for the whole account of James being a Christian interpolation is very strong: not so much, as Schürer argued, because Origen had a different recollection of what Josephus had said on the subject, but simply because of its startling divergence from the previous assessment (in a case where Josephus is not transcribing a source), and its harsh criticism of the Sadducees, and of the Sanhedrin. Furthermore, the James passage seems to suppose in the reader some knowledge of the man 'who was called the Christ', so that anyone who takes the view, as many do, that Josephus' reference to Jesus (the '*testimonium flavianum*') is completely an interpolation, should find difficulty in accepting the account of his brother. Yet it has been unfashionable, of late, to doubt the James passage; but cf. Schürer-Vermes-Millar, vol. 1, p. 430, n. 1.

towns and villages, the war party fought it out with the peace party. This was the heyday of *stasis* outside Jerusalem. The men who now entered the city tend to be referred to by Josephus as 'brigand chiefs' and 'brigands', and it is probable that their sentiments to- wards men of property were more vindictive than those of the Jerusalem rebels. Social distress and the effects of bad harvests must have been worse in the country, for the towns were relatively un- developed and did not contain a real urban proletariat. Land- owners, however, must often have lived in town (cf. p. 119), and there they could be attacked. John of Gischala had speculated in olive oil during the Galilean troubles, and, on the strength of this, some have described him as a wealthy merchant.[74] But bandits quite often turn to business, and have to be in touch with 'the wider economic universe';[75] John's capital could have come from plunder. It is doubtful whether there were many merchants of any kind in first-century Palestine, let alone ones with substantial means. His association with Josephus in the Galilee and with Simon son of Gamaliel in Jerusalem might incline us to deem him more respect- able than other rebel leaders, yet these could equally well have been brought about by political necessity (see pp. 160–5).

The irruption into the city led to the wholesale destruction of the old ruling class, and to what seems to have been quite a systematic take-over of the organs of power. Both are adequately documented by Josephus in the first part of Book 4 of the *Jewish War*. What is taking place now begins to look like a revolution.[76] Men of royal blood or high reputation were arrested, and when the risk of their families' vengeance seemed too great, they were done away with and the crime concealed. A new high priest was chosen by lot from within a particular priestly clan, so that the claims of those families out of which the post had regularly been filled (and which had now fallen into dissension) were deliberately overlooked, in favour of individuals without birth or reputation (*BJ* 4.147ff.). The new, last ever high priest was a villager, Pinchas ben Samuel (by Josephus called Phanni, in the Aramaic fashion), and he, according to Tal- mudic literature, worked as a stone-mason. Josephus' harsh and

[74] So H. Hoehner, *Herod Antipas* (1969), p. 71; M. Stern, 'Zealots', *Encyclopedia Judaica Year Book* (1973), p. 148.
[75] E. J. Hobsbawm, *Bandits*[2] (1981), p. 85.
[76] Cf. Roth, op. cit. (n. 62), pp. 519ff. Also, the same author's 'The constitution of the Jewish republic of 66–70', *JSS* 9 (1964), pp. 314–19; but here he tends to exaggerate the regular and ordinary working of the revolutionary 'government'.

indignant dismissal of him as a boor and an ignoramus contrasts most instructively with the Talmudic reports, which seem designed to minimise the importance of Pinchas' humble background, and which make no suggestion that he lacked knowledge or dignity. His poverty is altogether refuted once, in a relatively early passage which may be factually inaccurate, but whose thrust is quite clear: he is described there as a son-in-law of the 'house' of the head of the Sanhedrin, the Nasi. More often, we are told simply that his fellow priests saw him hewing stones, and, because they knew that a high priest should be rich, they filled his quarry with 'golden *denarii*'. The story, if not a satire on the high priests and their acquisitiveness, at least carries the implication that there were in principle no insuperable obstacles to a man who was originally poor being allowed to fill the post.[77] The contrast with Josephus offers a clear demonstration of the historian's prejudice.[78]

When Ananus, as official leader, begins to make a partial recovery, winning some support among the populace, and isolating the war-mongers in the Temple, he is falsely denounced to the Zealots as a traitor. Josephus' story is that the man responsible was John of Gischala, who until this moment had appeared to co-operate with the official leadership. On John's motives it is as usual hard to adjudicate in the face of Josephus' patent malice (cf. p. 161). But the sequel is clear: an army of Idumaeans is called in by the Zealots. They come as kinsmen of the Jews and defenders of the Temple, set to challenge Rome; but it is immediately apparent that they have been dragged into a civil war. The peace party does not scruple to try and turn them against their Zealot patrons; however, their sense of identification with the popular side is for some reason closer.[79] It is fortunate for Josephus that he is safely out of the way when Ananus and his party are accused by two priests, persuaded by what John has said, of planning to betray the revolt: one of the

[77] *Tos. Yoma* 1.6 (the son-in-law); *Midrash Rabbah, Leviticus* 26.9; *Tanhuma* 48a; *Yalkut* 1.63.1; cf. Dérenbourg, op. cit. (n. 64), p. 269 and n. 2.

[78] Yet, strangely, his assessment has tended to be accepted without question; the notable exception, not unexpectedly, is J. Klausner, *History of the Second Temple* (Jerusalem, 1952; Hebrew), vol. 5, pp. 207–9. The motif is reminiscent of how the throne of Sidon (or in other sources, wrongly, Tyre) and the royal regalia were bestowed by Alexander the Great's friend Hephaistion on a water-drawer in rags named Abdalonymus: Diod. 17. 74 etc.

[79] Perhaps because they are poor. Their forcible Judaization, which had occurred some two hundred years earlier (*AJ* 13. 257–8; 15. 254ff.), seems no longer to be resented.

two is Eleazar son of Simon, who had stopped the sacrifices (p. 129). The suspicion is understandable, whether or not the charge had any validity, and Joshua ben Gamala's strenuous defence saves neither himself nor Ananus from the savagery of the enraged and temporarily wild Idumaeans. Now follows the arrest and torture by the Zealots of numerous 'young nobles', as well as the establishment of what we might call a counter-Sanhedrin of 70 men, and the show trial of a rich citizen (*BJ* 4.305–25, 326–33, 334–44). Josephus speaks also of further trials which he regards as farcical mockeries. In this particular case, the accused is acquitted by the court, but none the less he is promptly despatched, and his body thrown into the ravine under the Temple; the judges are struck with the backs of swords. It is significant that Josephus describes the victim as a 'lover of liberty', just as he had eulogised Ananus as a passionate devotee of freedom and an adherent of democracy. Here he seems to reflect the ideological conflicts of the moment: since 'freedom' was a watchword of the revolt, it makes sense that the opponents of revolt should appropriate the term and put their own meaning to it.[80]

If so, this did not convince the original lovers of liberty. It was at this time that Niger the Peraean and Gorion son of Joseph were also put to death, while Simon son of Gamaliel disappeared from view (*BJ* 4.355–65). The witch-hunt against 'virtue and good birth' intensified after the Idumaeans, or some of them, regretted their involvement and withdrew;[81] and the revolutionaries seemed determined, in Josephus' words, 'to leave alive no one of influence'. The humble were not touched (*BJ* 4.357, 365). This is a true reign of terror, the Jacobin phase of revolution. Many Jews deserted at this time, if they could buy their way past the guards. In this different way, it was the poor, unable to offer a bribe, who suffered most (*BJ* 4.378, 397). Their attempt to escape indicates, of course, that they did not approve of the Zealots; and it is not surprising that, as the excesses increased, a growing number of ordinary citizens lost sympathy.

But now we witness the fragmentation of the revolutionary party

[80] On revolutionary 'freedom', see p. 139. On Josephus' fondness for this sort of 'reverse polemic', where the arguments of the revolutionaries are turned against themselves, see D. M. Rhoads, *Israel in Revolution: a Political History Based on the Writings of Josephus* (1976), pp. 166–7.

[81] They cannot all have gone, as Josephus carelessly states, since some are still there later: see *BJ* 5. 248, 290.

itself—a *stasis* within a *stasis*, Josephus calls it. This must have been as much the consequence of tensions accumulating during the period when the Zealots had unhindered control of the capital, as of any fundamental differences of approach.[82] Josephus dwells mainly on the resentment felt in all quarters at John of Gischala's dictatorial authority. The arrival of *sicarii*, men of violence who had been conducting local raids from the fortress of Masada, also contributed (cf. p. 84). There was also Simon bar Giora: he was a Gerasene who had been expelled by Ananus from Judaea, and had gone first to Masada, and then into the hills; now, arriving to join the *sicarii* in Idumaea, he even won over some notables for a short period. They presumably hoped, in their desperation, that if he established a strong enough power base in the country, he might put a stop to the Zealot frenzy within the walls: this is a frenzy which Josephus might seem to exaggerate, but such moods often grip participants during the 'crisis phase' of revolution.[83] When Simon was established outside the walls, it was a high priest, Matthias son of Boethus, who admitted him—only to be murdered later by his ungrateful prótege, after watching his three sons die (*BJ* 4.574–6). Again, Eleazar ben Simon pretended to a deep revulsion when he seceded from the Zealot party; and he, likewise, had at first the support of individuals of significance, including two notables (*BJ* 5.5).

It was partly in pursuance of what was now a tripartite conflict among the extremists, but clearly also in a spirit of vindictiveness against the rich, that John and his people burned most of the city's supplies of corn and other commodities, thus greatly reducing her ability to withstand the siege when it came. To this stage of revolution the most acute expressions of class struggle are appropriate. For Josephus, the wanton destruction is beyond comprehension.[84] So disturbing was this irrational act, that it is recorded by widely differing authorities; it found its way on the one hand into Tacitus' *Histories*, on the other into Rabbinic recollections of the revolt, few

---

[82] As assumed by Applebaum, 'The Zealots: the case for revaluation', *JRS* 61 (1971), pp. 163–6.

[83] Simon's creation of a disciplined people's army is stressed, with some exaggeration, by O. Michel, 'Studien zu Josephus; Simon bar Giora', *NTS* 14 (1968), pp. 402–8, especially 403.

[84] Roth, op. cit. (n. 62), is as perplexed as Josephus, and suggests a religious motive—that the aim was to gain divine favour by a demonstration of faith. The explanation is hardly necessary.

though these are. In that tradition, while the details have been reduced to a childish simplicity—as is often the case—the basic story seems to be preserved: for the conclusion of the passage about those three magnates of Jerusalem whom we encountered earlier, and who, from their stores, could have kept the city supplied, each with one vital commodity, for twenty-one years, is that when certain citizens wanted to come to terms with Rome the men of violence (*biryonim*) refused, and responded by burning up all the provisions. This tradition, it should be noted, is as disapproving of the revolutionaries as is Josephus (see Chapter 1, nn. 45 and 46).

The consequence of this destruction was a terrible famine, whose effects are described at intervals by Josephus, in a graphic and observant way. Moreover, John of Gischala and the Zealots had by now lost all restraint; they had been stripping the houses of the rich, and were going around drenched in perfume and dressed in female clothes (down to painted eyelashes), as though in a parody of the occupants' behaviour. Josephus takes some delight in comparing the city to a brothel, though he goes on to say that the scene was a far bloodier one (*BJ* 4.560–5).

Once Simon bar Giora was in town, the elimination of the upper class seems to have gained added momentum, if that was still possible (4.577ff.). Simon has been taken to be the most extreme of the leaders, on the reasonable assumption that his liberation of slaves and prisoners would have been in part ideologically motivated. Later in the narrative his extraordinary powers of leadership are attested when Josephus says that his followers so admired and feared him that they would gladly have committed suicide at his bidding (5.309). Neither Eleazar's temporary involvement when he held the Temple, leaving John in the outer courts and Simon in most of the city; nor his defeat; nor the eventual unification of the remaining two factions made much difference to the primary conflict within Jewish society. Cruelty and vindictiveness continued to characterise the revolutionaries' treatment of their former superiors (5.433); though it was perhaps not quite indiscriminate, for Josephus' parents were put in prison and yet, at least for a time, not harmed: if the author is to be believed, his mother was even in a position to converse with her guards (545–7).

As famine spread, anyone in possession of corn was a wanted man. Yet Josephus observes the remarkable fact that, even at the extremity of the hunger, the poor and the rich were not equal: the humble might be tortured for food, but the rich and the powerful were charged with conspiracy or desertion by suborned informers (5.439, 527–30, 567; 6.112ff.). One way or another, members of the upper class, including (still) high priests, were deserting whenever they had the opportunity. Provided they had not resisted, they were welcomed by the Romans and generally allowed to go free, with promises for the return of their property. Some were despatched to Gophna, but only for their own safety, Josephus assures us (5.422; 6.115). We cannot discount the possibility that the historian's personal intervention may have played a part in securing favourable terms for some of the escaping individuals. In one exceptional case, however, some 2,000 deserters came to a gruesome end, on account of the very wealth which should have been their salvation. They had swallowed gold coins, which they proposed to recover after their escape, but some Syrians and Arabs noticed what they were doing, and ripped their stomachs open, without further ado. For Josephus, this ranks as the most horrible of all the war's atrocities; but he takes care to dissociate Titus from it (5.548–52). Some potential deserters were thus deterred, and in spite of Titus' admonitions there were isolated cases in which this brutality was repeated; but still Josephus is able to document a succession of desertions, taking place both before and after the mishap, and to name the prominent members of each group. The poor, instead, were simply crucified, if, foraging for food outside the walls, they were picked up by Romans soldiers and put up any kind of struggle.[85] He also notes that within Jerusalem the rich generally received burial, the poor did not.

It is fair to suppose that a large number of people on both sides had not been, or had ceased by now to be actively involved in either the revolt or the civil war. To have remained in Jerusalem was not necessarily an indication of commitment; and by now the city also contained newcomers, who had found their way there as refugees. So Josephus may be quite justified in firmly distinguishing the *dēmos* (people) of Jerusalem from the insurgents (*stasiastai*) at this stage, even if the distinction did serve particularly well the interests of his argument that the revolt was the work of a wild minority (people from across the Jordan—*BJ* 6.201). Yet the special treatment meted

---

[85] *BJ* 5. 447, On crucifixion as the penalty first for slaves, and later for the lower classes in the Roman empire, P. Garnsey, *Social Status and Legal Privilege in the Roman Empire* (1970), pp. 126–7.

out by the Romans to the notables and the wealthy, but not extended to the whole *dēmos*, was based on a general view of the roles of the two sections of society vis-a-vis Rome, formally expressed as a military policy of excusing deserters but punishing belligerents; fundamentally, this view was not unrealistic. Thus it occurred that, in the very moment of the city's ruin, the wheel was coming full circle: the rich were winning back their rapport with Rome, while the poor were again victims.

This powerful portrait of revolution in a city under attack is not easily rejected, Josephus weaves these developments into his more dispassionate account of the Roman army's progress; thus it is while the tripartite conflict is at its height inside, that Titus and four legions encamp outside Jerusalem, causing a temporary unification; while the climax of the terror and the famine coincides with the completion of the huge earthworks constructed by Titus. It is after the Romans decide to build a complete wall of their own around the city, and do so in three days, that Simon murders the high priest Matthias son of Boethus, and the 2,000 Jewish deserters are ripped open by the Syrians. The famine increases relentlessly, and desertions proceed apace, while the Romans demolish the Antonia fortress, make a road up to the Temple, and burn its porticoes. Desertions are still recorded during the final conflagration in the Temple and the attack on the upper city. Only when the upper city has been taken, and all Jerusalem is in flames, does the inner turmoil cease.

There is plainly a literary purpose in Josephus' exploitation of the two contrasting themes: aware that his strange position has given him an unusual knowledge of the two different worlds, he designs a form of narrative which can incorporate this. His interest in the vicissitudes of the beleaguered Jews is wide and varied; his penchant for the sensational does not exclude real observation, especially of the psychological effects of hunger. His information, whether derived mainly from deserters or rather from what he himself could observe during his perambulations on the walls (when he was at close enough range to address the inhabitants and be knocked out by a rebel stone (*BJ* 5.541–7)), is evidently close and accurate. He even knows the nicknames that the Jewish fighters used for the Roman battering machines (5.272, 299). This makes interesting history; but Josephus also has, in recounting what happens to the Jews, a specific point to bring out about the breakdown in the Jewish social and political order. We have already analysed his line of thinking, and it has emerged as an approach which may, without hesitation, be classed as political.

Equally, it can scarcely be doubted that the actions of the revolutionaries took clear social and political forms, and must have had social and political objectives, even if these were vague and ill-defined. Few leaders, let alone followers, know where they expect to arrive when they start a disturbance; and vagueness was in this case compounded by the general lack of a conscious revolutionary ideology in the ancient world, as well as by the particular circumstances—the fact that attention was diverted to the Roman war. In so far as political aims were expressed, we may assume them to have taken the form which was standard in the Greek world—demands for the abolition of debt (and we recall the destruction of the money-lenders' bonds in the archives) and for redistribution of land (on which Josephus does not comment).[86] The one slogan which is well attested is the single word 'freedom', and that from coinage,[87] as well as Josephus. Theologically-minded commentators on Josephus (and they are the majority) have read this eschatologically, as referring to the conditions which will arise at the End of Days. Yet even in such circles, more balanced opinion, by taking the actions of the rebels into proper consideration, has allowed that the kind of freedom of which they dreamt—whenever they meant it fully to materialise—must have had as a prominent component the practical liberation of the oppressed. Some of the reactions to oppression expressed in apocalyptic literature have seemed comparable.[88] And we can also say that the zealots (in the wide sense) paralleled Josephus in being, for all their piety, political animals.

This is not to deny that there was a powerful religious element in the behaviour and attitudes of both sides, inextricably bound up with the political, as is to be expected among the Jews; even

---

[86] On the emergence of these ideals, in fourth century B.C. Greece, M. M. Austin and P. Vidal-Naquet, *Economic and Social History of Ancient Greece: An Introduction* (transl. and rev. Austin, 1977), pp. 138–40. This is the sort of area where we should expect Josephus to be incomplete.

[87] L. Kadman, *The Coins of the Jewish War, 66–73, Corpus Nummorum Palestinensium*, vol. 3 (1960) is the most exhaustive collection. See also C. Roth, 'The historical implication of the coins of the First Revolt', *IEJ* 12 (1962), pp. 33–46.

[88] A welcome corrective to the emphasis of Martin Hengel is provided by G. Baumbach, 'Das Freiheitsverständnis in der zelotischen Bewegung', *Das Ferne und Nahe Wort* no. 105, *Beihefte zur Zeitschrift für die Alttestamentliche Wissenschaft, Festschrift L. Rost* (1967), pp. 11–18 (also in *ThLZ* 92 (1967), pp. 257f.).

Josephus does not obscure its existence. The rebels, like their opponents but with greater intensity and rigidity, saw themselves as
defenders of the purity of the Temple and of correct observance in
such matters as the Sabbath and dietary law.[89] Coins of years one
and two of the revolt carry the legends 'Jerusalem is holy' and
'Jerusalem the holy'.[90] Hostility to figurative representation, and
particularly to the appearance of images in holy places, had already
been more acute among the forerunners of these rebels than in other
sections of Judaism.[91]

Prophecies and prophetic leaders were also an influence, as we
have discovered (see p. 90). Nevertheless, the received opinion that
the Jewish revolt was essentially a millenarian movement, whose
followers were awaiting imminent salvation, has less than might be
expected to recommend it, unless it be the evident fact that the first
century of the Christian era was a uniquely fertile one for millenarian expression.[92] Prima facie, we would be inclined to suppose
that coherent political action will be an alternative outlet for frus-
trations which might give rise to fervent expectation and spontaneous, undirected Messianic agitation, or else a development
replacing such agitation. There is nothing like a universal rule, but
there is some support for this observation in a wide variety of
instances, both past and contemporary.[93] We are speaking here of
powerful Messianic enthusiasm: it is of course true that, if tension
is great, some sort of generalised fervour about the future, carrying
some religious overtones, is to be found even among the most secular
of protesters; all the more so in a Bible-centred society, since, as
Christopher Hill has observed 'any careful reading of the Bible
gives thoughts about the end of the world'.[94]

Beyond this, Messianism does not appear to figure very largely

---

[89] M. Hengel, *Die Zeloten* (1961), pp. 229–234.

[90] *Jerushalem Kdosha* and *Jerushalayim Hakdosha*: see Kadman, pp. 96–8, 124–8, 152.

[91] Hengel, loc. cit. (n. 90).

[92] Hengel emphasises this aspect, pp. 235–307. An example of the kind of assumption made is provided by N. Cohn, loc. cit. (n. 22): 'there is evidence that the
party of the "zealots" was a truly millenarian movement, obsessed by such fantasies
. . . and convinced of the imminent coming of a supernatural messiah.'

[93] E. J. Hobsbawm, *Primitive Rebels* (1959), ch. 4; Worsley, op. cit. (n. 21), pp.
231ff.

[94] C. Hill, *The World Turned Upside Down* (1972, repr. 1975), p. 95. And it is
undeniable that its religious component makes the Jewish revolt unique in the
Roman empire: S. Dyson, 'Native revolts in the Roman empire', *Historia* 20 (1971),
p. 273.

in the Jewish rebellion as a whole. None of its leaders, however charismatic, presented themselves, or were received as Messiahs, unlike Bar Kochba who led a second revolt less than a century later. Nor do they look like precursors of a redeemer to come, analogous to John the Baptist. Now it is conceivable that Josephus so far suppressed, concealed or misunderstood the dynamics of the movement he opposed that they have vanished beyond recall; we have certainly seen that when it comes to his enemies, his present-ation must be deemed somewhat deficient. But it rather seems that his offence is less grave, and that, after making some allowance for partisanship and temperament, we are still able to follow him in discounting millenarian expectation as a major factor behind the revolt.

The case against Josephus has rested on shaky foundations. Sometimes his own words are used against him; for when he writes about prophecies which had been current among the Jews before the outbreak of war, he remarks that 'what incited them most to fight the war, was an ambiguous oracle, found also in the sacred books, that at that time a man from their country would become ruler of the known world'. Yet there is no doubt that in this sentence the adverb 'most' is to be understood in relation to other prophecies which have just been discussed: this was not, for him, the principal cause of the war, simply the most influential of a series of utterances of a particular type. In any case, this prophecy is not in the full sense Messianic.[95] A good deal has also been made of the personality cults surrounding Simon bar Giora, and, earlier, Menahem; it has seemed to some a short step from charisma and from alleged kingly pretensions to Messiahship. But the gap is a decisive one.[96] Next, it is possible to interpret the ideal of the fourth philosophy and the *sicarii*, to be ruled by none other than God, as universal rather than national in intent and, once again, as implicitly eschatological, a reference to the 'kingdom of heaven'.[97] Yet, had this been the sense of the doctrine, it could without difficulty have been expressed by Josephus. Most tangible, and also most important, because for once

---

[95] He applied this oracle to Vespasian, and it is discussed in Chapter 8.

[96] E.g. to M. Stern, reviewing Hengel, *JRS* 52 (1962), p. 259. For Simon's 'char-isma', see more fully, Stern, op. cit. (n. 22), p. 284, where, however, he is more reserved about Messianic claims. The Messianic interpretation is criticised well by Kreissig, op. cit. (n. 40), pp. 103, 132–3, 141.

[97] Again, Hengel is the most thorough, original and influential exponent: see pp. 308–14.

the evidence comes from outside Josephus, is the slogan on the reverse of the bronze coins of year four of the revolt. The bronze of years two and three had borne the caption 'the freedom of Zion'; year four, while retaining on the obverse some of the same Jewish symbols, changes the caption to '*for*' or '*of* the *redemption* of Zion'. This issue has been linked with the period of the faction fighting between the rebel leaders, and especially with the time when the magnetic Simon bar Giora was dominant.[98] But it is noteworthy that neither Simon nor any other potential Messiah figure is represented on any of the coins. And to make the best sense of the variety of forms of expression found on the different types, the slogan of year four should be taken together with the date on the obverse: this is year four *of* the redemption. And the redemption now has to be something which is already in force: not a hope of salvation, but a name for the new régime.

The picture we derive through piecing together the available information is thus one of men whose beliefs may well have encompassed the expectation of a Messiah sooner or later; but whose minds in 66–73 were mostly fixed on other things, and who hoped to achieve for themselves a better lot in this world before contemplating a terrible new one.

It is true that the writing in Greek of a Greek-style history of a war puts particular emphasis on political and military aspects. We have to take this into account; but at the same time to acknowledge that form will not have dominated content totally in the historian's writing, and that due weight should be given to the terms in which this contemporary writer conceives of what happened.

If Josephus, himself a first-century Jew, was able to keep his feet on the ground and his mind on the issue at hand when it came to action or describing action, those whom he opposed and denigrated could also have done so. To have decided on revolt when they did, with the emperor degenerating and the empire in crisis, it was not necessary to be dreamers or visionaries. If they were aided by the conviction that God rewarded the righteous, this was faith but not

---

[98] B. Kanael, 'The historical background of the coins year four of the redemption of Zion', *BASOR* 129 (1953), pp. 18–20. For numismatic arguments against the view that the coins are an emergency issue of much debased shekels, A. Kindler, 'Numismatic remarks on Jewish minting at the end of the Second Temple Period', part 1, in A. Oppenheimer, U. Rappaport and M. Stern (eds), *Jerusalem in the Second Temple Period: Abraham Schalit Memorial Volume* (1980; Hebrew with English summaries), pp. 271–8.

Messianism.[99] In practice, powerful armies could be held at bay for long periods with guerilla warfare; and the memory of Judas the Maccabee's success rendered a new attempt not entirely foolish.[100] Far less was it vain to think of trying to eliminate the Jewish ruling class, when Rome herself seemed to be rejecting them. In the event, however, the collapse of the first objective, and the Roman victory, rendered the attainment of the second, internal, goal quite futile. What is more not only the corrupt high priesthood, but the Temple itself collapsed in ruins; and there would never be another one. The effects of the revolutionaries' actions on the course of history was thus incalculable, beyond what anyone could have expected. And the last word on the revolution remained to be written from Rome by a member of the old aristocracy who had the good fortune to survive.

In the next chapter, we shall go back to scrutinise that survival, and Josephus' individual part in the revolt.

---

[99] See W. R. Farmer, *Maccabees, Zealots and Josephus* (1956), pp. 175–80. But we do not have to accept Farmer's theory of a direct connection between the Maccabees and the Zealots.

[100] To this limited extent, Farmer's association has value.

CHAPTER SIX

Josephus and the Civil War in Galilee

Josephus has a capacity for the unexpected. But the picture which emerges from his *Life*, of him scurrying among the towns and villages of lower Galilee, usually on horseback and often followed by a motley crew of partially armed Galileans, is one of the most amazing we have. He never specifies who these 'Galileans' were, and it is, of course, to his purpose to imply that the best part of the region's population is to be numbered among his supporters.[1] Those behind his enemy, John of Gischala, are, on the other hand, 'bandits'. In fact, however, the people who attach themselves to Josephus when he first appears in the area seem to be not very different in kind from the followers of John and of other local leaders. They are poor, volatile, and given to raiding; they are enemies of the town whether Jewish or Greek. Josephus tells us early on in the *Life* about brigands whom he could not disarm, and whom he therefore bound to himself as mercenaries (cf. p. 158). It is a known and not surprising fact that local administrators or commanders, especially if they are weak, will seek to benefit from an accommodation with bandit groups.[2] But what is happening here goes further than that; and to find himself the aspirant leader of something like a band of wild men, swollen with homeless peasants and angry villagers, must have been for Josephus bizarre, not to say frightening. Not only was he unaccustomed to such company, but, as a Jerusalemite, he was far removed from Galilean *mores*[3] and the intricacies of local feuds.

---

[1] S. J. D. Cohen, *Josephus in Rome and Galilee* (1979), pp. 206–14, is right in suggesting that they will have been largely Jewish peasants, from lower rather than upper Galilee, and that their numbers were never large. For bandits in Josephus' forces, Cohen, p. 212; but Cohen is (unusually) too credulous when he draws the line between ordinary people and bandits exactly where Josephus does.

[2] E. J. Hobsbawm, *Bandits*[2] (1981), pp. 89–95.

[3] On the gap between Galilean and Judaean Jewry, G. Vermes, *Jesus the Jew* (1973), pp. 42–57.

It must be remembered that it had been Jerusalem, without consultation, which had declared war on Rome, so that when Josephus reached Galilee it was not yet clear whether the rest of the country would revolt, and, if it did, under whom, with whom, perhaps even against whom the revolt would be.[4] Josephus had to assert Jerusalem's control over Galilee, and this was necessary, whatever shape the future might take.[5] His difficulties may be better imagined if three points are kept in mind. First, that the removal of Roman authority (however inadequate) from the region, and the total uncertainty as to its future, opened the door to the instant and forceful expression of a multitude of domestic controversies and rivalries: the question of war or no war was simply a new bone of contention, and old quarrels were revitalised around it. Second, although his former position and attitudes were well known, he had to present himself now as organiser of revolt, and to associate himself with elements who would be likely to assist that cause. Yet the hope of sustaining such a role was slim indeed for a man of his background and persuasions; to gauge the extent of his commitment, his every action would be watched by those who were sincerely dedicated to revolt. Last, he had his own associations and affiliations in the region, with officers and subordinates of the client king Agrippa II, for example, and with men of property.[6] Since they had not been exposed to the pressure of events in Jerusalem, and since, for some of them at least, the prospect of Agrippa's military and diplomatic protection was available, they would hardly have been drawn to the view held by Josephus and his friends, that it was no longer possible to stand in the way of the war. He could understand them well enough; yet to be lenient would make him vulnerable to fire from other quarters, and so he would find himself in embarrassing opposition to them.

---

[4] Note that, in A.D. 132–5, Galilee seems for the most part to have kept out of the revolt of Bar Kochba: S. Applebaum, *Prolegomena to the Study of the Second Jewish Revolt (A.D. 132–5)* (1976), pp. 22–5.

[5] And whether or not it is true that it would still have been possible to stop the revolt, as Josephus several times claims in the *Life*.

[6] For example, the four prosperous citizens of Tiberias, mentioned at *V* 33–4 as being firmly for peace and for a continuation of the city's allegiance to Agrippa II. Josephus had to instruct these people to destroy Herod's palace—*V* 65. Of Agrippa's men, he seems to have had some connection with Philip son of Jacimus, an official whose exploits he recounts at length (*V* 46ff., 179ff. and see Cohen, op. cit. (n. 1), pp. 160–8 for the story). It may also be significant that he tried, it seems, to save the stolen goods of Ptolemy, the overseer—*V* 126ff., and see p. 163.

Thus, while Josephus may have had personal qualities which did not readily inspire trust, these are by no means the principal source of his difficulties. In the other areas of command, Idumaea, Peraea (across the Jordan), and the various sections of Judaea, there are likely to have been comparable tensions, but it happens that we hear scarcely anything of them.[7] Josephus' account of these years in the *War* deals mainly with the Galilee, partly because that is where the author was, partly because when he started to compose the *War*, there were already calls on him to defend his own record,[8] and partly because Galilee proved crucial—Vespasian began his reduction of the country there, and there the longest resistance before that of Jerusalem occurred. The *Life* is concerned solely with that area. We know that Josephus was criticised; but such other organisers as survived may well have been similarly treated.

It was the fact that Josephus arranged for his own survival and flourished afterwards, which ensured that the controversy about his activities remained alive: verbal assaults were still being made on him under Domitian, and mutual recriminations seem to have been in full spate some twenty years after the events (*V* 429). Part of the argument survives for us in the form of his second account of the Galilean period, which occupies most of the *Life*, and which was composed, as we have seen, for the purpose of refuting written attacks. The most notable was that of Justus of Tiberias, a local politician, who in due course sought refuge with Agrippa II and after the war became his secretary and a historian of some kind. Justus had reason to hate Josephus as responsible for imprisoning him and his father.[9] From Josephus' reply, it is possible to ascertain some of the contents of these attacks.

There is no chance, however, of reaching a secure verdict about the literary relationship between Josephus' two narratives, and there is nothing to be gained by involved speculation. But a working hypothesis, the simpler the better, is needed, and it must incorporate

[7] We know only that in Thamna, the north-western corner of Judaea, the commander John the Essene perished in a very early action (*BJ* 3. 9ff.), a seemingly foolhardy attack on Ascalon; and there cannot have been much resistance when Vespasian rapidly reduced this area, in spring 68 (4. 444ff.).

[8] See p. 150, and also *V* 416, 423—criticisms after the fighting was over.

[9] On Justus' career and the evidence for his writings, T. Rajak, 'Justus of Tiberias', *CQ* 23 (1973), pp. 344–68; the imprisonment, *V* 175. Justus' brother-in-law was murdered by militants, and his brother had his hands cut off by 'Galileans': he may have held Josephus, as organiser of the war in Galilee, responsible for these misfortunes (*V* 177, 186).

the following facts. First, it is immediately clear, and natural enough, that there is much material in the *Life* which had not appeared in the *War*. Then, there are some disparities between the two accounts, both in the chronological order of events and in factual detail: in many, but not all, of these cases the *Life* appears to be the more correct, as though Josephus has been able to, or has had to, improve his first story. Yet, while each account carries its own one-sidedness in presentation, that in the *Life* is the more insistent, since a case for the defence is there being argued in a sustained way (the contradictions are discussed below). And each account has, in view of all these features, its own kind of claim to superiority. It is possible to go further, and analyse their biasses. But what is principally needed is some sort of explanation of the changes found in the *Life*. Various hypotheses can be put forward, as well as a mixture of all of them. At one extreme is the unprovable notion that Josephus retained in his possession a report or old notes from the year 67, which may or may not have been drawn upon for the *War* but were, in any case, exploited in the *Life*. Then there is the idea that, when his memory was jogged and he was compelled to concentrate more closely on what had happened, he reached a more accurate view, or that, by discussion or reading, he encountered the truth in what was said by friends or adversaries. Finally, we have the harsh view that he was aware of the truth all the time, but in one of the works offered a series of falsifications. The first hypothesis has been developed at great length more than once, without leading anywhere.[10] The last is hard to credit in the case of the many divergences between the two versions which appear unmotivated. We may safely settle for a blend of the middle options, amply supported as they are by common sense.[11] Also in their favour are the allusiveness and seeming incoherence of parts of the

---

[10] It was originated by R. Laqueur, *Der jüdische Historiker Flavius Josephus* (1920), chs 3 and 4. M. Gelzer changed Laqueur's formal document into a *hypomnēma*, which is seen as the historian's preliminary draft: 'Die Vita des Josephus', *Hermes* 80 (1952), pp. 67–90. Cohen, op. cit. (n. 1), pp. 80–3, suggested a *hypomnēma* used by Josephus on both occasions, but modified less in the *Life*; this meets some of the obvious objections to the earlier theories, but, as a tool, the *hypomnēma* now becomes useless. The notion that the early nucleus should be distinguishable within the *Life* seems extraordinary.

[11] For the possibility of Josephus coming upon fresh revelations, see H. Luther, *Josephus und Justus von Tiberias* (Halle, 1910), p. 15. On error in a man's recollections of his own military activities, see the apt remarks of J.P.V.D. Balsdon, *JRS* 45 (1955), p. 161, where the writings of Winston Churchill serve as an example.

Life, which suggest that the matters discussed there were much rehearsed over the years and that Josephus could expect his readers to be familiar with the events he was talking about.

The amount of controversy and re-interpretation which came out of the war in Galilee is entirely intelligible in the light of the multitude of divisions, arguments and internal battles which took place there at the time—together, of course, with the fact of ultimate Jewish defeat. The fissures opened in Jerusalem were multiplied in Galilee. All three initial major groupings, created by the issue of whether or not to fight, succumbed to internal splits: the party of Agrippa, who had taken the Roman side after his persuasions for peace failed, in the shape of a deadly feud between two of his functionaries, Philip and Varus; the moderates, or reluctant war-mongers, in the quarrel between two men, Josephus and Justus, whose positions, ambivalences and future careers were remarkably similar—and even their social backgrounds, for we notice that Josephus personally gave dinner to Justus and his father when they were his prisoners and spoke to them about the revolt in a way which suggested a basis of shared assumptions;[12] and not least the militants, some of whom at first also adhered to Josephus, while others hitched their waggons immediately to the star of John of Gischala. Through all this, Jews and Greeks (the latter being, in fact, mainly Greek-speaking Syrian natives) fought a running battle in a number of urban centres. Countryside and town were in conflict, with bands of Jewish peasants falling upon pagan centres and attacking even the city of Tiberias, where the population was essentially Jewish, for all that the public buildings looked quite Greek.[13] The overseer Varus turned renegade, conspired against his master Agrippa, and made raids on Jews in Caesarea and on a Babylonian-Jewish settlement in Trachonitis, to the east of the Sea of Galilee (*V* 48ff.). Neighbouring towns, as so often happens, took up arms against each other—Tiberias against Sepphoris (each one claiming to be the capital of the region); Tiberias against Tarichaeae (both lakeside towns); Tiberias against the territory of Scythopolis. Within cities, the war party was in conflict with the peace party, while those in the middle kept changing sides, and repeated shifts of local policy were manifest.[14] Local bandit chiefs or armed strong

---

[12] Rajak, op. cit. (n. 9), p. 353.
[13] *V* 26, 99, 375, 381ff.; on the character of Tiberias, Rajak, op. cit. (n. 9), part 1.
[14] *V* 37, 97–8, 42, 162; for inter-city trouble. Internal war: *V* 32–6, 125, 155, 185–6, 353.

men attached themselves and their troops to whichever faction they fancied. A certain Jesus, for example, was a brigand chief who controlled territory around Acre, and put 800 men at the disposal of the pro-Roman Sepphorites (*V* 105).

The class dichotomy, so visible at Jerusalem, is obscured here, where there is at least as much division within classes. But elements of it can be perceived. The destruction of the Jerusalem archives and the Herodian palace there is foreshadowed in Galilee by the firing of the palace of Herod the tetrarch at Tiberias and the appropriation of the wealth found in it. This money later came into Josephus' hands, causing him great embarrassment. There was also the ambush on Agrippa's prefect Philip (or his wife), caught trying to get their possessions out of the country—with, again, the unwilling involvement of Josephus. One might also add to this list of actions originating in class hatred some, even if not all, of the attempts to murder the general, Josephus (see pp. 162–3).

The methods used in pursuing all these animosities were brutal in the extreme. It seems that the punishment of cutting off the hand or hands of a supposed malefactor or a personal enemy, was the standard practice among all parties. It is used as freely by Josephus as by the insurgents, and recorded as something which does not need an apology (*V* 171ff., 177).

It is no wonder, then, that Josephus had to struggle simply to assert his authority. When he says that his main objective was to keep the peace in his region, the statement is indisputable in at least one sense, whatever it implies, or is meant to imply, about his attitude to the war against the Romans (*V* 38). His skirmishes with detachments from Agrippa's forces seem to be almost a diversion. That is why it is so hard to gauge Josephus' true intentions with regard to the revolt, using the evidence of Galilee alone.[15]

His most painful quarrel, and the one which he is still conducting in the *Life*, is with men of his own political colour, those whom we have called upper class moderates, for want of a better term. We have seen enough of Palestinian Jewish society, and of the origins of the revolt, to understand their importance in its early stages, and to reject any notion that they could be a self-justifying invention of Josephus (on this notion, see p. 106). That quarrel, together with

---

[15] Not that this has prevented scholars from trying: for an interesting conspectus of the history of the debate see Cohen, ch. 1. Recent opinion has tended to the view that Josephus' aim was to avoid fighting, but Cohen attempts to reverse this.

the length of time that had elapsed since the events, explains his consistent tendency to stress that, through all the vicissitudes he had endured, he had dissociated himself as far as possible from acts of violence and had never been responsible for fanning the flames of insurrection. He acknowledges—he can hardly deny it—that he had performed the role assigned to him as organiser and 'general'; but he disclaims any enthusiasm for it. He goes so far as to assert that he played, if not a double game, at least some sort of a waiting game. How true this is we shall never know. What is interesting is the very fact that he wishes us to believe it.

But the *Life* is centred, in fact, on a more specific argument. There is one incident which caused our author more discomfort than any other in his career, more even than the Jotapata defeat and deception, which he had narrated fully and unashamedly in the *War*, and to which he apparently had no need to return in his second apologia (*V* 412; see pp. 167ff.). This incident is the call for his removal from the Galilean war-command made by the Jerusalem authorities themselves. The charge, which he of course denies, was essentially one of incompetence; but from his incidental claims at various points in his recital we can guess that other complaints, of vindictiveness and venality, authoritarianism ('tyranny') and impiety, were also involved.[16] The dishonour of being rejected by his own associates was hard to live down. Simon ben Gamaliel, a man of great repute, was the main advocate of Josephus' dismissal: so well-known was Simon, that Josephus felt he had nothing to lose in acknowledging his opponent's distinguished descent and scholarly pre-eminence. Ananus and Joshua ben Gamala, the two high priests, were, it is said, somewhat resistant to the measure, but had to go along with it. Others of their party (*stasis*), which was also Josephus' party, were also caught up in this. It looks as though a vote in the Jerusalem *koinon*—evidently some sort of provisional assembly—went against Josephus, though, perhaps deliberately, he is not explicit on this point. The commission of four, despatched with an escort of a thousand armed men to unseat the general, are three of them Pharisees like himself, while one comes of a high

---

[16] *V* 79–83, 100, 260–1, 293ff. Note also how Josephus rebuts such charges when he stresses his moderation, honesty, clemency and religious correctness: 100, 102–3, 110–11, 159, 265, 275, 321, 329–30, 379–80, 385ff. These issues are brought out by H. Drexler, 'Untersuchungen zu Josephus und zur Geschichte des jüdischen Aufstandes 66–70', *Klio* 19 (1925), pp. 277–312, section 2; and by A. Schalit, 'Josephus und Justus', *Klio* 26 (1933), pp. 67–95.

priestly family. To make it worse, one of the three Pharisees—his name is Joazar—has exactly the same background as Josephus, being priestly and upper class: a contrast is drawn with the other two Pharisees, who are *dēmotikoi* (men of the people).[17]

Josephus does what he can to rescue his reputation in recounting the incident: John of Gischala, who was an intemperate revolutionary and a personal enemy, had instigated the whole thing. According to the *War*, those in power in Jerusalem responded because they were jealous. The *Life* has it that gifts had changed hands, and that Ananus had proved susceptible to bribery. Yet even the elaborate defence in the latter account cannot conceal the conviction and the resolve with which the measures were adopted. The embassy was given orders to capture or kill him; many messengers were sent out to seek assistance from the Galilean towns (*V* 203). Much of the *Life* is really concerned with the activities of the embassy, and of John, its engineer and accomplice. We are regaled with an assortment of ingenious manoeuvres by which Josephus and his followers avoided and wore down the ambassadors, until he could corner and trap them, and then insist on his reinstatement. The face-to-face encounters between Josephus and the little party from Jerusalem are dramatic high points in the narrative. The desperate devotion of his 'Galileans', dubious characters though they were, is mentioned time and again, and used to show why he was unable to leave the district. And this self-justification is reinforced by the introduction of a pathetic letter from his sick father, pleading for his return, which demonstrates that Josephus personally had every possible motive for departure; if he stayed on, it could only have been to help others (*V* 207, 244, 250). A key position is assigned to a dream, which came to Josephus at his headquarters in the plain of Asochis (near Sepphoris, and not far from today's Nazareth), in which a voice told him to remember that he would have to fight the Romans before he could achieve greatness and happiness. This exculpatory device, exactly comparable with the vision of Jotapata,

---

[17] *BJ* 2. 626ff., *V* 189–202; on the embassy, cf. p. 31. Note that Simon is praised by Josephus here, in spite of the way he had treated him. No general comment, either negative or positive, is made about Ananus. These two facts together make it improbable that Josephus' resentment against Ananus was so great after this affair as to move him from adulation in the *War* to the vicious criticism of *AJ* 20. 200–6. And, in any case, for this view to be tenable it would also be necessary to suppose that when he wrote the *War* Josephus had not yet known the full extent of Ananus' betrayal. The *Antiquities* assessment may be part of a Christian interpolation.

forwards with brilliant economy (even if less than complete persu-
asiveness) Josephus' double objective in the *Life*: first, to explain
why he hung on to his command after having been formally stripped
of it; and secondly, to justify what might have appeared to be an
excess of anti-Roman zeal.[18] There were, he claims, superior orders
to be followed.

The whole tenor of the *Life* indicates that it was addressed to
readers whose political cast of mind was essentially that of Josephus.
This seems undeniable, in spite of the awkward fact that he evidently issued the work as an appendix to the much larger *Antiquities*,
and therefore formally addressed it to a pagan audience (see p.
228); these were people whom he wished to reconcile with the Jews
in their midst, by acquainting them with that people's traditions
and institutions. We do not need to be disturbed by the apparent
contradiction, and the best solution seems to lie in the supposition
that, throughout, two kinds of readers were somewhere in Josephus'
mind. Of course he wanted to reach and impress the learned pagan
public; but this was not the safe readership, the one he could fully
rely on. Many a modern academic writer has the same sort of
ambivalence of intention about the books he writes. The significance
of this for the *Antiquities* is a complex matter. For the *Life*, it simply
means that we need not hesitate to rely on the internal evidence
which it offers us, and to accept that it was designed for people
intimately involved with the events of 66–7, mostly (though not
necessarily exclusively) Jews; and, what is more, for people who
were to a great extent like its author. They had been influenced by
Josephus' critics; the record therefore had to be set straight, and
the critics pulled up.

One prominent adversary was Justus of Tiberias (see p. 146).
But it is helpful to realise that Josephus need not be replying to
Justus alone, and that the notion that his whole polemic relates to
points made by Justus is a pure assumption.[19] Justus' account of
the events is first mentioned in passing, when he is introduced as
an actor on the political scene. It does not come in again until much
later. If we look at the passage which has conveniently been dubbed
the 'great digression' against Justus, appearing near the end of the

---

[18] *V* 208–10. For the comparison between the Asochis and the Jotapata visions,
see Cohen, op. cit. (n. 1), p. 160, n. 188.

[19] I depart here from my earlier reconstruction, op. cit (n. 9).

Life,[20] we see that it begins with a statement which tends, if anything, to suggest that only now is Josephus turning his attention to
accusations from that quarter: 'having come to this point in my
narrative, I propose to address a few words to Justus, who has
produced his own account of these affairs, and to others who purport
to be writing history.' Justus' claim that Josephus had been responsible for the revolt of the city of Tiberias, is thrown back at him;
the main political disagreement between these two ex-moderates, in
a period when zealotry had naturally become more discreditable
than ever, was on the question of who had been more of a warmonger.[21] But, beyond this, the rest of the digression concerns, in
a fairly general way, the rival claims of the competing authors' war
narratives, and aims to devalue Justus' whole enterprise. Josephus
is no longer talking exclusively of his own command, for he makes
the point that Justus had not been in a position to follow events
either in Galilee *or* in Jerusalem. Naturally Galilee is a significant
part of the argument—they had been there together, and quarrelled
there, and it is Josephus' strongest suit in claiming superior knowledge, because, as commander, he had a better overview than Justus, and had remained longer. But it is not the whole debate.

The evidence of the 'great digression' is consistent with the otherwise plausible idea that Justus had written a fairly general account
of the war, perhaps even a brief one; such a work could have had
room in it for other material and could thus accommodate the
excursus on the Jewish kings ascribed to Justus by the Byzantine
scholar, Photius, who must have seen Justus' opus in its entirety.[22]
Galilee will, then, have appeared in brief, and Josephus might have
come in intermittently, or even momentarily. We do know that
Justus had written of Jotapata; but that Josephus does not trouble
to engage him on this subject is another sign that the *Life* has
preoccupations which extend beyond replying to this single individual. Although some perceptive scholars have noticed that the case
presented by Josephus is a unitary one, and cannot easily be separated, as their predecessors thought, into a succession of different
extracts from different sources,[23] it does not follow that the whole
of it looks towards one single target. Apart from anything else, it is

---

[20] The term is Cohen's. See *V* 40 and 345–67.
[21] Rajak, op. cit. (n. 9), pp. 355–6.
[22] Photius, *Bibl.* 33; Rajak, op. cit., section 4.
[23] Especially Schalit, op. cit. (n. 16), pp. 68ff.

probable that there was not enough material in Justus to generate the *Life*. It is within a wider milieu, the surviving or regenerated Jewish aristocracy in the years after 70, and especially that part of it which was to be found in the Diaspora, that we must locate the dispute about Josephus in Galilee. And this explains admirably the lack of interest at this stage in his going over to the Romans at Jotapata. These aristocrats all understood the political quandary which had given rise to the action, and they knew that they might well have done just the same. There had been, of course, a morally dubious aspect to such a change of sides, and to Josephus' friendship with the Flavian generals. These had caused something of a stir in the seventies (see p. 171). But by the nineties they were of less moment than questions like whether the revolt could have been prevented, or, if it had to happen, whether it could have been better organised; and why the moderates had not managed to grasp hold of the situation, and to retain their grip. These were the more painful and far-reaching subjects, which continued to be disturbing; and, in this context, Josephus' failure to master the Galilee, and his rejections as an official commander by Jerusalem were the major issues.

The upper class attitude underlying the *Life's* Galilean narrative turns out to be the same as that displayed in the *War* to the revolt as a whole; and there is no reason to think that Josephus greatly changed his view of what had happened between the publication of the two works. In spite of some tendentious statements in each, they spring from the same overall assessment of the situation.

So far, in discussing Josephus' confused and confusing Galilean escapades, I have relied largely on the *Life*. It remains to tie this in with what is recounted on the subject, much more briefly, in the *War*; and to justify this reliance by showing that the much-vaunted inconsistencies between the two versions are not such as should substantially discredit one, or both of them. Particularly, we need to test the reliability of the *Life*, on which, because it is fuller, our dependence is greater. My claim is that what discrepancies there are, beyond the trivial and the accidental, can be explained in terms of the literary form, and purpose of the narratives, and that it is inappropriate to speak of persistent, wilful distortion. In fact, in many cases we are dealing not even with real inconsistencies, but with shifts in emphasis.

For a variety of reasons, we would expect there to be some

differences between the two accounts. First, there is the contrast in purpose: for while the *War* naturally presents Josephus' campaign to advantage, it is only the *Life* which is entirely motivated by the need for self-defence. This need had called it into being; and in any case it was a usual tendency in ancient writing of an autobiographical kind. When it comes to form, the *War* has to subscribe to firmer conventions, those current in the classical world for writing the well-established genre of war histories. For autobiography, on the other hand, there existed little by way of direct precedent; and from this, perhaps, arises the curious lack of proportion and of connection in Josephus' autobiography.[24] There is also the sheer difference in scale, which makes the *War* version necessarily more simplified and condensed: some sort of omission is unavoidable. Finally, we should not forget that when two accounts of the same set of events are to be offered, there arises the simple need to avoid repetition: some details will be suppressed, others offered in their place.

Since, as we have said, Josephus is writing a war history, the *War* account presents his activities as part of a formal and properly organized defensive campaign. A tendency towards emphasising the war as a major military event can be traced right through the work. Indeed, the very first line of the whole history goes so far as to claim the Jewish revolt as virtually the greatest war ever fought: this literary conceit, inspired and made legitimate by the model of Thucydides, admirably reveals Josephus' frame of mind as he embarked on his composition. The Jews are to emerge as worthy opponents of the mighty Roman army, whose strength is surveyed in a famous speech, and whose structure and campaign formation are described in a famous digression (cf. pp. 160 and 180). The Jewish general has to be correspondingly impressive, and it is not vanity on Josephus' part that makes him dignify his own role.[25] So much is he influenced by literary exigencies, that he has no inhibitions about proudly claiming that he had fought his Roman patrons well. In the *War*'s Galilean narrative, incidents are explained in simple, bold and almost crude terms, and, apart from admiration, excitement is

---

[24] On these aspects of ancient autobiography, see A. D. Momigliano, *The Development of Greek Biography* (1971), pp. 89–91.

[25] As Thackeray thought; see the introduction to his translation, Loeb *Josephus*, vol. 1, p. xiv. This view also ignores the ancients' lack of inhibition about boasting, on which see E. A. Judge, 'St. Paul and Classical Society', *JbAC* 15 (1972), pp. 35–6.

the main response Josephus seeks to evoke from his readers.[26] Few
comments are made about his intentions or expectations, or about
any doubts he may or may not have had, for the account describes
action rather than opinion. There are two principal themes: the
vigorous preparatory measures taken by Josephus as commander,
and—told at greater length—the intrigues of his adversary, John of
Gischala, with his own counter-machinations. But we do not learn
nearly enough to understand what was going on beneath the surface.
When these two themes have been dealt with, we have only to hear
about the entrance of Vespasian's army into Galilee, and about the
end of the resistance, both of Josephus and of the district.

A reader does not have to be especially attentive to notice that,
in contrast to all that we have just seen, when it comes to the *Life*
Josephus makes a point of demonstrating that his mission to the
Galilee had initially been a pacific one. First, unlike the *War*, the
later work concentrates on the precise manner in which the Jerusalem leaders made their *volte face* and became organisers of revolt,
for this is indispensable to an explanation of Josephus' own position.
He says that after the fiasco of Cestius the militants in Jerusalem
took up arms and the notables were in danger. Learning that there
was a significant peace party in Galilee, they sent Josephus, along
with two other priests, to try to control the rebels in the area. These
were to be persuaded to put their forces at Jerusalem's disposal,
making it possible to wait and see what the Romans would do, and
to avoid precipitate action. This, then, is the background to Josephus' commission (*V* 28). Next, we hear something of what he
discovered when he got there: the situation in the towns of Sepphoris, Tiberias, Gischala and Gamala, as well as a retrospective
account of the trouble caused by Agrippa's overseer, Varus. As
soon as Josephus had grasped what was going on, he wrote to the
Sanhedrin at Jerusalem. Instructions came that he was to remain
and make provisions for the area. His colleagues could stay if they
wanted to; as a matter of fact, they returned shortly afterwards (*V*
63). The Sanhedrin letter constitutes Josephus' official appointment.
Later in the work, although not at this point, he describes himself
as the recognised 'general' of the Galilee (*V* 135, 176, 230, 250).

The *War* simply says that some unspecified time after Cestius
Gallus' flight, the respectable Jews still remaining in Jerusalem

---

[26] Notwithstanding that in one or two cases the *Life* has a more thrilling account
of an episode, the balance is normally the other way.

were brought over to the war party either by persuasion or compulsion and assembled in the Temple to appoint generals for the war: Josephus was given the two Galilees and Gamala. On arrival, he sought to win the affection of the population, and he made various appointments (*BJ* 2.562–71). What has happened is that all those preliminary activities described in the *Life* have been omitted in the *War*, so that Josephus goes straight to his official appointment; this corresponds to the Sanhedrin instructions which, according to the *Life*, were received in due course, and which left him in sole control, even if his two companions delayed a little before returning. The *Life* has them active for a short while at Gischala, and then going back. The activities ascribed to them occur also in the *War*, but, since there are no companions there, Josephus makes himself wholly responsible for carrying them out: as he was now in official control, this is not incorrect, though it is incomplete (*V* 70–7).

This disparity between the two accounts is the most famous of the alleged inconsistencies in Josephus.[27] But if it is realised that the *War* merely omits a few of the events for which the *Life* finds room, then the inconsistency dissolves. All that is necessary is to see that *War* 2. 568, corresponds not to section 28 but to section 63 of the *Life*. There are other episodes in this phase of the war which are not central enough to figure in the shorter account—the Tiberian attack on Sepphoris, the destruction of the Herodian palace, and the massacre of the Greek inhabitants of Tiberias (*V* 37, 64, 67). The only implication there which might be considered misleading is that Josephus started to make his dispensations as sole commander as soon as he arrived in the area; but his words do not suggest that he intends to be chronologically precise: and, indeed, the whole *War* narrative tends to organise events around themes, and to be less concerned with placing them in time.[28]

The information passed over in the *War* is simply irrelevant there—and that includes the details about the way he took up his appointment, and about his companions. But it is material to the *Life*, with its special interest in the wrangles over Josephus' command, and there every internal political manoeuvre is spelled out. Nevertheless, it remains true that the same picture of the mood and

---

[27] Thackeray presents, on this, the conventional wisdom: *Josephus the Man and the Historian* (1929), pp. 10–11; cf. p. 5. For a more detailed exposition, Drexler, op. cit. (n. 22), pp. 209–302.

[28] This aspect of the *War* is handled by Cohen: see especially pp. 67–77.

attitudes of Josephus and his colleagues is painted in the two accounts. That they went unwillingly to war is quite evident from both (cf. p. 129). And so it is of little moment that a short-lived expedition, sent out to discover whether the revolt in Galilee was still small enough to be stifled, and accomplishing nothing, does not rate a mention there.

The same pattern continues in the relationship between the versions. When the *War* tells how Josephus, once appointed, strove to win the favour and support of the Galileans, that is simply a vague and euphemistic way of describing what is explained in the *Life*: the rebels could not be disarmed, so they were taken on as 'mercenaries', in an attempt to bring them under the official umbrella. According to the *War*, seventy distinguished magistrates *(archontes)* and seven petty judges *(dikastai)* for each town were appointed by Josephus, so that Galilee might manage its own affairs; he himself remained responsible for serious cases. Reading the *Life*, we are amused to learn that these officials were simply the old Galilean functionaries, taken hostage by Josephus, retained beside him, and allowed to judge cases in order to keep them happy. By exposing the motives behind the decision, the *Life* attaches flesh to the bare bones (*V* 77–9).

It is also to be expected that the *War* should place more emphasis on the Jewish fortification of Galilee. This is achieved by putting the operation among the general's first activities, and offering immediately a list of sites which were supposedly fortified against external attack, either by his own doing, or (in two cases) under his auspices. In the *Life*, Josephus at first says vaguely that he took steps to obtain arms and strengthen the towns; somewhat later, we read about the organisation of protection and supplies for a variety of settlements, many of them the same as those mentioned in the *War* (2.573; *V* 187–8). Again, the worst offences committed in the early account are a disregard for chronology in the interests of its thematic arrangement, and a certain literary over-simplification, leading not so much to falsehood, as to a picture which is a little too glamorous. Josephus' defensive strategy must have in fact been a scrappy affair, if, indeed, it is right to speak of a strategy at all. The list of places fortified is a mixed bag, including villages, prominent urban settlements, a scattering of high points in both upper and lower Galilee, which were protected by their position and capable of withstanding a siege, and some places of refuge down in the rift valley.[29] The fortification must in many cases have been very limited. But a general requires a strategy, and Josephus conceives of himself as having had one.[30]

In just one case he is carried away into making an apparently incorrect statement: he says that he allowed the population of Sepphoris to construct its own walls on the grounds that, as well as being wealthy, it was eager for war. Yet in the parallel account in the *Life*, and everywhere else in both *Life* and *War*, the pro-Roman inclinations of the city are emphasised.[31] It would seem that Josephus has been swept away by his own picture. But this is a minor point.

In the *Life*, the rebels were described as Josephus' mercenaries, a description which brings out the lack of common purpose between him and them, while the *War*, instead, is concerned with another facet of the preparations, and tells, in a well-known excursus, how he trained his men and attempted to turn them into a replica Roman army. There is nothing in the *Life* which makes this incredible. In itself it is plausible, apart from the extraordinarily large figure given for the number of troops at Josephus' disposal: they amount, if the manuscript tradition can be trusted, to sixty thousand of infantry alone, which is more than ten Roman legions (*BJ* 2.576–

---

[29] Avi-Yonah's view, that a complete protective circuit was provided for the region requires a conjecture to provide even one fortress blocking a Roman advance from the direction of Acre: 'The missing fortress of Flavius Josephus', *IEJ* 3 (1953), pp. 94–8. M. Har-El, 'The Zealots' Fortresses in Galilee', *IEJ* 22 (1972), pp. 123ff., assumes, without demonstration, that the siting of the fortresses was based on a carefully planned, fully integrated defence system. The haphazardness of the Jewish defences is well brought out by Y. Levinson, 'Vespasian's advance from Acre to Jotapata', *19th National Congress for the Exploration of the Land of Israel and its Antiquities* (Jerusalem, 1965; Hebrew). Useful points in B. Bar-Kochva, 'Notes on the fortresses of Josephus in Galilee', *IEJ* 24 (1974), pp. 132.

[30] Cohen, op. cit. (n. 1), pp. 91–7, explores Josephus' depiction of himself as a great general.

[31] *BJ* 2. 574; *V* 30. Sepphoris as anti-war also at *BJ* 2. 511; 3. 30, 61; *V* 38, 104, 346–8, 373ff., 394ff. An unusual coin of 67–8, mentioning Vespasian and apparently entitling Sepphoris 'city of peace' (*eirēnopolis*) points the same way: H. Seyrig, 'Irenopolis-Neronias-Sepphoris', *NC* (6th ser.) 10 (1950), pp. 284–9; together with 15 (1955), pp. 157–9; Y. Meshorer, 'The coins of Sepphoris as a historical source', *Zion* 43 (1978), pp. 185–6 (Hebrew); Cohen, pp. 245–8. The reasons for this loyalty are not entirely clear, and some unconvincing explanations have been offered, such as the vulnerability of the city's water supply (S. Yeivin, *Excavations at Sepphoris* (Michigan, 1937), vol. 2, pp. 23–4); or the large number of priestly families there (S. Klein, *Miscellaneous Essays in Palestinian Research* (1924; Hebrew), Zippori, pp. 55–6—but why should all the priests have been from the upper stratum?).

84): this is the 'ideal general' motif run riot.[32] Otherwise it is an obvious move for an inexperienced fighting force to imitate the methods of its adversary. We are told that Roman techniques were adopted by an earlier leader of revolt against Rome in a different part of the empire—Arminius the German, of whom we read in Tacitus (*Ann.* 2.45). The wisdom of such an approach, instead of the more irregular guerilla tactics which can harass formal armies for years on end, is another matter. And it need hardly be said that we should not expect Josephus' army to have acquired, in the short time available, and in those confused and equivocal circumstances, much of the Roman discipline and organisation for which he expresses such enthusiasm. Like the American army of the Revolution, they were in reality little more than 'a rabble dignified by the name of army'. But the Jews had less working in their favour. In fact, through all the subsequent events, their lack of planning, skill and equipment were to be disastrous. Josephus will point out their difficulties repeatedly, and it is evident that he was always deeply aware how unfit the Jews were to face the Romans.[33] We may like to think that the detailed digression, appearing at a slightly later stage, about the way the Roman army functioned, springs from his own fascination with it, as much as from the intrinsic suitability of the subject for cultured Greek readers, or the desire to imitate Polybius, or the wish to convince subject peoples that the imperial power was invincible (*BJ* 3.70–109; Polyb. 6.26ff.).

It is a fusion of the two representations—the aspirations to order embodied in the *War* and the underlying anarchy exposed in the *Life*—which brings us close to grasping the real situation in Galilee. If the *War* shows what Josephus tried to make of things, the *Life* reveals how many obstacles stood in his way.

In both accounts, John of Gischala dominates the events that follow, but in somewhat different ways. In the *War*, the over-simplification stands out at the start. The responsibility for the revolt against Josephus, throughout his district, is laid immediately at the door of this one man, said to be the most unscrupulous and crafty of all. An abusive, but unspecific portrait of him follows, in which he is drawn as a standard villain: this portrait invites comparison with the characterization of the rebel Catiline by the Roman his-

[32] On the motif, loc. cit. in n. 30.

[33] E.g. *BJ* 3. 113–14, 153, 270, 475. Tacitus says that it was only after repeated campaigns against Rome that the Germans became more disciplined.

torian Sallust.[34] Blaming everything on John might excuse Josephus; and at the same time this concentration on one personality is a solution to the problem of reporting in brief what was actually a very involved political episode. In the *Life*, the trouble in Josephus' province can no longer be explained in such simple terms—it is one of the main topics under investigation, and the details now have to be scrutinised. However, it is clear from that account too that John was a power to be reckoned with, and the fact that Josephus sought him out as soon as he arrived suggests that he was regarded as the principal local leader.

But the fact that the *Life* has to be more explicit on the subject of John means that there is also room for more distortion. Josephus has acquired a new concern, to show that he had never willingly collaborated with John, and to explain away the co-operation which appears temporarily to have existed between them. So there are problems with both accounts. The truth of the matter is that, by the end of his Galilean period, Josephus thoroughly detested John, and he cannot talk about him without a high degree of emotion. A historian writing of events in which he was involved will be weakest when it comes to personalities. The two accounts are not altogether consistent, particularly in the realm of motives and intentions. We will never disentangle the whole truth, and do best simply to note the general drift of what he says. But it would certainly be wrong to maintain that the way he shifts his ground about John is characteristic of his writing.

The defamatory set piece which introduces John to the reader of the *War* describes him as a brigand, who had been plundering Galilee and terrorising its people. But the whole passage is so full of exaggeration and stock denunciation that the reader can hardly be expected to take what is said at face value. In the *Life*, the suggestion is that John at first tried to restrain the people of Gischala from revolt. It was to resist raids from various Greek cities that he took up arms, and when his town was destroyed he rebuilt it. This seems to be part of the attempt to justify the good relationship that Josephus initially had with John, a relationship which is revealed

---

[34] *BJ* 2. 585–8: 'a ready liar and clever in obtaining credit for his lies, he made a merit of deceit and practised it upon his most intimate friends; while affecting humanity, the prospect of lucre made him the most sanguinary of men; always full of high ambitions, his hopes were fed on the basest of knaveries' etc. (Thackeray's translation; the Sallustian comparison appears in Thackeray's notes).

and vouched for also by the *War*, where we learn that because
Josephus had at first admired John's energy, he had put him in
charge of constructing walls for Gischala (2.590). That this was
later an embarrassment for Josephus, comes out in the *Life*, when
he distributes the blame by asserting that his two colleagues (who
had not yet returned) were putting pressure on him at the time.

Thus, while we cannot be sure quite what John was up to, it is
plain that Josephus did at first try to work with him, and that later
John revolted. This is stated by both works, the first time in a
straightforward fashion, the second with considerable unease. What
seems to have happened is that John moved from the fairly moderate
position which he took up when it was still unclear what would
happen in his area, and when his friendship with men like Simon
son of Gamaliel was of advantage to him, to a patently revolutionary
one soon afterwards, when the middle ground in the Galilee began
to fall away.[35]

The two versions agree that it was with Josephus' consent that
John was able to make profitable speculations in olive oil, cornering
the market and selling to Syrian Jews (who would not use pagan
oil) at a vast profit. Apart from details, such as the exact numerical
relation between the buying and selling prices of the oil, the only
difference is that in the *War* Josephus does not explain why he
permitted this while in the *Life* he says he did it because he feared
reprisals from the mob (*BJ* 2.591; *V* 74–6). The *Life*, then, offers
excuses once more for Josephus' co-operation with John. The *War*
simply ignores the problematic aspect of the relationship until the
moment of John's revolt, leaving us under the impression that
John's true nature was unclear before that.

Both versions recount at some length a plot by John to have
Josephus assassinated at Tiberias (*BJ* 2.614–18; *V* 85–96). The *War*
makes of it an exciting story, in which the villain, while pretending
to take the waters, displays his limitless ingenuity. For the *Life*,
there are the additional purposes of making it doubly clear that
John and Josephus were not secret allies, and of excusing Josephus'
own ruthless stratagems. There are two differences, neither at all
substantial. In the *War* the incident is less plausibly put after John
has publicly denounced Josephus at nearby Taricheae, when Josephus would have been unlikely to trust him enough to fall into his

---

[35] On John as a moderate, and the relationship with Simon, see p. 132.

trap. No particular motive for this reversal is detectable, and the explanation may be that the emphasis which Josephus places in the *War* on the confrontation at Taricheae misleads him into giving it also chronological priority. The second difference is that the earlier account is more melodramatic, the later more realistic. In the first, Josephus does not discover the plot until, addressing the Tiberians, he turns round to find a blade at his throat. Then he jumps straight onto the beach, from a hillock six cubits high, and leaps into a conveniently waiting boat. In the second, armed men approach the stadium where he is speaking, so he jumps off the parapet on which he stands, and is conducted by his bodyguard to a lake, where they pick up a waiting boat. John's followers pursue, until frightened off by a menacing proclamation.

Now many of the Galilean cities reject Josephus' leadership. The *War* puts this down to a case of stolen baggage. An employee of Agrippa II, one Ptolemy, had been ambushed while trying to escape from the war, and his valuables had then been seized from the robbers by Josephus. The Galilean people suspected (rightly, by his own admission) that he wanted to return them to their owner, and that he would be reluctant to endorse hostilities against Agrippa and his interests. He narrowly escaped having his house set on fire, and succeeded in getting a public hearing at Taricheae. There he distracted the local crowd by playing on its hostility towards the neighbouring Tiberians, but could not pacify people from elsewhere. Even when he promised to use the money to wall their towns, his life was in danger, and he was pursued by armed men. In the *Life*, the incident of the valuables, there described as belonging to the wife of Ptolemy, does not stand out in the same way (*BJ* 2.595ff.; *V* 126–31). It had clearly been an over-simplification to ascribe the whole anti-Josephus movement—which was so intense, he tells us, that he had to take Tiberias by storm four times (*V* 82)—to this one event. In the *Life* he could not get away with it. What is more, John is not mentioned there as an inciter of the mob in the hippodrome; he is no longer a figure of such interest, not being, this time, the source of all evil. The whole affair now has a different function, for critics had evidently accused Josephus of intending to put the stolen wealth towards the revolt, and he therefore denies this even more emphatically than he had in the *War*. Twice instead of once he shows us how it had only been to save his own skin that he had pretended the money would be used to build defences. To underline his true intention, he reminds us that the Jewish law abhors theft, even from an enemy (*V* 128).

This, then, is another case where the *Life* pursues a generally similar line to that of the *War*, but accentuates it differently. Whether Josephus' assertions are true is a question we cannot answer. They are quite credible, but the involvement of Agrippa, still alive when the *War* was written, and at that time a patron and correspondent of Josephus, makes the self-defence in the *War* somewhat suspect, since it could be contrived to appeal to him. What is more, we know that Agrippa was given to occasional hostility towards Josephus. On the other hand, by the time that the *Life* was published, he was dead, so that this motivation cannot explain the appearance of a similar version there.[36] Perhaps the reality was that Josephus had never even got as far as deciding what to do with the stolen goods. In any case, we can imagine how disagreeable it must have been to him to act as though he was countenancing the theft, and to be implicated in just the kind of attack on property which he so much deplored.

Not all the revolts were by militants; and loyalists could put Josephus in equally awkward positions. The *War* tells us that when Tiberias appealed to Agrippa for help, Josephus tricked the city into submission. He approached with a few boats that were made to look like a large fleet, arrested the whole town council (respectable men no doubt), and forced the instigator of the disturbance to cut off his own left hand (*BJ* 2.632–46; *V* 155–78). The charges made by Justus, whatever they were, probably emphasised his own home town, and that may be why its vicissitudes figure rather largely in the *Life*, and why Josephus takes great care there to justify his somewhat irregular actions. The device of the mock fleet was necessary because the Sabbath was approaching, and his troops had been dismissed; Clitus volunteered to cut off his own hand when the man who was bidden to do it blanched at the prospect. Moreover, when Tiberias had revolted again and had been recaptured by Josephus, he inflicted severe punishment—according to the *Life*—on the troops who looted the city. But the disparity of the two accounts is of marginal significance outside the context of the personal anatagonisms expressed in them.

[36] *AJ* 16. 187: Josephus has on occasion provoked the descendants of Herod to anger by telling the truth about them. Agrippa as patron and correspondent: *V* 362–7. His death: see Appendix 3.

The outcome of all these troubles was, as we know, that Josephus was unable to do his job. Each account offers its own explanation for his temporary loss of his command (*BJ* 2.626ff.; *V* 189–335). Their origin, according to both, lay in John's malicious scheming. According to the *War*, the Jerusalem leaders were jealous of Josephus. For the *Life*, as usual, something a little more convincing is needed, and Josephus falls back on the stock allegation that some of the leaders were bribed. This bribery enabled Simon ben Gamaliel to carry the day against Ananus and against Josephus' other supporters. In reality, Josephus' failure to master the situation would seem to be enough to explain the attempts to remove him. The disgrace, as we have seen (pp. 150–1), is central to the *Life*, and there we hear a good deal about the activities of the four ambassadors, and the escapades by which Josephus thwarted them, until, finally, a new decision arrived from Jerusalem. Neither side comes very well out of the affair, and in this account, more than in the earlier one, we are made to realise how close Galilee was to total anarchy.

Yet there is no question of the embassy's being excluded from the *War*, and it is hard to find much meaning in the small discrepancies which exist. Thus there seems to be no particular reason why the chronological relation between the activities of the embassy and the different revolts of Tiberias should have been altered. In the *War*, the first revolt occurs after the embassy's arrival and the last after its departure. Perhaps this assists in creating the simplified picture that this intervention, and so, at one remove, John, was responsible for originating the difficulties. In the *Life*, the first revolt occurs well before the embassy (and even before Taricheae, as we have seen, pp. 162–3), while the city is finally captured just before the embassy leaves. There is also a curious discrepancy in the names of the participants of the embassy: the Judas son of Jonathan named in the *War* is replaced in the *Life* by his father; and the father is assigned so prominent a role that it is hard to see how Josephus could ever have forgotten it. We can accept that the son may have been involved as well; but it does look disturbingly as though Josephus chose to cut Jonathan the Pharisee out of the *War*. Our speculation might be that the man had been a respected friend of Josephus, who therefore found his opposition painful to recall—not to say undesirable, supposing Jonathan to be still alive in the seventies. By the date of the *Life*, the whole story had been brought into the open by others, and, in any case, Jonathan's behaviour may have ceased to bother him. If this is so, we must once again find Josephus wanting in his treatment of individuals, and especially so in his first account, which was written so close to the events. Attention is called for; but our scepticism should not spread over the whole narrative.[37]

The *Life* does not present any encounters between Josephus and Roman troops, although we hear of one battle which is avoided, and one almost victorious skirmish with Agrippa's forces, north of the Sea of Galilee. Here Josephus attacks a picket which is blocking his supplies, and comes away with a broken wrist instead of a victory (*V* 399f.). He announces that he will pass over Vespasian's arrival, his own engagement with him at the village of Garis, the siege of Jotapata—which led to his own capture, imprisonment, and subsequent liberation—and his activities during the rest of the revolt: all these have been described in detail in his previous work (*V* 412).

He now moves on to provide a formal but cursory conclusion to his 'autobiography'. This contains, on the one hand, some general biographical detail, in the shape of seemingly insignificant facts about his three marriages (with the provenance of each wife), and the names of his sons (one of whom was called Justus); and, on the other hand, dutiful reference to the liberality and protection afforded him by all three Flavian emperors (see pp. 194–5). Here, above all, it becomes apparent what a curiosity this work is, in formal and structural terms. And if we want to know about the actual war in Galilee, it is to the earlier account that we must turn.

Josephus' view of his own role continues there unchanged. He believes that, like Ananus in Jerusalem, once war was clearly unavoidable he had done his best and taken all the appropriate steps (see the citation at Chapter 5, pp. 130–1). In fact, it is apparent

---

[37] A few other disparities may spring from Josephus' personal relationships. Thus in the *Life* Agrippa's official, Philip, leaves Jerusalem early, is sent by the king to pacify Gamala, and then again by him, and, on Vespasian's recommendation, to Nero; in the *War*, he does not leave Jerusalem until Cestius' withdrawal, and it is Cestius who sends him to Nero, to accuse the procurator Florus. Here the *War* seems to err, as a result of omitting the Galilean material in which the *Life* is rather interested; but on both occasions Josephus seems, in different ways, to be protecting or defending Philip: *BJ* 2. 556–8; *V* 59–61, 179–84, 407–9; discussion in Cohen, op. cit. (n. 1), pp. 160–8. But there are others without significance: Ptolemy's baggage was consigned to one named man in the *War*, to two in the *Life*; John sold oil to the Jews of Caesarea Philippi in the *War*, Syria in the *Life*.

that, minor provocations apart, the only action he ever seriously contemplated was defensive action, and that, even in the sphere of defence, no plan was devised for withstanding the weight of the Roman legions, or for disrupting the systematic Roman advance towards Jerusalem, beyond putting the enemy to the inconvenience of conducting a siege like the one at Jotapata.[38]

Throughout Josephus' narrative, the sense that the war was both pointless and hopeless is not lost, and it co-exists with his insistence that, being committed, he was loyal to those he led, and gave conscientious service. He tells how, at Garis, near Sepphoris, his men fled before ever the Romans arrived. Taking the outcome to be a foregone conclusion, he took refuge in Tiberias and wrote to Jerusalem, making, as he says, a frank statement of the position. He plausibly points out that he could have deserted at this stage, but writes, somewhat over-effusively, that he would have preferred to die many times rather than abandon his command and betray his country (*BJ* 3.137). The protestation may be absurd, and per-haps partly an apology for the length of time he persisted in revolt; but his portrayal of the choice which confronted him at the time seems entirely realistic. It is not altogether preposterous that he should congratulate himself on continuing with the fight, on throw-ing in his lot with the defenders of Jotapata, and on organising the construction of their defences (*BJ* 3.141ff.). He admits that after this he did contemplate leaving the town; but he bowed to the entreaties of a population that believed its safety to depend on him. So he stayed, to conduct the town's resistance under siege with, as he describes it, vigour and energy, and he managed to inflict con-siderable damage on the Romans outside the walls. Here we have a vivid, even if rather favourable, depiction of a proponent of peace reacting to a war in which he had become caught up: obligations had to be fulfilled (even if only for his own present security), yet personal disentanglement at the earliest possible opportunity was desirable. This is the natural consequence of a state of affairs which had been in existence ever since the Jerusalem leaders had joined the revolt.

[38] Cf. p. 155. On Vespasian's well-managed reduction of the area, J. Nicols, *Vespasian and the Sortes Flavianae: Historia Einzelschriften* 27 (1978), pp. 48–52; and (for the later stages), Z. Safrai, 'Vespasian's campaign of conquest in Judaea', A. Op-penheimer, U. Rappaport and M. Stern (eds), *Jerusalem in the Second Temple Period: Abraham Schalit Memorial Volume* (1980; Hebrew with English summaries), pp. 178–90.

There are more irregular facets, perhaps, to Josephus' subsequent survival: his avoidance of suicide after the fall of Jotapata, and his reception by the Roman generals. What happens to him is still, in part, a reflection of his class position and attitudes; but we have also to reckon, now, with individual, personal attributes. Ingenuity, quick thinking, unscrupulousness and good fortune all contributed to the way he came out of the affair. It was a sequence of events which had the effect of detaching him finally from his fellows; and a degree of uneasiness is shown up by his tendency to keep examining his actions.

Many of his own picked men had committed suicide during the last battle at Jotapata (*BJ* 3.331). He had found forty notables hiding in a cave. These were people who would once have been as reluctant to fight as Josephus himself: but now they saw their failure as total, and though they were far from being zealots, suicide seemed the only honourable course. They tried desperately, and even with violence, to press it on Josephus too (3.355ff.) His narrative contains, either implicitly or explicitly, three kinds of excuse for his rejection of this course. One is practical, one moral, and one relies on supernatural sanction. All of them seem to look towards Jewish readers, for there is no suggestion that to attach himself to the Romans was in itself respectable or tempting. He makes a point of showing how his position was a special one: for him, in contrast to the others, there was a guarantee of safety, and Vespasian had made a gesture towards the Jewish general by sending down to him a tribune, Nicanor, who was Josephus' friend, and who brought an invitation to surrender. It was when Josephus stepped forward to do this that his companions set upon him.[39] But he believed that heroism in battle was one thing; futile self-sacrifice after defeat another; if the enemy offered clemency, there was nothing to be gained by refusing. In a speech allegedly delivered to his colleagues, he tried to distinguish between dying fighting and killing oneself, and, again, between deserting to escape a battle, and surrender after an honourable defeat (*BJ* 3.356–86).

Such rational contentions were reinforced by a strong condemnation of the act of suicide as such: it is offensive both to nature and to God, since the soul is immortal, and is a part of God within us; not without reason are suicides consigned to the underworld. In

[39] *BJ* 3. 346–55. Nicanor is probably the same man who is described as a friend of Titus at 5. 261. Cf. pp. 54–5.

the way he writes of the soul, Josephus is inclined to echo Plato. Yet this speech is in no way as Hellenized as its contrasting counterpart, the second Masada oration ascribed to Eleazar.[40] Josephus quite deliberately invokes Jewish practice: 'with us it is ordained that suicides should remain unburied until sunset', and that is why, he goes on to say, the legislator has arranged to have them punished. The legislator referred to must be not the designer of the imaginary state in Plato's *Laws*,[41] but his own Moses, the composer not only of the Pentateuch—which does not consider the problem of suicide—but also of the oral law—which, in later times, explicitly forbade it.[42] And although the condemnation is not articulated in any surviving text of Josephus' day, we can quite well accept his statement that it was already current then, at least in some quarters. It looks in fact as though the issue was an open one, and debated at the time. Certainly, it is not uncommon for early doctrines or traditions to appear in writing only in later texts. Josephus' argument against suicide is, then, one which could have found a real response in an audience of moderate Jews. It is rhetorical, but not solely rhetoric. A personal and comical twist is added to it by Josephus, when he says that, in beating off his angry comrades, he is doing his duty by his God, who would wish him at least to transmit a correct view of the ethics of suicide before his demise.

In case, however, this should not convince, a more direct form of divine endorsement is claimed; for prophetic dreams had come

[40] On the pairing, see p. 89. On classical, especially Platonic citations in the Masada speech, W. Morel, 'Eine Rede bei Josephus', *RhM* 75 (1926), pp. 106–15. It is paradoxical that Josephus' thinking should come out as less Greek than Eleazar's, but there is not enough to support the attempt to read it in Greek terms made by D. J. Ladouceur, 'Masada, a consideration of the literary evidence', *GRBS* 21 (1980), pp. 250–1.

[41] *Laws* 10. 873c–d. So Ladouceur, criticising the Jewish interpretation in the commentary of O. Michel and O. Bauernfeind, *Flavius Josephus, de Bello Judaico, der jüdische Krieg*, II, 2 (1969), p. 276ff. These authors argue that even in the second Eleazar speech, the Hellenization is compartmentalised, and there are significant Jewish traits: see also their 'Die beiden Eleazarreden in Jos. bell. 7, 323–6; 7, 341–88', *ZNTW* 58 (1967), pp. 267–72.

[42] The Rabbinic tradition is ignored by Michel and Bauernfeind. The first explicit condemnation is in the post-Talmudic tractate *Semahot (Evel Rabbati)*; it excludes certain very extreme circumstances: see *Enc. Jud.* s.v. 'suicide'. It has been suggested that the preference of suicide to captivity is implicit in the tenet of the Fourth Philosophy to recognise no master but God: I. L. Rabinowitz, 'The suicide of the Zealots at Masada', *Sinai* 28 (1964), pp. 329–32 (Hebrew). For additional material, L. H. Feldman, 'Masada: a critique of recent scholarship', in J. Neusner (ed.), *Christianity, Judaism and Other Greco-Roman Cults: Studies for Morton Smith at Sixty*, vol. 3 (1975), pp. 239–43.

nightly to Josephus, informing him of the destinies of Jews and of Roman rulers, and now he recalled them—and was happy to find in them an encouragement to surrender. This private matter does not figure in the speech he makes; but, before that, writing of himself in the third person, as he always does in this work, he imparts it solemnly to his readers. He also presents a short prayer: 'I testify that I go not as a traitor, but as your minister' (*BJ* 3.351-4). Before long, this inspiration is to have a dramatic sequel, in the prophecy of future sovereignty which Josephus is able to utter when he is brought face to face with the Roman general Vespasian. The prophecy will enable the prisoner to catch his captor's interest straight away, but its full impact will only be realised later (see p. 186).

Josephus professes moral convictions and deep religious experience; but he cannot shake off altogether the imputation of cynicism and hypocrisy. Even if we bear in mind that religious language of this kind must have come naturally to a first-century Jew as a dress for quite ordinary statements, and therefore refrain from reading too extensive a meaning into his description of himself as a prophet,[43] still, we cannot but suspect that to introduce these profound sentiments at this point has an element of calculation. This suspicion is strengthened if we remember that Josephus does not speak of himself as a prophet in any other context than that of his embarrassing transition to the Romans.[44] He has been recently compared, in an interesting way, with the prophet Jeremiah, who also foresaw the destruction of the city of Jerusalem, and advised a course of political prudence. Josephus, on a different occasion, and perhaps more than one, perceived this similarity himself; and the second destruction of Jerusalem undoubtedly evoked the first.[45]

[43] For interpretations which emphasise these descriptions, see J. Blenkinsopp, 'Prophecy and priesthood in Josephus', *JJS* 25 (1974), pp. 239-62; W. C. van Unnik, *Flavius Josephus als historischer Schriftsteller* (1978), pp. 41-54, esp. 46.

[44] Blenkinsopp's view, op. cit., pp. 241-2 and 256, that Josephus saw his role of historian as a prophetic one, is not supported by any of the author's statements.

[45] The Jeremiah parallel is worked out by D. Daube, 'Typology in Josephus', *JJS* 31 (1980), pp. 18-36, where Josephus' address to the besieged from the walls of Jerusalem is cited: ' "for, though Jeremiah loudly proclaimed that they would be taken captive unless they surrendered the city, neither the king nor the people put him to death. But you assail me with abuse and missiles, when I urge you to save yourselves." ' (*BJ* 5. 392ff.). Cf. Jer. 27.12ff. On pp. 26-7, Daube gives several interesting non-Biblical details in Josephus' portrayal of Jeremiah which may arise from a blurring of his own career with the prophet's. For Jeremiah's rejection of the king's offer, see Jer. 40.1-6 (Daube, p. 26). Against the parallel, H. Lindner, *Die Geschichtsauffassung des Flavius Josephus im Bellum Judaicum* (1972), p. 73, n. 2.

But to say this is still far from establishing that he consistently saw himself as a man carrying out a prophetic mission. In any case, Jeremiah turned down the king of Babylon's offer of hospitality, so the parallel failed at the crucial point.

Josephus said he felt that God had delivered him, but he did not deny the part played by his own inventiveness (*epinoia*). When entreaty had failed with his colleagues, he devised a scheme by which the group should draw lots for the order of suicide (*BJ* 3.387–92). This, we may infer, gained him time, and left him with some hope of extracting himself. There was sense in it, even without counting on the ideal outcome which in fact materialised, that of being one of the last two to be drawn, and then being able to persuade his companion to renege on the pact. Admittedly, to have been drawn first would have meant the end; but any other position offered the chance of trying his persuasive powers again, on a smaller group, and one shaken by the sight of colleagues' suicides. So, if the story he tells us is true, he had engaged in a worthwhile gamble. There is yet a further possibility: if the chosen method of selection was a circular count, rather than normal sortition, then it would have been possible for a clever manipulator to arrange the right outcome, through what mathematicians today still call a 'Josephus count'.[46] And, whatever kind of draw was performed, it would be possible to claim that the result was, in a special sense, the will of God. That the story is a complete fabrication remains, of course, a remote possibility, especially since Josephus' fellow survivor seems immediately to have disappeared into total oblivion. But this is a possibility which it is fruitless to explore.

The true mystery about the episode lies not in what happened in that cave, but in Josephus' subsequent attitude. It seems strange that he sees fit to give us all the particulars of his discreditable action in the *War*, where he could have avoided it, but then excludes the whole business from the self-defence in his *Life*. Yet even this can be understood. He himself tells us that the news of what he had done spread rapidly after Jotapata: Jerusalem was ablaze with indignation and resentment; he was castigated as a coward and a traitor (*BJ* 3.432–42). The *War* apologia is designed to counter these two charges. For this reason it stresses the courage and tenacity with which the general resisted the Romans until the last moment.

---

[46] A popular explanation in M. Gardner, *Aha! Insight* (1978), p. 84ff.

Several times, he insists that he did not expect them to spare him,
and the purpose of this assertion is to make it absolutely clear that
there had been no kind of deal with them. Those who saw him as
a traitor will have had in mind not so much the act of submission,
as its implications for what had gone before. For any arrangement
made previously with Rome would have involved throwing away
the lives of his comrades—some of whom, no doubt, had friends
and relatives who survived the war. Such suspicions will have disturbed even those who had been opposed to the revolt. The words
'traitor' and 'treachery' appear five times in this portion of the *War*;
three of the instances are denials, while in two of them the author
pointedly applies the slurs not to what *he* had done, but to what is
most abhorrent to him.[47] The probability that some political machinations were, at a later time, behind his transactions with Vespasian made matters even worse (see p. 187). But Josephus wishes to
make it very clear where his limits are drawn: the one true treachery
would be to fight alongside the enemy, and this he would never do
(*BJ* 3.381).

It is thus with the aim of reinstating himself that Josephus offers
a series of justifications designed to appeal to Jews who were not
fanatics. Zealots could never be convinced. We cannot suppose that,
by the time he wrote the *Life*, all those who mattered to him had
been persuaded; this would seem improbable, when accusations of
so many varieties were still being levelled at him. But the passage
of time reshapes our picture of past conflicts. In due course, Jotapata
became just one part of the whole reckoning, while the argument
over the Galilean commission had festered.

To us, Josephus' tenacious clinging to life is somewhat unattrac-
tive. But we will always remain excluded from this central moment
in his career:[48] its psychological interpretation must, to some extent,
elude us; and, after all, in the realm of motives, we are often enough
at a loss even over our own contemporaries, where the information

---

[47] 3. 354, 359, 361, 381, 439. The same preoccupation with leaving his colleagues
to their fate presumably still underlies the paragraph in the concluding section of
the *Life*, where he tells how he had used his good graces with Titus to save compatriots: an unspecified number freed; then a successful petition for his brother and
fifty friends; then, after a distasteful survey of the captive women and children in the
Temple, the extraction of some hundred and ninety friends and acquaintances;
lastly, three men whom he had known cut down from crosses at Tekoa, and one of
them saved by the attentions of a doctor.

[48] As William Whiston, Josephus' eighteenth-century translator wrote, 'the personal character of Josephus may be regarded as an historical enigma'.

is so much more complete. More can be learnt about Josephus when we investigate not his personal reactions when he is isolated, but rather the links between him and the world around him. These are fortunately quite extensive, reaching in many directions.

CHAPTER SEVEN

Josephus as an Aramaic Writer

It is hard to envisage Palestine in the immediate aftermath of the great revolt. In none of his works does Josephus discuss anything there later than the reduction of the Judaean desert fortresses by the Roman legate L. Flavius Silva, and that was over in A.D.73.[1] Presumably the historian was not personally involved in the post-war re-allocation of land by the Romans, or in such rebuilding as the administration had to undertake.[2] For we find him making a vague, and almost certainly inaccurate statement to the effect that the whole country was turned into imperial property as a kind of punishment; all the territory was then, he says, to be leased out by a procurator. In reality, such a measure will have applied, at the most, to rebel zones,[3] and Josephus' vagueness suggests that he had relatively little interest in the process. For our part, we do not know when or how it was that Vespasian presented him personally with new estates 'in the plain' to replace holdings near Jerusalem now occupied by a Roman garrison (V 422). But Josephus' removal of 'sacred books' from Jerusalem to Rome, with Vespasian's express permission (V 418), seems to symbolise well his shift of focus away from Palestine; and at the same time the fact that he was not

[1] For this operation, see E. M. Smallwood, *The Jews under Roman Rule* (1976), pp. 334–9; or Schürer-Vermes-Millar, vol. 1 (1973), pp. 608–12. For the date of the fall of Masada, I accept what appears to be Josephus' chronology, and follow G. W. Bowersock, reviewing Schürer-Vermes-Millar, vol. 1, *JRS* 65 (1975), pp. 183–4, in rejecting the arguments for 74 proposed by W. Eck on the basis of two inscriptions which record Flavius Silva's career: the ordering of posts might easily be disorganised in these inscriptions. Documentation in W. Eck, *Senatoren von Vespasian bis Hadrian* (1970), pp. 93–103.

[2] Reconstruction: Smallwood, op. cit., pp. 342–3.

[3] *BJ* 7. 216–17. See Smallwood, pp. 340–2; S. Applebaum, 'Judaea as a Roman Province: the Countryside as a Political and Economic Factor', in *Aufstieg und Niedergang der Römischen Welt* 2.8 (1977), (ed. H. Temporini and W. Haase), pp. 385–9, especially on the relation of this ruling to the obscure Talmudic law of *sikarikon*.

discarding a Jewish for a Roman allegiance, simply transferring an old one to a new location (cf. p. 225).

In any location, however, it must have been difficult in the years between A.D. 70 and 80 to turn to thoughts of religious or political re-orientation. There is no evidence that the work of building Rabbinic Judaism, initiated at Yavneh (Jamnia) by Johanan ben Zakkai had gained any kind of momentum so soon after the fall of the Temple and the loss of the cult.[4] Even a man as hard-headed as Josephus will have been prone to look backwards, and his first preoccupation was the attempt to grasp and absorb the destruction and the loss of the Jerusalem which he had so much admired.[5] Indeed, it is dubious whether he was ever able fully to shake himself free of the impact of the disaster (see p. 226).

Josephus' first known action after his move to Rome is entirely in keeping with such a mood. He composed an account of the recent war and sent it to people who would not have known the details of what happened. The account is now lost, but we know a little about it from what he tells us. In the preface to the Greek *War* he says that its predecessor, written in his own language, had been sent to the 'barbarians in the interior' (of Asia). Rather curiously and inappropriately, he uses the term 'barbarians' here in an entirely Greek way, to refer to all who are not Greeks. Even his own nation is numbered among them, as emerges a few sentences later, when he gives a closer definition: the recipients are to be Parthians, Babylonians, and the furthest Arabians; but also the Jews who lived across the Euphrates, together with the people of Adiabene. He wanted them all to have the real story of the war, of its beginnings, of the sufferings it brought, and of the way it ended (*BJ* 1.6). The barbarian label, then, is not to be taken seriously: these were people with whom Josephus had some affinity. The native language in which he writes for them must be Aramaic, rather than Hebrew, for all the peoples addressed came within the vast area, of which Palestine was a part, which extended through Syria to Arabia, and on the east to the Tigris, and which had one form or another of Aramaic as a spoken and as a semi-official language. In these countries, at about this time, Aramaic was making its debut also as

---

[4] It is telling that very few facts are known of the latter part of Johanan's career, and its very duration is obscure; the small number of *halakhot* ascribed to him are of limited import compared to those of his successors.

[5] On Josephus' lamentation, see p. 79.

a literary language.[6] Greek, by contrast, had made some inroads under Alexander the Great's successors, but in spite of the foundation of many Greek cities, it had not penetrated very deep.[7]

Josephus' Aramaic war narrative was thus in some sense the precursor of the later Greek *War*.[8] But there is no reason to think that the first work bore much similarity to the second in scope or literary form. The fact that the Aramaic version was not preserved in the eastern Christian tradition points to its having been a slight production. Speeches and digressions, characteristic formal features of Graeco-Roman historiography, are likely to have been absent. If there were any prefatory remarks, they would have had to have been different.[9] We may guess that the Aramaic *War* was in the nature of a plain report, with perhaps some passages of lamentation. An element of personal self-justification may also have entered into it.

The word used by Josephus to describe the conversion of the one work into the other is *metaballein*, to change, or even transform. This figures on several occasions in his writings in the sense 'to translate', and there are several instances from Christian texts of a later period where it has this meaning. But it is by no means the normal word for the translation process. Nor is it any kind of technical term. In fact, it leaves entirely open the relation between the versions.[10] Josephus' words on the subject might be rendered thus: 'I adapted to Greek the narrative which I had previously composed and sent to the barbarians of the interior.' The Greek text that we have bears no mark of Semitic antecedents, and there could never be any question of seeking to reconstruct the Aramaic original, in the way that some ingenious investigators try to do for the Gospels. Aramaic versions of proper names and Aramaic forms of some quasi-tech-

---

[6] For Josephus' native language, see Appendix 1.

[7] A. H. M. Jones, *Cities of the Eastern Roman Provinces*[2] (revised, 1971), chs 9 and 10; useful notes on Greek among the Parthians in A. Momigliano, *Alien Wisdom* (1975), pp. 137–40.

[8] On the chronology of publication, see p. 195.

[9] So already B. Niese, 'Der jüdische Historiker Josephus', *Historische Zeitschrift* 76 (1896), p. 201.

[10] G. Hata, 'Is the Greek version of Josephus' "Jewish War" a translation or a rewriting of the first version?', *JQR* 66 (1975), pp. 89–109, goes too far in claiming that *metaballein* necessarily *means* 'to transform utterly', but he collects useful material. Also far-fetched is a claim that the word refers specifically to the physical process of conversion from one script into another, made by A. Pelletier, *Flavius Josèphe adapteur de la lettre d'Aristée: une réaction atticisante contre la koiné* (1962), pp. 22–4.

nical terms, such as the names for the high priest's vestments, are found in far greater profusion in Josephus' later work, the *Antiquities*.

The composition of the Aramaic *War* suggests that Josephus, though cut off from Jerusalem, and undoubtedly disturbed, was not culturally quite homeless. His native language offered him potentially wide perspectives. There was, first, the connexion with those eastern Jews for whom he wrote. The Babylonian communities, though they had not yet reached their great days, were already prosperous, numerous and influential; earlier in the century, two Jewish strong men from Neardea had been able to make themselves masters of an independent territory in Mesopotamia, with the consent of the Parthian king (*AJ* 18.314–73). As for the inhabitants of Adiabene, who occupied what had once been Assyria, it is not clear whether Josephus is listing them as Jews or not; but without doubt a number of them had earlier in the century followed their ruling house in its conversion to Judaism, just as, in the eighth century A.D., the Khazars were to follow their king. The Adiabenian monarchs had gone on to make marriage connections with the Herods, and to leave their mark on the Jerusalem scene with the palaces and elaborately constructed rock-cut tombs that they built there.[11] Then there was a second, more tenuous link, that between a former Jerusalem notable and the members of other Aramaic-using, partially Hellenized, middle-eastern élites. Although it will emerge that Josephus' professed hope of a reading public in those quarters has to be taken with a pinch of salt (p. 181), still it is significant that he is able to go so far as to make this rhetorical claim and wish that Parthians and their subjects might be interested in what he has to say. Evidently he was speaking of a part of the world which came naturally within his mental horizons.

For the next stage in his career, Josephus would take yet another small step, and find that he could address easterners (as well as others) through writing in Greek, a language which was more appropriate to an author at Rome, and which, also, was quite within his reach. Greek was more versatile than Aramaic, and it was certainly not unsuitable for literature directed to the east. Josephus' last book, *Against Apion*, was to have a distinct eastern orientation: it was to be preoccupied with relating the Jewish past to other

---

[11] On the conversion, J. Neusner, *A History of the Jews in Babylonia*, vol. 1 (²Leiden 1969), pp. 62–7; see especially *AJ* 20.17ff.; monuments: *BJ* 4.567; 5.55, 119, 147, 252–3; *AJ* 20.95.

reliable oriental traditions, and indebted to a species of native chronicler, Babylonian, Phoenician and Egyptian, who recorded in somewhat bare Greek prose his own local history.[12] The Aramaic *Jewish War*, Josephus' very first work, in a way looks forward to that end point.

I would argue, in fact, that the Jewish Diaspora was always the primary setting for Josephus as a writer. In Rome, he had gradually to start seeing himself as a Diaspora Jew, and this will have made him more conscious of his fellows throughout the Mediterranean world. We may remember that his second wife was an Alexandrian Jewess, his third wife a Jewess from Crete. Indeed, it was not unnatural even for the old Palestinian Josephus to communicate with fellow Jews and, in reporting the war, it was essentially as a Palestinian that he must have presented himself to them. For there was a strong tradition, in Judaism, of communication between the centre and the periphery. Correspondence between Jerusalem and the Diaspora, especially Babylon and Alexandria, is well-attested, and probably occurred regularly.[13] Usually a question of law or observance is involved, but sometimes just news is transmitted, or else there is news as well: the latter is the case in the two letters which form the opening of the Second Book of Maccabees, which instruct the Jews of Egypt to celebrate the festival of the purification of the Temple in honour of the Maccabean victory. What is more, the first letter refers to a previous notification about recent persecutions, and thus indicates that there was a background of such exchanges. Again, when Paul visits the Jews of Rome, they say that they have not received any letter about him, implying that it would have been normal for them to have had one (II Macc. 1;7–8; Acts 28:21). So there could be nothing more natural than that worshippers abroad should be told how and why the Temple had fallen. Their financial contributions and their pilgrimages had done much to support it. At the very least, they needed to know when to set a day of mourning or fasting. Josephus had no official status, apart from being a priest; but he did have better information on the events than other survivors. We can understand his motives for sending a report to the east.

---

[12] The principal figures were Berossus of Babylon, Manetho the Egyptian priest, Menander of Ephesus and Dius the Pheonician. Our knowledge of them derives largely from references in *Against Apion*, or in Josephus' *Antiquities*. See below, pp.225–6.

[13] Neusner, op. cit. (n. 11), pp. 44–6.

Nevertheless, the lost Aramaic *War* of Josephus has normally been seen in a very different light, as satisfying the needs not of its author, but of his supposed master, the Roman emperor. The initial mention of Parthia evokes almost automatically the history of confrontation between Rome and her eastern rival. Those who see the lost work in this way are able to observe that the peoples addressed by Josephus fell, more or less, under Parthian control. The only possible exception are the Arabians; for if it is the Nabataeans who lived on Syria's western margins who are intended in this vague allusion, then they were ostensibly independent; but even they came alternately within the orbit of each of the great powers, and therefore looked to Parthia at least as much as to Rome.[14] And since Josephus speaks about distant Arabs it could be preferable to point to Edessa (Osroene), remotely situated in northern Mesopotamia, and ruled by Arab kings under Parthian influence; or to Palmyra, the great oasis of the Syrian desert, which had a strong Arab element in its population, and which also produced an Arab dynasty and depended on Parthia.[15] Thus, a context of international *realpolitik* is provided for Josephus' little book. Vespasian's purpose, it is alleged, was to demonstrate the might of the Roman empire to those who lived around its eastern periphery, so as to deter them from attacking Rome, in association with Parthia. Josephus was, on this view, merely Vespasian's agent.[16]

Evidence both internal and external is adduced to support such theories. But it is not evidence which stands up to any kind of scrutiny. The internal support has to come from Josephus' later Greek *War*, and from the supposition that the arguments believed to underlie that work were those which dominated its predecessor. This supposition would perhaps be acceptable, if only the later work contained what it is alleged to contain.

A remark in Josephus' preface is crucial to the claim. He says that at the time of the Jewish revolt the whole eastern empire had

[14] The Nabatean kingdom formed, in A.D.106, the basis of the Roman province of Arabia. Strabo, a few generations before Josephus, took Arabia to extend as far as the Northern reaches of Mesopotamia. He says that in his day its chieftains were free, with some inclinding to Parthia and some to Rome: Strabo 16. 1.28 and 16.4.1.

[15] However, the word 'distant' used of the Arabians may be no more than a literary epithet.

[16] R. Laqueur, *Der jüdische Historiker Flavius Josephus* (1920, pp. 126–7; H. St. J. Thackeray, *Josephus the Man and the Historian* (1929), ch. 2; and the same in almost every work of scholarship.

hung in the balance, for the Jews had been expecting help from their compatriots beyond the Euphrates, and Rome had been occupied elsewhere (*BJ* 1.5). Here, it is believed, lies proof of the connection between the revolt in Palestine and an eastern threat; and it follows that the tale of the revolt's crushing defeat would serve to deter future enemies from making trouble. The Greek work is supposed to contain the same warning, directed this time towards Greek-speaking regions, for the most part under Roman control. Agrippa's province-by-province survey of the empire, with its stress on Rome's work of subjection, and Josephus' long digression on the efficiency of the Roman army are adduced; and the chief witness is the sentence with which Josephus closes that digression, when he says that he hopes what he has just written might deflect others from revolt (*BJ* 3.108). These words are taken as a sort of manifesto, a desire close to the heart of the author. In fact, they are an isolated statement, and at no other point does Josephus say anything comparable. Moreover, its context makes it a statement of very little importance: Josephus offers a number of conventional justifications for his digression, and this is just one of them (cf. p. 160). It is far from being a definition of the work as a whole; even for the digression, it is a fairly perfunctory and formal explanation. That Josephus chose, at this one point, to express the hope that other nations might in future hesitate before challenging the great Roman machine, does not mean that he had been concerned about this all the time. And the substance of the Greek book does not suggest concern. We earlier found that the military excurses reflects the author's own interests; while Agrippa's speech, by bringing out the futility of a Jewish revolt, serves to justify Josephus' personal position as a Jewish politician whose commitment to war was less than total.[17]

In the case of the Aramaic book, there are even more serious difficulties. We return now to Josephus' statement about its intended recipients, and ask how much weight may be placed on it. It is in reality improbable that all those mentioned could have managed Josephus' Aramaic with any ease. He will have written in that Palestinian western Aramaic dialect which has sometimes been called Jerusalem Aramaic. Few instances survive, and the badly-preserved *Genesis Apocryphon* from Qumran Cave I is the most substantial; its language is still a matter for intense debate. This dialect

---

[17] On such use of speeches by Josephus, see p. 80.

is made less mysterious, however, by the fact that it is a prototype of the better known Galilean form, the branch of Middle Aramaic in which, from about A.D.200, the Aramaic parts of the Jerusalem Talmud and other Jewish literature was composed.[18] Already in the first century, Jews everywhere could probably have understood any Aramaic which had a strong Hebrew content. Parthians and Arabians, on the other hand, will have spoken and written quite differently, using an eastern branch of the language, mixing it with words from their own, and, what is more, often reading it out to sound like their own, as had been done with the old imperial Aramaic in the days of the Persian empire.[19] We have, then, to take it that Josephus is fancifully exaggerating or engaging in a certain amount of wishful thinking when he extends his prospective readership beyond his own people to the oriental world at large.

Apart from the problem of the language, there is that of the contents, and it is hard to see how Josephus' subject-matter could ever have served to deliver a short, sharp message to the east. It is hardly plausible that the news of Rome's effective suppression of a petty province in revolt would have much impressed the ruler of a great empire like Parthia.

The question can also be approached from another angle. If we hold that Josephus' original book was used by the emperors as a form of propaganda, directed behind the enemy's lines, then we assume that there really was an enemy. So we have to ask whether Parthia was at this time perceived by Rome as an active threat. The evidence is sadly fragmentary—indeed, for the Vespasianic period, most of it comes out of Josephus himself—and we cannot entirely exclude the possibility that Parthian movements caused serious worry in the seventies. But the picture which seems to come together is one of suspicious diplomacy, without overt hostility or likelihood of war.[20]

---

[18] See C. Rabin, 'Hebrew and Aramaic in the first century', *The Jewish People in the First Century, Compendia Rerum Iudaicarum ad Novum Testamentum* 1. 2, ed. S. Safrai and M. Stern (1976), pp. 1007–39; E. Y. Kutscher, *The Language and Linguistic Background of the Isaiah Scroll* (1974), pp. 8–14. Rabin holds on linguistic grounds that the Genesis Apocryphon was designed for the eastern Diaspora, like Josephus' Aramaic *War*.

[19] See Rabin, op. cit., pp. 1025–6.

[20] See N. C. Debevoise, *A Political History of Parthia* (1938), pp. 196–202; G. W. Bowersock, 'Syria under Vespasian', *JRS* 63 (1973), pp. 134–5; K. H. Ziegler, *Die Beziehungen zwischen Rom und dem Partherreich* (1964), pp. 78–81. But the latter tends to overestimate the belligerency of both sides.

The Parthian king of this period, Vologaeses, had, according to Tacitus, a long-standing and almost immovable determination to avoid war with Rome (*Ann.* 15.5). In 66, his brother Tiridates, whom the Romans had originally opposed as a candidate for the throne of Armenia, travelled to Rome with his veiled queen and his train of Magi, nailed his dagger to its sheath, and was crowned with a diadem by Nero, in an ostentatious ceremony which was in reality a sort of compromise.[21] In July 69, after Vespasian had been declared emperor by the legions at Alexandria, he sent an embassy to Vologaeses. In response. the king offered 40,000 Parthian horse to assist in the Jewish war (Tac. *Hist.* 2.82, 4.51). Vespasian's rejection of this aid did not discourage Vologaeses from sending Titus a golden crown, and congratulations on the final victory (*BJ* 7.105). Not long afterwards, in 72, Vespasian annexed the two client kingdoms which formed buffers between Rome and Parthia— Commagene and Lesser Armenia. He also changed the status of Cappadocia, which lay to the west of them, and which had been a Roman province without a garrison, into an armed province under a prestigious, consular governor. Such actions admittedly look as though they were designed for protection against Parthia, and they did bring Roman troops to the Euphrates. But the situation was a complicated one. In the case of Commagene, we have a hint of the surrounding circumstances from Josephus. We are told that Caesennius Paetus, the legate of Syria, had accused Antiochus, the petty king of Commagene, of intriguing with the Parthian Vologaeses and planning to defect from Rome. What deserves attention is the way Josephus follows this up: he adds that the allegation was considered quite likely to be false, but that Vespasian could not risk inaction; and it is striking how little hostility Josephus himself shows towards Parthia in narrating these events.[22] We also learn from him that this jockeying for position did not embitter Vologaeses. For, in 75 or thereabouts, when tribes of Alani from across the Caucasus invaded Parthian territory, the Parthian ruler felt quite able to request Roman help. This must have been the occasion of the well-known haughty communication which caused such amusement

---

[21] Tac. *Ann.* 15. 29; Dio Epit. 63. 1; Suet. *Nero* 13; perhaps referred to by Josephus in Agrippa's speech, *BJ* 2. 379

[22] *BJ* 7. 219ff.; on the annexations, Bowersock, loc. cit. (n. 20); R. D. Sullivan, 'The Dynasty of Commagene', in op. cit. (n. 3), pp. 790–4.

at Rome; and perhaps its tone explains why his petition was turned down (*BJ* 7.244–51; Suet. *Dom.* 2.2; Dio Epit. 66.11.3).

At any rate, the only suggestion of a really hostile relationship occurs in a late source: Aurelius Victor, in the fourth century, writes that the Parthian king was forcibly pacified (9.10). Another historical summary, dependent on Victor, and known as the *Epitome de Caesaribus*, inspires more confidence when it speaks of pacification by intimidation alone (9.12). Whether Victor's statement has some kind of basis in truth, and, if there was an incident, whether it occurred before or after the invasion of the Alani, it is beyond our power to decide. At most, an isolated encounter might have occurred, small enough to leave little impression on the record. All in all, the balance of power in this decade was such that it is hard to imagine a Parthian threat prompting Vespasian to decide to drive home by literary means the lesson of Rome's might.

Apart from the Parthians, there were Josephus' Jewish readers, and for them an explanation in terms of Flavian *Realpolitik* has also been offered: the eastern communities might now make trouble for Rome, either out of loyalty to Parthia or else out of solidarity with Palestine; and so they should be shown the consequences of aggression.[23] Again, the hypothesis is an improbable one. It is true that the embers of the great revolt were slow to die, and smouldered in various places. *Sicarii* fled from Palestine after the fall of Masada, and it is rather surprising to find them continuing their resistance in Egypt; the prefect, Tiberius Julius Lupus, had to take the drastic step of demolishing the Temple of Onias at Leontopolis, for centuries a cult centre for Egyptian Jews. In Cyrene, other escaped *sicarii* stirred up the poorer section of the Jewish population, and, to Josephus' indignation, brought the governor's vengeance upon rich and poor alike.[24] But it is one thing for the old disturbance to linger on, another for a new spirit of resistance to arise. We should hardly expect a violent response to the defeat of the revolt from people who had had scarcely any contact with it. The Jews of Babylon and Adiabene had been noticeably inactive. Help had been expected, but had failed to materialise, just as Agrippa had predicted. Only a few members of the Adiabenian royal house and one or two private individuals had taken up arms, and probably only

[23] See e.g. J. Neusner, 'The Jews east of the Euphrates and the Roman empire, I, 1st–3rd Centuries A.D.', op. cit. (n. 3) vol. 2. 9.1 (1976), p. 54.

[24] *BJ* 7. 410ff.; on the Cyrene incident, see further pp. 221–2.

because the war happened to catch them in Jerusalem.[25] After the loss of the Temple, the mood of the time was despondency and a sense of powerlessness, finding expression in apocalyptic visions of the future (see p. 99). When, in A.D.115–17 the Jews of the east did finally revolt, simultaneously with those of Egypt, Cyrene and Cyprus, it was for some a response to Trajan's invasion of Mesopotamia, and for those within the empire a consequence of almost half a century of humiliating payment of the Jewish tax.[26] It may be tempting, but it is entirely misleading, to imagine that the Trajanic revolt could just as well have erupted under the first Flavian.

There is a limited amount that can be said about a book (or booklet) of which not a word survives, and for which the only direct testimony is a passing allusion by its author. Speculation, in any direction, is hard to avoid. It is most reasonable to conclude that what Josephus wrote was a report on a tragic event, issued for those who were interested, not propaganda to suit the requirements of the Flavian emperor and the Roman administration. After we have examined the curious relationship between emperor and Jew more closely, as we shall do in the next chapter, it will become even clearer why Vespasian is not to be freely invoked in explaining Josephus' major choices as a writer.

[25] Expectations: *BJ* 1. 5; embassies seeking help: 6. 342; Agrippa: 2. 388–90; individual participants: 2. 520; 5. 474; 6. 356. Adiabenian participation is much exaggerated by J. Neusner, op. cit. (n. 11), pp. 67–70.
[26] The revolts are described by Smallwood, op. cit. (n. 1), ch. 15. The tax was imposed as a consequence of the first revolt.

CHAPTER EIGHT

Flavian Patronage and Jewish Patriotism

After surrendering at Jotapata, Josephus saved his own life and, in due course, transformed his status by prophesying that the general Titus Flavius Vespasianus would become Roman emperor. Within two and a half years, there was a revolt in Gaul, Nero had committed suicide, Galba, Otho and Vitellius had all tried in vain to hold on to the principate and to control the empire, and Vespasian, the chosen candidate of the legions at Alexandria, took power at Rome. As Josephus tells the story, his prophecy served him extremely well; and understandably so, for, when it was fulfilled, Vespasian was both impressed and flattered.

In this curious manner the Jewish ex-general bound himself to the Flavian emperor-to-be, with the fortunes of the one at their lowest, and those of the other about to reach their peak. Again, personal aspects of the relationship are virtually impenetrable. Less so is the nature of Flavian influence on Josephus' work, and how far this has distorted, dominated or even dictated the character of the *Jewish War*. This is a central question; for if there were good grounds for suspecting a strong imperial stamp on the book as a whole, our assessment of it would have to be reshaped to allow for this. Fortunately no such drastic action will be necessary. Josephus is not an objective writer; but the Palestinian prejudices described in previous chapters have a deeper effect on his writing than the Roman bias which tends to be automatically ascribed to him. It has been taken for granted that the *Jewish War* is to be explained as a wholly Flavian history; but that too is perhaps little more than a prejudice, harboured in this case by the historian of modern times.

The prophecy is the best starting point. Josephus' report is narrated with care and to be found in Book 3 of the *War*. When he appeared in the Roman camp, the Jewish leader whom all had been seeking, object of the troops' fascination and the officers' pity, it

was only a sudden burst of compassion by Titus which prevented
him from being removed there and then. He asked for an interview
with Vespasian, and during this interview he was moved to utter
a prediction: the Roman general would wear the purple, and be
master of the human race. Vespasian was interested, if not greatly
impressed; but from other prisoners came favourable reports of
Josephus' skill as a prophet, and especially of how, as leader of the
besieged Jews, he had correctly predicted that Jotapata would fall
after precisely forty-seven days. Therefore Vespasian decided not to
send this important captive to Nero, as intended, but kept him and
treated him rather well (*BJ* 3.392–408). In summer 69, Vespasian
was acclaimed emperor in Alexandria, and consequently in the rest
of the east, and he was amazed to find that the man who had
correctly foretold this was still a prisoner. At Titus' insistence,
Josephus' chains were ceremonially severed with an axe, a symbolic
action which made the imprisonment as though it had never been.[1]

The story is not without its difficulties. Rational calculation can
hardly have led a man, even one much more involved in Roman
politics than was Josephus, to conclude that Nero would be toppled
and eventually replaced by none other than Vespasian. It is true
that the eruption in 65 of a conspiracy in the capital headed by the
well-connected C. Piso, and the widespread disgust evoked by the
emperor's long sojourn in Greece with its undignified theatrical and
athletic appearances seemed to foreshadow a crisis (Tac. *Ann.*
15.49ff.; Dio *Epit.* 62.8–19). And what may have pointed towards
Vespasian in particular was the way in which he seemed to be
taking over the nexus of friends and associates built up by another
great man, Domitius Corbulo: in 67 the Flavian may even have had
for a time Corbulo's enlarged eastern command; and it was well
known that, during its tenure, Corbulo had been perceived by Nero
as a serious threat to his régime.[2] In retrospect these were all
pointers, yet at the time of their occurrence they cannot have con-
veyed the same clear meaning. None the less, we find Josephus
firmly putting his prediction immediately after his arrival in the
Roman camp, and elsewhere insisting that it had been made during
Nero's lifetime (*BJ* 4.623).

[1] *BJ* 4. 623–9. Josephus thus avoided having the status of an ex-slave: D. Daube,
'Three legal notes on Josephus after his surrender', *Law Quarterly Review* 93 (1977),
p. 192.
[2] J. Nicols, *Vespasian and the Partes Flavianae: Historia Einzelschriften* 28 (1978), pp.
114, 119–24.

Some may believe that our author truly had a divine prompting— or a brilliant hunch. Others will suppose that he pre-dated his prophecy to make it appear more impressive.[3] Others will go still further in this last direction, recalling the political machinations in the east during the troubled first half of the year 69, when, with a view to a seizure of power, an alliance between Vespasian and Licinius Mucianus, the man now in charge of Syria, was planned by Vespasian's elder son, Titus, and a compact was concluded with the once Jewish prefect of Egypt, Tiberius Julius Alexander. Queen Berenice, previously the wife of Tiberius' brother, and her own brother Agrippa II were also involved in some way. And Josephus, who had links both with the Herodian pair and with Alexandrian Jewry, may either have played a part of his own in these activities, or at least have been au fait with them.[4] We need not imagine him literally fettered at this time: in his late work, *Against Apion*, he says, referring back to this period, that he remained bound at first, but how long that lasted is unclear. He could have donned the chains again for his liberation ceremony. What is more, the statement in the *War* that Vespasian forgot about Josephus until he became emperor has also to be taken loosely, for in the later passage Josephus claims that he had remained always beside Titus (*CA* 1.48–9). So the prisoner could well have been active in the camp. And his prediction will then have been a performance rigged with his patron's connivance; or else a trick of his own devising. I shall not try to choose between the different possibilities.

It is good for rulers to be seen as marked out by destiny. In comparable circumstances, this point was appreciated, and similarly exploited, by the wily Arab historian Ibn Khaldun. In 1401, when he was left behind in Damascus after the withdrawal of the sultan, he won respect, assistance and gifts from the Mongolian conqueror Tamerlaine by applying to Tamerlaine's rise predictions about world history that he had learned in the Maghrib. However, Ibn Khaldun treats his readers better, recounting at length his

---

[3] As A. Schalit, 'Die Erhebung Vespasians nach Flavius Josephus, Talmud und Midrasch. Zur Geschichte einer messianischen Prophetie', *Aufstieg und Niedergang der Römischen Welt* 2.2 (1975), ed. H. Temporini, pp. 208–327. That the prophecy is entirely an invention is improbable but not wholly impossible: Schalit's endeavours to prove that it occurred are misguided.

[4] *BJ* 2. 309; 5. 1; Tac. *Hist.* 2. 79ff.; see Nicols, loc. cit. (n. 2), and, on Josephus' possible connection with an 'oriental group' in the Flavian party, J. Crook, 'Titus and Berenice', *AJPh* 72 (1951), p. 163, n. 9.

interview with the potentate, and exposing his motives with apparent frankness: 'because of this fear, I composed in my mind some words to say to him, which, by exalting him and his government, would flatter him.'[5]

At the same time, there lay even greater advantage for Josephus than for Vespasian in the recounting of this prophecy. It provided yet another justification for his dubious passage to the Roman side, and it perhaps served to cover up other dealings, less fitted for publicity. In the telling of it, it is clear that the author's concern is less with glorifying his patron than with speaking about himself. The account is subdued in character, and such enthusiasm as there is centres on his own brilliance and inspiration, not on Vespasian's great destiny. Josephus is preoccupied at this point with explaining his own escape. The fact that God had sent signs to indicate the Roman's future elevation is not ignored; but Josephus does not choose to expand upon that theme. There are two cryptic and scarcely noticeable references to omens which, like his own prophecy, had also pointed to the event; but they are not explicit enough to create any impression.[6] Half a sentence alone describes the power of the Roman emperor, and that half sentence puts Josephus in front of the empire: 'you are lord, Caesar, not only over me, but over earth and sea and the whole human race.'

There was a similar prediction ascribed in Jewish tradition to Rabban Johanan ben Zakkai, a leading scholar. And, just as with Josephus, when Johanan is reported as addressing Vespasian as emperor-to-be, this serves not to enhance the dignity of the conquering power and its general, but to cover up what must have been somewhat sordid realities in the sage's negotiations with the enemy. The four Rabbinic versions of the story differ so much from one another that it is hard to know what actually happened. But it is clear that a deal was made. Admittedly, Johanan had a better moral case than Josephus, for, apart from the personal conflicts of a political moderate (a position he probably shared with Josephus), he had an altruistic purpose: to found, or expand, an academy in the coastal area of Jamnia (Yavneh) where Vespasian had desig-

---

[5] The story is in Ibn Khaldun's Autobiography, which, exactly like Josephus', is a work without a title appended to a large history: see W. J. Fischel, *Ibn Khaldun and Tamerlane: their Historic Meeting in Damascus, 1401 A.D. (803 A.H.): a Study Based on Arabic MSS of Ibn Khaldun's 'Autobiography'* (1952), pp. 14–17, 34–7.

[6] *BJ* 3. 403–4; 4. 622–6. On Josephus' concern with himself, H. R. Graf, *Kaiser Vespasian: Untersuchungen zu Suetons Vita Divi Vespasiani* (1937), pp. 37f.

nated a refuge for loyalist Jews. Even so, the prediction did not come amiss in explaining how it happened that a favour was granted, and in legitimising the transaction. If God had singled Vespasian out for greatness, it was surely right for a pious man to strike an agreement with him. Even if much of the tradition is fictitious, and no more than an adaptation of the Josephus story, the point still holds; and though many things have been said of Johanan's prophecy, nobody would take it as propaganda for the Flavian dynasty.[7]

This Rabbinic story seems to have eluded Greeks and Romans altogether. Other eastern signs and predictions became famous, and some of these do seem to have been encouraged by Vespasian, or even deliberately sought, to forward a new dynasty's claim to the throne. It is worth looking more closely at this phenomenon, to see how far Josephus' prophecy should be assimilated to it. On one occasion, Titus went to consult Aphrodite's oracle at Paphos in Cyprus, ostensibly on the subject of his travels but also, in a private interview, about weightier matters. Then Vespasian visited a famous shrine on Mount Carmel, and its priest Basilides. Afterwards, discussing matters of state in the temple of Serapis at Alexandria, he miraculously saw the same Basilides. In the first two encounters, the future possession of empire was said to have been predicted behind closed doors. No doubt these manifestations helped to create the right aura around father and son in the crucial months of 69.[8] For notwithstanding his professed reluctance, Vespasian seized power with great boldness, becoming the first emperor to be made by the military outside Rome. He depended on the eagerness in the first instance of the Alexandrian legions and then of the army of

---

[7] There are various versions: *Avot de Rabbi Nathan* recension a (Schechter p. 22); recension b (Schechter p. 20); *Midrash Rabbah, Lamentations* 1.5; *TB Gittin* 56b. They differ in the political stance ascribed to Johanan, in the precise point where the prophecy is put, and in circumstantial detail: J. Neusner, *A Life of Rabban Yohanan ben Zakkai* ([2]1970), pp. 157ff.; *Development of a Legend: Studies on the Tradition concerning Yohanan ben Zakkai* (1970), pp. 228–34; A. J. Saldarini 'Johanan ben Zakkai's escape from Jerusalem', *JSJ* 6 (1975), pp. 189–204; P. Schäfer, 'Johanan ben Zakkai and Jabne', in op. cit. (n. 3), 2.10.2 (ed. W. Haase), pp. 43–101. For difficulties about the exact form of the request, G. Alon, 'Rabban Johanan ben Zakkai's removal to Jabneh', in *Jews, Judaism and the Classical World* (transl. I. Abrahams, 1976), pp. 269–313.

[8] Suet. *Tit.* 5.1; Tac. *Hist.* 2. 2–4; Suet. *Vesp.* 5.6; Tac. *Hist.* 2. 78; Suet. *Vesp.* 7; Tac. *Hist.* 4. 82.2. See K. Scott, *The Imperial Cult under the Flavians* (1936), pp. 2ff.; 'The role of Basilides in the Events of A.D.69', *JRS* 24 (1934), pp. 138–40; A. Henrichs, 'Vespasian's visit to Alexandria', *ZPE* 3 (1968), pp. 51–80.

Judaea. The Flavian family 'a warlike clan nourished on the berries
of the Sabine hills' also lacked distinguished birth. From every point
of view, a boost was needed.[9]

But it was enough for public interest to be aroused; curiosity and
rumour could be relied upon to do the rest. Once in power, the
dynasty could cease to take an active interest in preserving the
memory of the portents. The theme had such a fascination to a
superstitious world that its own momentum kept it alive and developed it further.[10] When we find that later a story grew up around
the itinerant miracle-worker Apollonius of Tyana, telling how he
had been summoned for consultation by the aspirant Vespasian,
then we are observing exactly such a process of evolution. According
to this story, which is mistrusted even by Apollonius' biographer
Philostratus, Vespasian was conducting the siege of Jerusalem at
the time, and wished to learn whether he should make himself
emperor. The chronology is garbled, but that is only to be expected
in a popular legend. And there is an amusing twist to the conclusion,
for Apollonius refused flatly to go to a country so polluted by the
actions and sufferings of its people (in this we catch a remote echo
of Josephus' attitude to the zealots), and that was why Vespasian
made his eventful visit to Alexandria. Tacitus, in a characteristically
terse sentence, brings out the psychology which allowed such *ex post
facto* tales to be generated: 'the secrets of fate and the signs and
oracles which marked out Vespasian and his sons for power were
believed once they had achieved it.'[11]

The omens had become truly a popular theme. The main surviving chroniclers of this period, Tacitus, Suetonius and Cassius Dio,
all report them, each in his own manner (Tac. *Hist.* 1.10; 2.4, 78;
Suet. *Vesp.* 4–5; *Tit.* 5; Dio *Epit.* 66.1). When Josephus mentions in
his preface that the signs of Vespasian's future rise will be one of
the themes covered by his history, he evidently expects his readers
to know just what he means (*BJ* 1.23).

Josephus' own prophecy, which figured among the famous por-

---

[9] *BJ* 4. 603–4; Sil. *Pun.* 3. 596; Cf. also Suet. *Vesp.* 1.1 and 7.2, on lack of distinction
and its connection with the portents; on the boldness, A. Briessmann, *Tacitus und das
flavische Geschichtsbild: Hermes Einzelschriften* 10 (1955), pp. 9–10; Nicols, op. cit. (n. 2),
pp. 94–5.

[10] Henrichs, op. cit. (n. 8), demonstrates an entirely spontaneous Egyptian contribution, arising from the characteristic forms of the local worship of Sarapis.

[11] Philostr. *VA* 5. 27 (with a diatribe on political philosophy in the succeeding
chapters).

tents, was subject to the same influences. Suetonius and Dio both have it, but each gives a slightly different story, and both differ in matters of detail from Josephus' account.[12] This shows that they did not take it from Josephus; and, more than that, it seems as though the story, once in existence, had a life of its own, on both oral and literary levels.

Josephus, then, had flattered Vespasian with his prophecy; and the telling of it would not have been displeasing. But with the Flavian family safely on the throne, insistence was no longer necessary, and the incident is prominent in the *Jewish War* principally as an explanation of the author's personal conduct. Josephus' literary handling of the motif does not suggest that he was at this point much preoccupied with giving Vespasian's reputation a boost, at Rome or in the empire.

There is a similar but distinct motif which occurs in Josephus, as well as in Tacitus and Suetonius, and which is all too easily confused with Josephus' personal prediction. Suetonius writes in terms very close to Josephus here, and so does Tacitus (who did not mention Josephus or the Jotapata incident). I am referring to the last of a series of prodigies and utterances which preceded the fall of the Temple, and are recalled by Josephus immediately after this event. An ambiguous oracle, discovered in the Jews' 'sacred texts', had announced that at that very time the future ruler of the world (*oikoumenē*) would emerge from their country. This, more than any of the other phenomena, had encouraged them to revolt, and yet (Josephus says) it pointed in truth to Vespasian's future rule. This oracle finds its place in the *Jewish War* long after the Jotapata episode, and Josephus himself makes no suggestion that it had formed the basis of his own prediction (*BJ* 6.288ff.). On the former occasion, he seems to have invoked no Biblical or other Jewish tradition to support him, merely maintaining that he had divined Vespasian's rule to have been pre-ordained by God. The two prophecies have been unjustly identified by readers, from the Byzantine Zonaras to the twentieth-century Thackeray.[13]

---

[12] Suetonius has Josephus repeatedly prophesying, and making the accession imminent. Dio has Josephus laugh when he speaks, and has him put the accession within the year.

[13] H. Lindner, *Die Geschichtsauffassung des Flavius Josephus im Bellum Judaicum* (1972), p. 70, sees that they are quite separate, but argues that the reader should make the connection. For assimilation, Zonaras 11.16 (Dindorf 3, p. 50); Thackeray, n. *ad loc.* in Loeb Josephus.

Furthermore, they have come to refer to the oracle of Book 6 as a Messianic oracle, implying that for Josephus Vespasian fulfilled the role of the awaited Messiah.[14] But the oracle is about a great ruler, nothing more—a man who might be seen as a forerunner of the eschatological end of days, but would not be marking that end. If we look for a Biblical text which fits the ambiguous oracle, we should go not to one like Daniel 7.14, which foretells the everlasting sovereignty of 'one like a man', but rather to a prediction of a powerful but transient power, as, for example, Balaam's prophecy about the star which will come 'out of Jacob' and 'smite the corners of Moab'. Again, Johanan ben Zakkai is an illuminating parallel, for his way of foretelling Vespasian's great future was allegedly by way of a reference to Isaiah's prophecy in which a conqueror: 'shall cut down the thickets of the forest with iron, and Lebanon shall fall by a mighty one.' This verse even has Messianic implications in many traditional exegeses, for it is followed by the famous passage about a 'branch from the stem of Jesse'; yet no one would suppose that the famous rabbi made Vespasian his Messiah.[15] In Josephus' case, there is no sense in conducting a search for the text which is the most likely candidate,[16] once we have seen that the author, though convinced in dismissing the zealot interpretation of such predictions, never himself goes so far as to treat Vespasian, or for that matter any other Roman, as the Jewish Messiah. His own interpretation is to be understood together with those judgments he makes in other places about the transference of Divine favour to the Roman side, and as a statement about the realities of power and about why revolt was fruitless. Here we have the same analysis— Roman superiority—with one additional element—that it was to come to fruition under Flavian auspices.

The prediction about the future ruler is the conclusion of a digres-

---

[14] An extreme example in W. Weber, *Josephus und Vespasian* (1921), p. 42; cf. also Schalit, op. cit. (n. 3), pp. 259–60.

[15] Num. 24.17ff. Johanan's citation: Isaiah 10.34ff. (present in some but not all the versions of the story); Neusner, *Life* (see n. 7), pp. 157–66; on the exegetical interpretation of 'Lebanon' as the Temple, G. Vermes, 'The symbolic interpretation of "Lebanon" in the Targums: the origin and development of an exegetical tradition', *JThS* N.S 9 (1958), pp. 1–12, also in *Scripture and Tradition in Judaism* (1961), pp. 26–39. The strongly Messianic reading at *TJ Berakhot* 2. 5a, is clearly post-destruction, when such tendencies increased.

[16] For other possibilities, J. Blenkinsopp, 'Prophecy and priesthood in Josephus', *JJS* 25 (1974), p. 245; M. Hengel, *Die Zeloten* (1961), pp. 244ff., who himself favours the Balaam oracle.

sion, a list of renowned prodigies which had appeared in the Temple or in the heavens during A.D. 70, or in the years before. There had been a star and a comet, the Temple gates had opened spontaneously, chariots and armed batallions had been noticed in the air, a cow had given birth to a lamb within the sacred area, voices had emerged from within announcing their departure, and for four years before the destruction a peasant prophet called Jesus son of Ananias had uttered persistent warnings of woe. After commenting on the Jews' obdurate failure to grasp that these messages portended disaster and not encouragement, he provided yet another two examples of gross misinterpretation. One concerned an old prophecy that the city would be destroyed when the Temple became square, which he believes was fulfilled during the siege, when the Antonia fortress was demolished. The other is the ruler oracle: 'but what incited them most of all to war was an ambiguous oracle . . . that at that time a man from their country would rule over the whole world.' [17]

These phenomena create an atmosphere of numinous tragedy around the fall of the Temple, and Talmudic literature has similar manifestations (*TB Yoma* 39b; *TB Pesahim* 57a). Most of the report is very immediate in character: we can picture the Temple officials' response to the sight of the gates opening, and we feel the impact of the relentless prophet's cries. Jewish observation rather than Roman seems to be behind these descriptions. It is true that Tacitus' *Histories* contain a very similar account of the prodigies, with the similarity running even to verbal echoes, but a dependence, direct or indirect, on Josephus is the best way of explaining this.[18]

[17] *BJ* 6. 288–312. The prophecies are analysed in the commentary of Michel and Bauernfeind 2.2 (1969), excursuses 14–16, and by A. Schalit, op. cit. (n. 3), pp. 269–76.

[18] Tac. *Hist.* 5.13; chariots and the clash of arms in the sky, flashing light, the spontaneous opening of the doors, and the voices of the departing Deity—'et audita maior humana vox excedere deos; simul ingens motus excedentium.' Tacitus' interpretation also echoes Josephus: 'pluribus persuasio inerat antiquis sacerdotum literis contineri eo ipso tempore fore ut valesceret Oriens profectique Iudaea rerum potirentur.' For the last sentence, cf. Suet. *Vesp.* 4.5, which is almost identical. E. Norden argued, in my view unconvincingly, for a different source behind Tacitus on the basis of minor differences in formulation: 'Josephus und Tacitus über Jesus Christus und eine messianische Prophetie', part 3, *Neue Jahrbuch für das kl. Altertum* 16 (1913), pp. 637–66; repr. in A. Schalit (ed.), *Zur Josephus-Forschung, Wege der Forschung* 84 (1973), pp. 27–69; and in E. Norden, *Kleine Schriften* (1966), pp. 241–75. Schalit, op. cit. (n. 17), p. 218 follows Norden. M. Stern takes a similar view, rejecting Lehmann, Schürer and Dornseiff: *Greek and Latin Authors on Jews and Judaism* 2 (1980), pp. 3, 61–2. A. M. A. Hospers-Jansen, *Tacitus over de Joden* (1949; Dutch with English summary) is undecided.

Suspicions have been voiced that pagan religiosity has intruded into
Josephus' descriptions, especially where he, like Tacitus, speaks of
the departing Deity in the plural.[19] Yet this plural would seem to
be just the decent vagueness with which Josephus clothes a reference
to a Deity whose name may not be spoken, a Greek form of allusion
to the numinous Hebrew *Shekhinah* (Divine Presence).[20]

The list of Temple prodigies is, then, most likely to be Josephus'
own; on the one hand, it serves a literary purpose at an important
moment in the narrative, on the other, it provides a way of making
a political and religious point against the rebels. After Josephus has
described some strange manifestations, he is led, when he explains
them, to the subject of Vespasian and to an interpretation which,
once again, will have gratified the emperor. But this time too the
interpretation is a by-product of an important argument between
Josephus and other Jews. At the end of it all, the reader's mind will
remain with the delusions of the rebels and with the Temple in
flames, not with Flavian claims. Josephus invokes prophecy not for
Vespasian's sake, but because he is dealing with a grave moment
in Jewish history.[21] What is said about Vespasian plays a minor
role. Only later was the motif transferred out of its Judaean context
into one of Roman imperial history, and for that Josephus was
scarcely responsible.

It is time to move on from the moment of Josephus' liberation
and the cancellation of his enslavement (see p. 185). The benefits
conferred upon him did not end with those acts, and are striking in
their generosity. Titus' protection throughout the war saved the
renegade from his irate countrymen, and it seems to have been
safest for Josephus never to leave Titus' side. He accompanied the
young Roman to Alexandria and eventually to Rome. There Josephus lived in Vespasian's old house (its location is unknown) and
the emperor had still to play the part of protector as did his successors, Titus and Domitian. The expatriate Jew was not only kept
in asylum during these years, but even honoured: he received
Roman citizenship, together with the Flavian name that was its

[19] The Greek reading is either *metabainomen* (we are departing) or *metabainōmen*
(let us depart). see O. Weinreich, 'Türöffnung im Wunder-, Prodigien- und Zaub-
erglauben der Antike des Judentums und Christentums', *Genethliakon Wilhelm Schmid*
(1929) section E, pp. 271–9.

[20] Cf. Michel and Bauernfeind's commentary (see n. 17), excursus 13, where the
interpretation is in Jewish not pagan terms.

[21] On Josephus' attitude to prophecy, cf. pp. 18–19.

conventional accompaniment; he was given a house, a pension, new estates in a fertile part of Palestine to replace some that he had lost; he clearly wanted for nothing.[22]

What services were rendered to earn all this? The prophecy, on any interpretation, was scarcely sufficient. The idea that the expatriate was paid for his historical writing therefore suggests itself, and seems to reinforce the characterisation of Josephus as Vespasian's official historian. The fruits of the emperor's investment would have been first the Aramaic report; and then, when this proved satisfactory, the seven books of the *Jewish War* in Greek.

The war history is certainly a Vespasianic work at least to the extent that it appeared in time to be presented to that emperor, and so while he was still alive and ruling. We cannot date it exactly, but it belongs to the latter part of the reign, after the dedication of the Temple of Peace in 75.[23] In a wider sense, however, it need not be Vespasianic. Josephus never explicitly suggests that it was his literary output which earned him his keep. And it is obvious that during the war there had been various ways in which he would have been helpful to the Roman generals once he had abandoned the revolt and won their confidence; some of these are described by him, others can safely be surmised. As we know, Josephus did his utmost to persuade the besieged Jews to submit while favourable terms were still available ((*BJ* 5.114, 261, 361ff., 541ff.; 6.94ff., 365), and was severely wounded in the process (*BJ* 5.541–7). This policy suited his own inclinations, but it also served the Romans well, for a hasty end to the war was most desirable. Sometimes, it was a message direct from Titus which Josephus took to the Jews (*BJ*

---

[22] *BJ* 3. 396ff.; *V* 415–16, 422–5, 428–9. On Josephus as landowner, pp. 24–5.

[23] For the *termini*, *V* 361; *CA* 1. 50; *BJ* 7. 158ff.; Dio, *Epit.* 66. 15.1 (dating of the Peace temple); B. Niese, *Josephi Opera* 6 (1894), *praef.* 4. A date rather close to the end of the reign is suggested by Josephus' treatment of the Flavian supporter Caecina Alienus as a traitor; only after Caecina had conspired against Vespasian is Josephus likely to have written in this way, and Suetonius and Dio put this conspiracy late: Dio 66. 16.3; Suet. *Tit.* 6; Briessmann op. cit. (n. 9), pp. 32f. The suggestion is rejected by G. E. F. Chilver, reviewing Briessmann, *JRS* 46 (1956), pp. 203–5, with the weak argument that it would be hard to find time between the conspiracy and Vespasian's death for the publication of the *Jewish War*; in fact Dio assigns no precise year to the conspiracy. See also M. Stern, 'The date of the composition of the Jewish War', *Proceedings of the Sixth World Congress of Jewish Studies* (1976). S. J. D. Cohen, *Josephus in Galilee and Rome* (1979), pp. 87–9, suggests a Domitianic date for Book 7, largely on the basis of Domitian's more frequent appearances there; but these appearances are due simply to the increase in Flavian subject matter: cf. p. 216 (on Book 7); and p. 218 (on Domitian).

5.325; 6.129). In such cases he was essentially an interpreter. There were no doubt many occasions when he did various less salubrious jobs, which he does not wish to specify. Years later, arguing in the *Against Apion* that he had been better placed than other historians to observe the war, he lets out the information that he had at some time been assigned the task of interviewing deserters (*CA* 1.49). In addition, Josephus was able to be an interpreter in a wider sense, guiding the Romans on Jewish habits and on the topography of the city and the country as a whole. We can understand his silence on such subjects. And finally, it was no doubt to Vespasian's advantage as well as Josephus' that the Jew accompanied him when he went to Alexandria to secure the empire. That Josephus had established, or could easily establish contacts with the upper stratum of the Jewish community in Alexandria is clear from the fact that on this journey he contracted a new marriage there, having dismissed his ex-captive wife some time before.[24]

Each of these acts was a signal service to the Roman generals. Quite apart from any services rendered, Josephus was in his own right a political figure of importance, once a leader in his country, now a distinguished exile, who would naturally be treated in a manner fitting to his station. We may recall that even the British rebel Caratacus had been allowed to go free, to be a witness to Roman generosity (Tac. *Ann.* 12.38). That Josephus took advantage of his sheltered (and idle) situation to become a writer may have given some additional satisfaction to the emperors; although, even then, it is unlikely that his origins permitted him to penetrate as an equal into any favoured literary coterie.[25] Anyway, to talk of imperial pleasure is not to say that the emperors paid the man to write his history.[26]

Some might still wish to say that in the end it does not make very much difference what a writer is officially paid for, and insist that it is the very fact of being in another's pay that determines the relationship; Josephus, they will point out, was obligated to Ves-

---

[24] *V* 415–6. On the earlier marriage, see pp. 20–1. On the intrigues, pp. 214–15.

[25] Z. Yavetz, 'Reflections on Titus and Josephus', *GRBS* 16 (1975), pp. 431–2; 'he was never awarded the official title of *amicus Caesaris*. He was not among his *comites*. He must have been a member of the lower entourage, in the same category as doctors and magicians, philosophers and buffoons.'

[26] Cf. Niese in *Hastings' Encyclopaedia of Religion and Ethics* 7 (1914) s.v. 'Josephus': 'it would be a mistake to regard the work as being an official chronicle. Josephus had no Government commission for his task, but wrote entirely on his own initiative.'

pasian, and that was that. Yet, while pecuniary obligation creates pressures, conflicts and embarrassments, an ambivalent situation of this kind is a far cry from simply writing under contract. There will be fewer positive constraints, even if as many negative ones.

Suetonius remarked (*Vesp.* 18.4) that Vespasian was the first emperor to pay orators out of the imperial purse and to reward distinguished poets. The single sentence in which he mentions this is a vital support for constructing Josephus as an official historian. No doubt Suetonius was alluding to important reforms, which served to encourage the arts and education throughout Italy, and perhaps the provinces.[27] But it would be absurd to think that the scheme was brought into existence just so that its beneficiaries could celebrate the imperial house with their creations, even if it is true that the poet Statius, whose estate near Alba was provided with water from Domitian's own, repaid him amply with poems about his equestrian statue, his seventeenth consulate, and the magnificence of his hospitality, palace and person, as well as with a series of lost works about his military exploits.[28] In any case, for our purposes the Suetonius sentence is irrelevant, for historians are not even mentioned in it. And if the suggestion is that Vespasian may have preferred not to make it known that chroniclers were refurbishing the image of his reign, then it is no longer possible at the same time to invoke Suetonius. In total contrast, the satirist Juvenal, referring probably to Trajan, took it as a known fact that it was ludicrously hard for historians to make a living, and implies that up to that time no sort of patronage had been forthcoming (without any suggestion that the situation had deteriorated since the Flavians) (*Sat.* 7.98ff.; cf. 7.5).

We might expect Vespasian, the most practical of men, to take care to direct the historians of his reign;[29] but it is only in the most limited sense that we find him actually doing so. True, Tacitus throws out a scathing dismissal of Flavian historiography, which is often quoted in this context; he says that it was perverted by adulation (*Hist.* 2.101). But this judgment is attached to the treatment of a specific and debated issue in the war of 68/9, and it is not clear

---

[27] M. P. Charlesworth, *CAH* 11 (1936), p. 16.

[28] *Silvae* 3. 1.61–3; 4. 5.1; 5. 3.36ff.; 1. 1; 4. 1 and 2. K. Scott, 'Statius' adulation of Domitian', *AJPh* 54 (1933) pp. 247–59.

[29] As maintained by H. Bardon, *Les empereurs et les lettres latines d'Auguste à Hadrien* (²Paris, 1968), pp. 294ff.

how wide a scope it is meant to have. In any case, the tone of the
statement is in keeping with this pessimistic author's general conviction that, since the late Augustan age, all imperial history was
distorted by fear if written during the lifetime of its subjects, and
by resentment if after their deaths.[30] Thus in no way is the Tacitean
dismissal intended to single out a feature unique to these years.
Moreover, what Tacitus actually asserts is that criticism of a member of the Flavian faction had been impossible: in other words,
historians had not been free to say all they wished. Therefore it is
again a question of subtle pressure, and this is different from an
overall control over what was produced, or an active policy of using
historiography for specific ends.

Pliny the Elder was the most prominent prose writer of the age.
Only his famous *Natural History* survives, but he also wrote a major
historical work in thirty-one volumes. This covered Roman history
from some point in the reign of Tiberius or of Claudius, where a
predecessor called Aufidius Bassus (also lost) had left off, down to
Pliny's own time, somewhere in the early seventies.[31] However, he
did not allow it to be published until after his own death. And he
tells us why: it was to avoid any possible suspicion of personal
ambition or of currying favour. Pliny, as we shall see, was a friend,
and it is probable that his work treated Vespasian and Titus
kindly;[32] and perhaps the Flavians for their part felt gratified that
this author would be presenting them to posterity in a favourable
light. None the less, they evidently did not expect him to enhance
their popularity in the immediate future, for they could not know
when he would die, and until that date the book was useless to
them.

It is remarkable that we know of the existence of various contemporary versions of the events of 68/9, but for the reign of the Flavians
which followed we can point only to Pliny on the first few years of
Vespasian. True, Tacitus' account of that period is lost, so that we
could hardly expect to possess the names of his sources. But there
is more to it: Tacitus' *Histories* once had either twelve or fourteen[33]

---

[30] Tac. *Ann.* 1. 1. And cf. *Hist.* 1, for a similar judgment on Augustan historians.
[31] On the end point of Pliny's history, R. Syme, *Tacitus* (1968), vol. 1, p. 288 and
appx. 38, p. 698. The whole work was finished and put away before Pliny wrote the
preface to the *Natural History*, which was published in 77: *NH praef.* 70.
[32] See below, pp. 200f. Pliny's reasons: *NH praef.* 20.
[33] Syme, op. cit. (n. 31), appx. 35; F. R. D. Goodyear, *Tacitus: Greece and Rome,
New Surveys* 4 (1970), pp. 17–20.

books, and more than four of those—the part which is extant—were occupied with the years 68–70. This meant that only some two-thirds of the work remained for the accounts of three entire reigns. Tacitus' account of Domitian's reign suggests that he had to collect most of his material himself;[34] and it looks as though the same was true for the era of Vespasian and Titus. The younger Pliny, in a discussion written in A.D.105 on the possible choices of subject for a history he is planning to write, says that recent, i.e. Flavian, history is a subject as yet 'untouched' (*Ep.* 5. 8.12). Cassius Dio's later account of the period is the only one we have today, surviving in a summary made by an epitomiser. This is short in comparison with the same author's summarised version of the years 68/9; and it is striking that within the brief narrative of 70–81 almost all the material is of an unusually trivial and anecdotal kind, except where the doings of the Stoic opposition to the régime are recorded.[35] Our overall impression is that before Tacitus came to the subject, very little had been written at Rome about the reign of any Flavian.[36] It was too difficult, too dangerous, or perhaps simply unfashionable.

On the other hand, there is no doubt that the Roman civil wars which led up to this period were an extremely popular topic. But it does not follow that this literature was orchestrated by the rulers; had that been the case, it would be inexplicable for them not to continue the practice into the subsequent years, and not to attempt to have the achievements of their years in power also enshrined in prose. We might rather suggest that people had written sponta-neously about the civil wars.[37] There was much in these years apart from the emergence of the Flavians. The troubles were an exciting subject for a memoir or a brief study. There would be information that people in Rome could not have had; they would want to hear about the turbulent and geographically widespread conflicts which had determined their destiny. Those who had participated in dra-matic incidents will have wished to describe them, and to read about them. And while an account of the rise of the Flavians might

---

[34] Syme, op. cit. (n. 31), vol. 1, p. 119.

[35] And these derive from a separate Stoic martyrology.

[36] The historians of Nero's reign, Cluvius Rufus and Fabius Rusticus, seem not to have gone any further.

[37] E.g. Vipstanus Messalla, a distinguished Flavian participant in Tacitus' *Dial-ogus* and brother of a notorious informer; C. Pompeius Planta, also on the Flavian side in the civil war, and later a procurator of Vespasian and perhaps prefect of Egypt.

figure as the culmination of such works, it would not be their *raison d'être*.

The Jewish war, with its effect on the fortunes of Vespasian and Titus, was in one sense an aspect of the civil war, which may be why various accounts were produced of the former as well. According to Josephus(*BJ* 1.2; *CA* 1.46), these were full of hearsay and gossip, and he contemptuously dismisses them as characterised by flattery of Rome and hatred of the Jews; had the emperors been involved, he could hardly have spoken so rudely of these accounts.

There is no doubt, then, that writers were stimulated by the upheavals in the empire. But the first Flavians appear to have left the historical record to take care of itself, only ensuring that it did not get out of hand. And when it dried up—for the main part of the reigns—they were content to do without it.

Our view of other authors cannot demonstrate conclusively anything about Josephus. Perhaps, it may be suggested, the Hellenized Jew could be brought to do, in Greek, what no self-respecting Roman would contemplate, abandoning even that vestige of independence which others strove to retain. Yet what the emperors did not require in Latin, they are unlikely to have commissioned in Greek. And it would have been strange had they abandoned their usual caution. It is far better to make the relationship between literature and patronage in this case fit in with the usual Roman pattern.

For the case of Josephus, we have just one hard fact as an indicator of that relationship. He himself, in a later work, describes the association of the first two Flavian emperors with the *Jewish War*: he presented it to them on its completion, and they both testified to its accuracy. Titus, he says, affixed his seal to the book and ordered it to be made publicly available, so anxious was he for it to be the only source of information on the war (*V* 361–3). Here the historian is engaged in contrasting the reliability of his own work with that of Justus of Tiberias, his troublesome adversary; hence his claims that his version was recognised as the only worthwhile one and his boasts about the recognition he had received are liable to be a little exaggerated.

A written recommendation attached to a text could mean that the text is to be regarded as an officially approved report. But it could have a slighter significance. From the elder Pliny's preface to his *Natural History* it appears that a work would be dedicated or offered to the Emperor as an application for an expression of his interest and satisfaction. He writes, addressing Titus, that his appeal to such patronage put him in a more exposed situation than the normal author; and he expresses his apprehension at having voluntarily submitted his work for judgment (*NH praef.* 6, 8). No doubt such a transaction was flattering to both author and emperor, and, if proclaimed, would increase the prestige of the published book (at least in some quarters). Pliny—like Josephus—was Titus' friend, and the pose in which he offers his book for scrutiny is that of a friend, even if he never really loses the consciousness of addressing an emperor.[38] It need hardly be added that there can be no question of the whole *Natural History* in all its variety being in any, except the most remote sense, a composition written to serve Titus.

Now Josephus' work was not formally dedicated to Titus as Pliny's was. But sending it to him is a comparable gesture. The affixing of the signature could serve the same function as did Pliny's explicit indication that he was counting on Titus' benign approval. Josephus simply resorted to a different form of presentation—perhaps a less impertinent one, for a newly created Roman citizen writing in Greek could not allow himself as much as a well-established equestrian Italian. None the less, Josephus too had chosen his judge; and it was the commendation of a literary *iudex* rather than the *imprimatur* of an autocrat which was attached to the *War*.[39]

The title by which we know Josephus' book is *The Jewish War*. This name is assumed to be the original one, and it is commonly taken to reveal that the author's standpoint was Roman: for the Jews are viewed as the opponents, just as the Gauls were when Romans talked of the Gallic wars. Josephus would then be identifying himself with the Romans and serving the interests of the emperors. However, the evidence indicates rather that the work possessed no title at all. Its first words: '(Since) the war of the Jews against the Romans . . .', would have provided an adequate means of labelling or identifying it.[40] In his later writings, Josephus refers back to his own work on the war in similar terms, speaking of his 'Jewish War' (*Ioudaïkos Polemos*) or his books 'about the Jewish

---

[38] 'Nobis ad colendum te familiaris audacia sola superest.'

[39] Cf. Yavetz, op. cit., (n. 25), pp. 430–1.

[40] It was normal practice to name the subject of a historical work in its opening sentence: D. Earl, 'Prologue-Form in Ancient Historiography', *Aufstieg und Niedergang* etc. (see n. 3), 1.2 (1972), pp. 841–4, 856. On the tendency for Greek prose books to want titles, *RE Suppl.* 12 (1970), 1108–9, s.v. 'Thukydides'.

War' (*AJ* 1.203; 18.11; 20.258; *V* 27, 412–13). Sometimes, however, he has simply 'Jewish Affairs' (*Ioudaïka* or *Ioudaïkē Pragmateia*),[41] suggesting that there was a habit of using this short name and so again, perhaps, that an official title was wanting. The manuscripts support this contention, for they too show no consistency.[42] Most have yet a different form of reference, one which finds no attestation in Josephus, and which looks as though it reflects Christian interest in the fall of Jerusalem—'(Book x of) Flavius Josephus' Jewish History about the Capture of Jerusalem'. There is one manuscript which twice corresponds with Josephus' opening, but the super-scription there is probably the work of an intelligent commentator or scribe (Cod. Par. 1425). The conflict in the tradition existed at an early date: of the Church Fathers, Jerome (in the fourth century) uses the first name, Theophilus of Antioch (in the second century) and Eusebius (in the fourth) have the second.[43]

But even if Josephus did not attach a separate heading to his work, it can be claimed that the way he chose to describe the subject proves the point. Yet the fuller version, which we find in the opening sentence, which includes the words 'against the Romans', hardly suggests, with its explicit mention of the Romans as the other side, the point of view of a Roman.[44] As for the shorter version which appears in other places, this says less about the author's attitudes than it does about the language he is writing in and about his readership. Presenting his work to the Greeks and Romans who inhabited the empire, he naturally gives the war the same name as they did. However patriotic a Jew, he could hardly have called it 'the Roman War'.

We are in the realms of fantasy if we conclude from a name—which is not even a formal name—that Josephus was playing the role of a Roman imperial historian. We must return to the reality of his relationship with Titus. When the emperor's son and co-ruler affixed his signature to Josephus' work he presumably liked what

---

[41] *AJ* 13. 72, 173, 298. Missed by Niese, op. cit. (n. 23), vol. 1 (1887), *praef.* 6. Recognised in vol. 6, *praef.* iii, where the author is consequently less confident about the possibility of discovering Josephus' original title.

[42] So Niese.

[43] Jerome, *Vir. Ill.* 13: 'septem libros Iudaicae captivitatis'; Theophilus, *ad Auto-lycum* 3. 23; cf. Eus., *Hist Eccl.* 1. 5.6; 2. 6.4. The sixth-century place-name list of Stephanus of Byzantium, s.v. Phasaelis, has just 'the war against the Romans'.

[44] Laqueur tried to explain this away by saying that the Romans were mentioned in those occasional contexts where Josephus found himself obliged to switch to a Jewish angle: *der jüdische Historiker Flavius Josephus* (1920), pp. 98, 255.

he had read there (or what he assumed he would find). The gesture conveys nothing more than that.

It is easy to understand why Josephus' book gave pleasure. There were many opportunities within it to present the persons of Vespasian and Titus in a glowing light, and these opportunities were not missed by the author. In this way he acknowledged his patrons, and rendered them ample service. This is the area within which the Flavians did influence the work, and exploration will show how far it extends.

We must remember that the successful termination of the Jewish war was a major achievement for the first two Flavians. Military glory mattered greatly to them, for it complemented supposed supernatural sanction to justify their seizure of power. The value attached to the Judaean triumph is graphically shown in Titus' Arch, a monument which, thanks to nineteenth-century restoration, is still to be seen at Rome, looking towards the forum from a spur at the top of the Sacred Way. The decorative sculptures which occupy prominent positions on both sides of the internal passage way survive in good shape. They are almost exclusively concerned with the conquest of Judaea, and the triumph of 71.[45] And yet the monument was not designed as a commemoration of that event: the total absence of Vespasian (even in a peripheral position) suggests rather that it was from the beginning planned as a general memorial for Titus,[46] and that the war was simply the most noteworthy theme of his career. The conscious desire to exaggerate this achievement emerges again in the preposterous claim of a dedication to Titus which is thought to come from another arch, and which is known because its text is recorded in an eighth-century itinerary: this asserts that Titus was the first man ever to capture Jerusalem—'he subdued the Jewish people and destroyed the city of Jerusalem, a task which previous commanders had either failed to accomplish or had not even attempted'. The claim is patently absurd, as even Josephus makes clear when he talks of the city's five previous conquests and one previous devastation.[47]

[45] S. B. Platner and T. Ashby, *A Topographical Dictionary of Ancient Rome* (1929), pp. 45–6; I. A. Richmond, 'Two Flavian Monuments', *Roman Archaeology and Art, Essays and Studies* (1969), pp. 218–21: S. Reinach, 'L'Arc de Titus', *REJ* 20 (1890), pp. lxv–xci. Illustrations: E. Nash, *A Pictorial Dictionary of Ancient Rome* (1961) vol. I, p. 133.

[46] Richmond, loc. cit. (n. 45).

[47] *CIL* 944 = *ILS* 264; Schürer-Vermes-Millar, vol. I, p. 509, n. 128; why there should have been two arches is obscure; the second was described some time before the ninth century (Dessau). Cf. *BJ* 6. 435–7.

Usually, however, when incidents in which Vespasian and Titus are prominent fall within Josephus' scope, he makes the most of them, and is not abashed by hyperbole. In addition, beyond what is strictly necessary, certain scenes which form a vital part of their rise to power are introduced, and sometimes described at length. We have to say that Josephus' Flavian portraits and episodes are orientated towards Rome and influenced by the imperial court in a way that none of the rest of his work is, but we should also add that they are an almost extraneous, detachable phenomenon. It may be correct to talk of propaganda here. The character of these representations scarcely needs to be spelled out.

Vespasian often plays an illustrious role; but the brightest aura surrounds Titus, in just the same way as it was Titus who in due course received a triumphal arch depicting the victory, who is represented as the only *triumphator* in the carvings of the north side of the passage way,[48] and who is the subject of the inscription which we have just referred to. The latter admits only grudgingly that the war had been fought 'under his father's instructions, guidance and auspices'. While it is true that Titus terminated the war on his own, there seems to have been a habit of ascribing even more, indeed as much as possible, to him personally at every stage. Thus Suetonius credits him with the capture of Gamala, which in reality was due as much to Vespasian (*Tit.* 4; *BJ* 4.4–83). Here, as elsewhere, Josephus is curiously in harmony with other presentations and, we should remember, far from unique in his forms of adulation.

Vespasian is accorded a more prosaic kind of praise. He is admired by Josephus for his military skill and for the same down-to-earth attributes as in Roman sources. In one speech of Titus he is talked of as a man to whom it was habitual to win victories, and in another, as a man who had grown old in warfare (*BJ* 3.482; 5.124). Josephus personally offers a similar description; and in that description he calls Vespasian the conqueror of Britain, when, in fact, the Flavian had commanded only one of the legions in Claudius' invasion. This exaggeration seems to be shared by a contemporary poet, Silius Italicus.[49] Vespasian's age is his principal advantage: when he is received by the senate as their new emperor,

---

[48] Richmond, op. cit. (n. 45), pp. 220–1.

[49] *BJ* 3. 4; Sil. *Pun.* 3. 589, on the assumption that by 'Caledonian' the poet means British: A. Momigliano, 'Panegyricus Messallae and "Panegyricus Vespasiani", two references to Britain', *JRS* 40 (1950), pp. 41–2.

they are glad that he is endowed 'with the dignity of age' as well as 'with the flower of military achievements'. Similarly Tacitus in his *Dialogus* has one of the speakers call Vespasian 'a venerable old man', and in the *Histories* a senator is made to remark, 'we have no fear of Vespasian, such is the maturity and such the moderation of our leader.'[50] It has been suggested that the three short speeches which Josephus puts into Vespasian's mouth have deliberately been written in the fluent but plain style of a man of action. There is little else, apart from Book 7, to which we shall come.

All this is extremely modest compared with what Titus receives. His personal valour as a commander in the battlefield is repeatedly described: his eagerness to be in the centre of the fray with his men and ahead of them into any new situation is stressed with rather tedious frequency. Thus he is the very first over the walls of Jotapata (*BJ* 3.324). He leads the charge against the Jewish troops outside Tarichaeae, and in the subsequent pursuit appears sometimes in the rear, sometimes out in front, and sometimes tackling groups of the enemy (*BJ* 3.485–502). Later, he is the first to enter the town, having just ridden his horse through the Sea of Galilee. On the approach to Jerusalem he is cut off with a small body of men from the main contingent, but shows supreme courage in proceeding into the midst of the enemy (*BJ* 5.58–66). God, too, is with him, and, of a rain of arrows, not one strikes home. After encamping on Mount Scopus, he rescues the tenth legion from a Jewish attack. Advised to retreat from yet another enemy charge, he stands his ground and, while his men are busy running away, he seems to hold off the opposition single-handed: 'thus to tell the truth without adding a word in flattery or suppressing one out of envy, Caesar twice rescued the entire legion when it was in jeopardy.' For all Josephus' disclaimer, the flattery is all too evident (*BJ* 5.81–4, 85–97). On yet another occasion, when facts forbid the assertion that Titus was first over the wall, Josephus finds an elegant face-saving formula, and says that Titus' good fortune (*tychē*) brought success to the man who was the first. Again, although Titus does not participate in the night attack on Jerusalem, this is not for want of eagerness, and he has to be held back by his friends and officers when already in arms.[51]

---

[50] *BJ* 7. 65; Tac. *Dial.* 8 (the words are ascribed to Julius Secundus; Tac. *Hist.* 4. 42.6 (Curtius Montanus).

[51] *BJ* 6. 132. Further examples of this kind in Yavetz, op. cit. (n. 25), p. 414, n. 13.

Courage is coupled with compassion in Titus; both in cases where mercy is granted, and in those where justice has to be exacted, or even cruelties to be perpetrated, the young man's humane and sympathetic sentiments are underlined. It is Titus' pity for Josephus which first leads Vespasian to spare the prisoner. Feeling sorry for the defeated inhabitants of Tarichaeae, Titus executes only the guilty among them (*BJ* 3.397, 501). He refrains from mass punishment when his troops entreat forgiveness after acting without orders—although here the picture is more realistic, and Josephus recognises the element of expediency, writing, with some honesty, that Caesar took into account both the men's pleas and his own advantage (*BJ* 5.128). Even anger does not deflect Titus from his habitual generosity, and he takes no reprisals against the sons and brothers of King Izates of Adiabene. Out of kindness he will even reverse his former orders and spare Jewish deserters. Thus while Josephus does not deny that the Romans were often savage, he likes to put Titus on a different plane of sentiment, if not of action. And so abundant is Titus' sympathy that when his father is struck on the sole of the foot by an arrow, as a son he experiences anguish (*agōnia*) (*BJ* 6.356, 383; 3.238).

But the most notable instance of compassion ascribed to Titus is the overwhelming concern he shows for saving the Temple. Josephus takes great pains to demonstrate that the conflagration was an accident and against Titus' express desires. He indicates in the preamble to his book that this will be a major theme (*BJ* 1.10, 27, 28). His obsequiousness is blatant, once again. What is more difficult is to determine whether there is any validity in the claims he makes on Titus' behalf. Josephus' critics maintain that here they have caught him red-handed in the act of distorting truth for the benefit of his patron.[52] This is a major issue in his history, and an interesting one; for if the charges are valid, then the blemish is far more damaging then the conventional embellishments and small flatteries which we have so far surveyed.

Josephus' story is that Titus strove to bring about a Jewish surrender before launching an attack on the remnant in the Temple area (*BJ* 6.124–9). Eventually he had to burn down the gates, but

[52] Accepted, among very many, by A. Momigliano, *CAH* 10 (1952), p. 862 and n. 1; and, in Hebrew, M. Stern, 'Josephus' manner of writing history', *7th Convention of the Israel Historical Society* (1962). It is extraordinary that the opposite view is described as a 'Handbuchweisheit' by I. Weiler, 'Titus und die Zerstörung des Tempels von Jerusalem—Absicht oder Zufall?', *Klio* 50 (1968), p. 139.

he immediately gave orders to extinguish the fire. At a council of war, he argued for leniency, on the grounds that so splendid a shrine was an adornment to the empire and that its ruin would be a disgrace to Rome; the building was to be saved, even if the Jews fought to the last ditch from the inside. The other officers were won over to this view, and again attempts were made to prevent a general conflagration. But the fire spread and was eventually brought into the edifice itself by excited Roman soldiers, who tossed in firebrands and rushed after them, mainly in the expectation of plunder. It was one of them who started the final and fateful blaze (*BJ* 6.228, 232ff., 249ff., 256–66).

This account is full of circumstantial detail and quite acceptable. The only ground for suspicion is the author's somewhat excessive insistence on Titus' goodwill: as we have seen, the point is already made in his preface—and there more than once—and later too the writer seems to protest too much.[53] But this is, after all, in keeping with the rest of his treatment of Titus; and it is improbable that it would have occurred to anyone to disbelieve Josephus, were it not for the existence of a rival account. A complicated set of hypotheses has been built upon this account.

In his Latin *Chronicle*, a universal history written in the late fourth century A.D., the Christian historian Sulpicius Severus describes Titus deliberating with his council about what should be done with the Temple, in similar terms to those of Josephus. But this time it is some of the other council members who feel that the building should be saved, and Titus who argues for its destruction.[54] The key question, from which all else follows, is whether this narrative contains real information, deriving from a good source other than Josephus, or whether it is simply Sulpicius' (or someone else's) imaginative adaptation of the Jewish author.

The German-Jewish philologist, J. Bernays, to whom we owe the development in 1861 of the 'sensational conjecture' that so greatly discredits Josephus, held that the character of Sulpicius' account suggests a well-informed source.[55] Bernays thought that it did not accord well with Sulpicius' general argument to make Titus the

---

[53] Apart from the preface, see *BJ* 6. 128, 216, 236, 240, 256.

[54] Sulp. Sev. 2. 30; text according to *CSEL* 1 (1866), p. 85.

[55] J. Bernays, 'Ueber die Chronik des Sulpicius Severus', *Gesammelte Abhandlungen* (ed. H. Usener), 2 (1885), pp. 159–81. The conjecture is thus described by A. Momigliano, 'Jacob Bernays', *Quinto contributo alla storia degli studi classici* 1 (1975), p. 146.

instrument of destruction, and that therefore he would have had no
motive for inventing the story. The exact opposite seems nearer the
truth. Although Severus, like most early Christians, is convinced
that the destruction of the Temple and the dispersion were punish-
ments of the Jews, brought about by their rejection of Christ
(2.30.8), he at the same time holds that the Romans' actual purpose
was a different one: they had really been attacking the Jews in order
to destroy the roots of Christianity, and that is what he says in the
passage quoted. In other words, this was just another in a line of
persecutions. In recounting persecutions, the habit of Severus and
other Christian writers is to ascribe each to the wickedness of an
individual emperor.[56] In the very next chapter of Severus we read
of the (supposed) persecutions of Domitian and Trajan. More than
that: Hadrian is there represented as doing just what Titus had
done, taking action against Judaism in at attempt to liquidate the
daughter religion, this time by turning the Temple into a pagan
shrine and banning Jews from Jerusalem.[57] Here too, the emperor's
personal thinking is made responsible. What could be more natural,
therefore, than to adapt Josephus' dramatic setting for Titus' decision about the Temple, but to stand the situation on its head?[58]
Josephus will have been familiar to Severus in the famous Latin
version which was known to the monk Cassiodorus and attributed
to Rufinus, Ambrose or Jerome;[59] that Severus *had* read the Jewish
historian is shown by the fact that his figures for total losses in the
siege and capture of Jerusalem derive from Josephus' figures, not
from those of Tacitus (*Chron.* 2.30.5; cf. p. 105 n. 1). So Josephus'
account must have precedence over Severus'.[60]

Bernays held that Sulpicius had as a source the now lost narrative
of the fall of Jerusalem from Tacitus' *Histories*. His proof was that
elsewhere Severus had patently borrowed from Tacitus' account of
Nero in the *Annals*.[61] But use of the *Annals* does not prove knowledge

[56] For this habit, T. D. Barnes, 'Legislation against the Christians', *JRS* 58 (1968),
p. 39, writing on the procedure of Melito and Tertullian.
[57] 2. 31.3, referring to the war of Bar Kosiba.
[58] H. Montefiore, 'Sulpicius Severus and Titus' council of war', *Historia* 11 (1962),
pp. 164–5, correctly analyses Sulpicius' tendency, but goes on surprisingly to conclude that, even if Sulpicius misrepresents what Titus said at the council, he correctly
reports his intentions.
[59] Cassiodorus, *Inst.* 1. 17.1 (ed. Mynors, p. 55).
[60] Cf. Weynand, *RE* 6 (1909), 2703, s.v. Flavius.
[61] Bernays, pp. 168–9.

of the same author's *Histories*.[62] An additional claim made in favour
of Tacitus as the source, that the *Histories* display a predilection for
depicting councils of war (e.g. 2.32, 81; 3.1), is worthless, when so
many historians, from Herodotus on, have used the same device.

Even if Bernays is right, and the story in Severus is Tacitean,
such origins would not endow it with authority, as Tacitus' sources
may well have been inferior ones. To counter this weakness, Bernays
made another proposal: Tacitus, he conjectured, used an eye-witness account of Titus' council of war. We find a mention in the
Octavius, a third-century dialogue of Minucius Felix, of one Antonius
Julianus, said there to be a Roman writer on the Jews, and we are
referred to this writer for further proof of the familiar punishment-
doctrine, that the Jews had deserved whatever misfortunes had
befallen them, and that they had ignored earlier warnings.[63] Who
was Antonius Julianus? The solution, adopted by Bernays, but
propounded already in Tillemont's great history of 1698, is that this
was the procurator M. Antonius Julianus, whom Josephus mentions
as having been present at the crucial council of war. This man *might*
have written an account of the fall of Jerusalem, and is conjectured
to have been Tacitus' source.[64]

In fact, of course, we must remain tentative about the identity of
Antonius Julianus.[65] There was a rhetorician of that name in Hadrian's period, contemporary with Aulus Gellius (*PIR*² A 844); but
we may well be dealing with a figure who is otherwise totally
unknown to us. Yet it is only the pure supposition that the procurator's account, through the mediation of Tacitus, underlies Sulpicius Severus' story about the destruction of the Temple which gives
the latter author any claim to be taken more seriously than
Josephus.

Apart from the literary construction, other types of argument

---

[62] All that can be said is that such knowledge was possible, since in the fifth
century, Orosius still had the *Histories*: see Tac., frag. 3 (Teubner ed., p. 238); C. W.
Mendell, *Tacitus* (1957), pp. 229–32.

[63] Oct. 33, 4: 'scripta eorum relege, vel si Romanis ante gaudes, ut transeamus
veteres, Flavi Iosephi vel Antonii Iuliani de Iudaeis require.' The text is generally
emended by transposing Josephus' name so that he should be classed as a Jewish,
not a Roman writer: 'scripta eorum relege, vel, ut transeamus veteres, Flavi Iosephi,
veil, si Romanis magis gaudes, Antonii Iuliani, de Iudaeis require.' Commentary by
G. Clarke, *The Octavius of Marcus Minucius Felix* (1974), pp. 348–9.

[64] *BJ* 6. 238. E. Hertlein, 'Antonius Julianus, ein römischer Geschichtschreiber?',
Philologus 77 (1921), pp. 174–93, argues against the identification.

[65] So Clarke, loc. cit. (n. 63).

have been used against our author in the wake of Bernays. There are deductions from other passages in the *Jewish War*, such as the various warnings expressed there that the outcome of continued Jewish resistance would be the loss of city and Temple. There is the Roman decision (not, be it noted, ascribed to Titus) to burn all the remaining outbuildings once the Temple was gone (*BJ* 6.281). There are imprecise phrases in other authors, and above all, Valerius Flaccus' description of Titus as 'blackened with the dust of Jerusalem, as he scatters firebrands and wreaks confusion over all its towers'. This poetic passage from the opening of a mythological epic is taken to show that Titus himself, through the mouth of a compliant poet, exulted in the deed of destruction.[66] But neither the portrayal of the Jews and of Josephus himself as fully aware that they risked their Temple by their obduracy, nor Titus' attempt to subdue them with threats, nor the effusive congratulations bestowed upon the conqueror after the events, serve to demonstrate that Titus had not aimed to keep the Temple standing.

Rabbinic literature and Jewish folk memory persistently represent Titus as the wicked agent of destruction, and stories have clustered around the theme of his punishment.[67] These are emotionally compelling, and they may even have had an influence on Bernays (who had been taught the Talmud by his father, the chief Rabbi of Hamburg).[68] But they arose from imagination, not knowledge. The Jews could have had no idea how the Roman decision was reached. Ironically, the same process of personalisation is at work here as in the anti-Jewish Sulpicius Severus. Its unhistorical nature will be apparent from one example: there is a Rabbinic text which tells that Vespasian was present at the siege of Jerusalem (in fact he had left for Rome), and that he attached messages to arrows and sent them to the Jews.[69] Such fictions are characteristic of Aggadic (non-legal) literature. And it is after all, in no way surprising that Jews and non-Jews alike should in retrospect regard the Roman commander as individually responsible for the destruction: for many purposes, it was what happened that mattered, not what nearly happened.

[66] Val. Flacc. 1. 13. These arguments are mustered by G. Alon, 'The burning of the Temple', op. cit. (n. 7), pp. 18–47.

[67] For the legend of the gnat which caused his death by creeping through his nose to his brains, see L. Ginzberg, *Legends of the Jews*, vol. 5 (1925), p. 60, n. 191.

[68] Momigliano, op. cit. (n. 91).

[69] *Avot de Rabbi Nathan*, recension b (Schechter p. 20).

A wider view of Roman policy and interests can show us what is possible, but cannot resolve this problem. In 73, Titus himself did order the demolition of the sectarian Jewish Temple of Onias at Leontopolis;[70] but then, after the main Temple had gone, there was naturally less incentive for concern. Again it could be said that there was evident advantage to Rome in eliminating the focus of Judaism. But equally it would have been in Titus' interest to obtain a Jewish surrender early in the siege rather than to have to fight to the bitter end for city and Temple. And at a later stage, a concession to the high priests and other aristocrats (many of them by now deserters)[71] could ensure their co-operation in the future administration of the country. It is perhaps partly the disappearance of this opportunity for his class (and himself?) which Josephus regrets when he harps upon what might have been. In any case, the balance of probabilities is an even one.

Therefore, as long as it cannot be convincingly impugned, Josephus' story, the best we have, is the one that should stand.[72] We do not have to believe that he knew all that was in Titus' mind nor all that went on at the private council of war. The description of the latter has a flavour of literary convention. Yet it is clear that Josephus would have had ample opportunity to discover the general direction of Titus' thinking—and might, indeed, have been consulted on some points. It is reasonable to follow him.

The theme of Titus' concern for the Temple is perhaps in the end less interesting for the light it sheds on the historical situation, or on Titus, than for what it reveals of Josephus. In his concern with demonstrating that Titus wished to save the Temple, he displays as much preoccupation with the vanished shrine as with Titus' reputation. Wilful destruction would, in Josephus' eyes, have been a great abomination: hence the kind of desperation with which he pleads Titus' innocence. This reflects an attitude which runs right

[70] *BJ* 7. 421–5. Further inconclusive arguments based on Roman strategy in Weiler, op. cit. (n. 52).

[71] Dio, in a plausible guess, represents Titus as offering clemency in order to make a quick end: *Epit.* 66. 4, 1. On desertions, cf. p. 134. Josephus singles out two remarkable men who could have deserted, but preferred to throw themselves into the burning Temple—*BJ* 6. 280; this was unusual. When Titus found priests (not described as high priests) holding out in the Temple, he had them executed, asserting that the time for pardon was over—6. 316–22; But these were probably from the lower ranks.

[72] Dio's story, *Epit.* 66. 6.2, that the Roman soldiers went into the Temple under Titus' orders, but there hesitated out of superstition, deserves no credence.

through his work: he has an attachment to the Temple which is striking and constant, and which survives long after its fall.[73] His respect for the cult as it had been and his distress at its disappearance are perceptible in many places in his writing. He evidently felt it still when he wrote the *Antiquities*—even if not to such an extent that we would class him with those mourners who are castigated in the Talmud for excessive grief.[74] For there is a notable moment in Josephus' rendering of Moses' last instructions to the Israelites, where the author makes a telling addition of his own: the Temple would be destroyed not once, but many times, yet God would restore it in the end (*AJ* 4.311–14, deriving from Deut. 28). This lies in the future. But here what must be recognised is that Josephus' own brand of national feeling, one centred on that established order of which the Temple had been a part, was not diminished by his commitment to the Flavians. And it is with justice that the unusually powerful and controlled description with which he concluded Book 6 of the *Jewish War* and which told of the holy city's final hours became one of the most celebrated in all his work.

We shall return to the loyalist sentiments of Josephus the Jew. Here it should be noted that the theme of Titus' anxiety about the Temple united Josephus' different interests in a rather convenient way. Looking again from the Roman angle, we observe that (irrespective of the truth about the incident), by making compassion (tempered with firmness) into one of Titus' principal attributes, Josephus was ascribing to him what was the monarch's virtue *par excellence*. A philosophical tract on clemency was composed under Nero by the philosopher and politician Seneca; there *misericordia*, perhaps the nearest Latin equivalent to Josephus' *oiktos* (pity) is repeatedly linked with *clementia*.[75] And nobody, at this time, would fail to realise that the display of both these attributes implied absolute power. Thus Josephus depicts Titus just as a fledgling emperor should be depicted. It is easy to exaggerate this point, and the portrait we are discussing is neither a philosophical manifesto, nor the ideal pattern for a *princeps*. Such characterisations are probably no more than an instinctive echo of themes heard by Josephus, at

[73] Evidence in H. Guttmann, *Die Darstellung der jüdischen Religion bei Flavius Josephus* (1928), pp. 27–32.

[74] *TB Baba Batra* 60b (Soncino translation, vol. 1, pp. 245–6).

[75] Cf. Yavetz, op. cit. (n. 25), pointing out that Titus as ruler had to overcome a reputation for viciousness and cruelty in his early life. On *clementia*: M. P. Charlesworth, *The Virtues of a Roman Emperor: Propaganda and the Creation of Belief* (1937), p. 11; A. Traube, *Clementia Principis* (1970), pp. 24ff.

court or elsewhere. None the less, the nature of the compliment which he pays to Titus is unmistakeable and characteristic of the literature of the period.

We are on more slippery ground if we seek the precise reason why Josephus (and others too) made the son and not the father emerge as the monarchical figure. That Josephus' history was published while Vespasian was still in power cannot be doubted (see p. 000). Did those who moved in imperial circles understand that it was politic to direct towards Titus that adulation in which the plain man, Vespasian, professed little interest? On Titus' position, after all, rested the dynasty's hope of continuance; and this was a matter of such importance to Vespasian that he was said to have burst into tears when his elder son's succession was challenged (Dio *Epit.* 65.12; cf. Suet. *Vesp.* 25). Or was it that in this case Josephus was influenced by his own personal relationship with the young man? The two explanations are not, of course, incompatible.

The *Jewish War* was not simply the scene of Vespasian's and Titus' great military triumph; it was also the spark which fired their ascent to power. Josephus had to decide whether to tell that story too, and how much space to give to it. One thing is clear. His work does not centre on the emergence of the new dynasty. The historian announces that he is summarising the upheavals in Rome and the successive seizures of power which followed Nero's death only so as to avoid breaking up his story; and that is on the whole a fair description of the situation (*BJ* 4.496). He does this by keeping track of Flavian movements; Titus is first sent by his father to acclaim Nero's successor Galba, but when news reaches him in Greece that Otho has taken over, he decides to go back to Palestine (4.491–502). The subject is taken up again a little later, when Vespasian, having reduced the surroundings of Jerusalem, hears that yet another emperor rules, Vitellius this time. This is the point at which Josephus puts the beginning of Flavian progress. The final eighth of Book 4 has Vespasian acclaimed emperor by the legions of Alexandria and Judaea, his first appointments and his journey back to Rome, as well as some major military and political developments in Italy.[76] We read about Vespasian's departure from Alexandria, with Titus left behind to finish off the Jewish war; and

---

[76] The defeat of Vitellius' men near Cremona; Caecina's treachery to Vitellius, and the sack of that city; the failure of Flavius Sabinus and Domitian to hold the Capitol; Sabinus' execution; Vitellius' degrading death; the arrival of Mucianus. See Briessmann, op. cit. (n. 9).

about the return march, and the many festivities which punctuated the new ruler's progress. Not until the last of Josephus' seven books do we pick up Vespasian again, still on his journey; and there we find Titus at Caesarea Philippi, where he has been throwing spectacles for the people in which Jewish captives played a prominent part, to celebrate an imperial birthday.

A historian whose angle was narrowly Jewish would not have recounted these events, or, at any rate, not in this way. Yet, while peripheral, they do offer information which the reader naturally seeks, for there is something remarkable and perplexing about the sudden elevation of the leading Roman in the war, and his consequent removal from the scene. Moreover, the story of Josephus' prophecy and its fulfilment has established a link between the fate of the emperor and that of the Jews. At the same time, Josephus could expect such non-Jewish readers as he had to find matter of such public importance a welcome diversion from Judaea and its problems. Josephus' access to Roman events is thus in some respects an asset to his narrative.

As for the detail of his account, it clearly represents a version of the story which is highly favourable to the Flavians, and sometimes untrue. Their seizure of power is described as a direct response to the state's needs: the inadequacies manifested by Vitellius during the few months of his rule had greatly distressed Vespasian; the rest was due to the troops. They felt that they had as much right as the German legions to choose an emperor, and would have killed their leader had he resisted. He himself would have preferred to remain a private citizen (*BJ* 4.588ff.). Alexandria followed Judaea, for when Tiberius Julius Alexander heard the news, he induced his two legions to take the oath of allegiance to the new emperor. We do not need Tacitus' rather different version to make us realise that the accession must have been designed with more forethought and deliberation than Josephus' account allows; and it emerges from between the lines that Titus' return to the east after Galba's death was a public declaration of Flavian ambitions. Tacitus makes this a turning point; and even Suetonius perceives that Vespasian's aspirations must have taken shape straight after the death of Galba.[77] Tiberius Julius Alexander's understanding with Vespasian

---

[77] Tac. *Hist.* 2. 6.2; Suet. *Vesp.* 5.1. Even earlier, the reconciliation between Vespasian and the legate of Syria, Mucianus, which Titus had effected, was a crucial first step: Tac. *Hist.* 2. 5.2.

is shown by these authors to have made such aspirations feasible, and Tiberius' troops are rightly said to have declared their will not after, but two days before the three Judaean legions.[78] Tacitus agrees with Josephus on only one point: that the declaration of the latter was spontaneous, and required no prearrangement.

Josephus' version of these political machinations is more pro-Flavian than any other which survives. But its twists and details are due as much to the author's source as to any deliberate argument on his part, and I do not think that Josephus personally had any concern with the finer points of the Flavian case or that he consciously contradicted other, less favourable accounts. The effect has come through his dependence at such points on source material of a pure Flavian character, and that material was probably the imperial records.

Josephus speaks once of the *commentarii* (notebooks) of Vespasian, citing them as authority for his own claim that his antagonist Justus of Tiberias had been implicated in a raid on the Decapolis region. He refers once to the 'notebooks of Caesar', as an authority which Justus had not consulted on the subject of the siege of Jerusalem. And on one occasion there is talk of the 'notebooks of the emperors' (*tōn autokratorōn*), described as a work which had been read by some of his detractors (*V* 342, 358; *CA* 1.56). This last reference suggests that the first part of the war had been covered by Vespasian, the second by Titus. The emperors' reports must have been available for consultation, even if not issued to the public. Although they are never mentioned in the *War*, it is more than likely that they were produced soon after the events with which they deal, and that our author had easy access to them because of his privileged position.[79]

He did not, however, over-use this source.[80] His criticism of Justus for ignorance of the notebooks does not mean that he himself was

---

[78] Tac. *Hist.* 2. 74, 79; Nicols, op. cit. (n. 2), p. 73; Henrichs, op. cit. (n. 8), p. 79.

[79] The argument of von Gutschmid, that Josephus could not have criticised previous historians of the war as sharply as he did in his preface had the *commentarii* then been known overlooks the point that generals' war reports were regarded not as history but simply as the raw material for historians; so Cicero, in a famous sentence, *Brutus* 261–2; see A. von Gutschmid, *Kleine Schriften* 4 (1893), p. 346.

[80] Weber's case for extensive utilisation, op. cit. (n. 14), rests on an elaborate series of hypotheses, developed through his book. Criticisms by R. Laqueur, *Phil. Wochenschrift* 41 (1921), pp. 1105–14. But Weber has been influential, and is now revived by H. Lindner, *Die Geschichtsauffassung des Flavius Josephus im Bellum Judaicum* (1970), esp. ch. 5.

slavishly dependent. Unlike Justus, he was either an eye-witness or
close to the crucial events almost all the time, and he was the last
person to need to plunder another account. [81] He confined his debt
to specific kinds of material. The Flavian passages are among the
most obvious, but military records could also provide exact information associated with the Roman campaign—measurements of
distance, dates, topographical descriptions, the names of Roman
soldiers (and perhaps even of Jews) who performed distinguished
feats of valour. Then there are Josephus' topographical excurses,
descriptions of the Jordan Valley and the Dead Sea, Egypt and the
port of Alexandria, Jerusalem and the Temple, Herod's palaces on
Masada, the fortress of Machaerus. Their level of accuracy is rather
high; and since, given the circumstances of composition, he can
hardly have surveyed the sites himself, these probably come out of
the Roman account. [82] All this was valuable, lending variety ot
Josephus' composition, and giving it the air of a proper war history.
But, whereas the *commentarii* were once thought to be the key to
understanding Josephus, it is now clear that such a key cannot
unlock so involved an author.

It is only when Josephus reaches the seventh and final portion of
his history that the Flavian material acquires a greater role in the
economy of his writing. One reason for this springs to mind. Book
7 opens with the razing to the ground of the holy city's defences.
Josephus' story is all but told. Book 6 has concluded with a solemn
epilogue, a retrospect on the history of Jerusalem from its foundation
by Melchizedek. And now he has to cast about for more material.
He needs to plug the surprisingly long gap between the fall of
Jerusalem and the subjugation of Masada in 73. [83] Reports of the
doings of Vespasian and Titus and members of their party, incidental to Josephus' main theme, come in very usefully for this
purpose. And Josephus manages to provide a satisfactory link by
making the events a reminder that Judaea was not at this time the
world's only trouble spot: every part of the Roman empire was in

---

[81] His advantage is pointed out by Josephus himself: *BJ* 1. 3; *CA* 1. 56.

[82] Nicols, op. cit. (n. 2), pp. 44–5, with a detailed and plausible argument as to
Josephus' dependence on the *commentarii* for his dates, which Nicols takes as trans-
literations of Julian dates. On topography, Weber, op. cit. (n. 14), pp. 142–8. The
excursuses, promised in Josephus' preface (1. 22), are at *BJ* 4. 471–85, 607–15; 5.
136–237; 7. 164–89, 280–303. But contrast 5. 570, where a different sort of 'precise'
figure, the number of corpses thrown out of the city, comes to Josephus directly,
from deserters.

[83] On this date, see p. 174, n. 1.

a state of turmoil and panic (*BJ* 7.79). So, after the capture of Simon bar Giora, we read about the Flavian family birthdays; the revolts of Classicus and Civilis in Gaul and Germany; and the Sarmatian attack on the empire, with the successful resistance of Domitian and of Q. Petilius Cerealis who was his relative. We also learn how Titus preserved the privileges of the Jews of Antioch, a theme rather more germane to the history and to its author.[84] However, there were also more acute and sensitive problems attached to framing a concluding book for the *Jewish War*. How was the Roman victory to be handled? There could be no evasion here. However free his patrons usually left him, Josephus could be sure that they would look for an account of the triumph in which *Judaea Capta* was the leading motif. This he did not deny them. The first part of Book 7 has two big set-pieces of description which make an important contribution to the total effect of his work. The first is the enthusiastic reception of the victorious Vespasian in Italy, the second and longer price is the triumph itself, at which Josephus may even have been present. Of these two scenes Vespasian and (in the second one) Titus are the resplendent centre-pieces, and we find in them an intensification of the aura which has throughout invested the imperial figures.

The Roman populace is overjoyed at Vespasian's return, and the whole of Italy begins to exult before he is anywhere to be seen. Senate, people and army are delighted with the *dignitas* and military distinction of their new ruler. The roads and the city are thronged with people. Vespasian is hailed as benefactor and saviour. There is feasting, libations are poured and prayers offered; we learn that this was the beginning of a new prosperity for Rome. The description is extravagant. It is echoed in briefer compass on Titus' return when, according to Josephus, a similar welcome was offered, better this time in that Vespasian could participate in it, and, since Domitian was present as well, all three Flavians were now reunited (*BJ* 7.63–74, 119–20).

The scene of a formal entrance (*adventus*) closely akin to these is depicted for us in another medium. It is to be found in stone, in one of the marble panels (B) discovered at Rome in the Palazzo della Cancelleria in 1938. The subject has been identified as Vespasian's return, and the contents are a fusion of Josephus' two scenes. As in Josephus, senate and people—here in the form of

---

[84] And pointing towards his future concerns, see p. 225.

figures representing the *genius senatus* and the *genius populi Romani*—
are there to greet him. At the same time, the theme stressed by
Josephus in connection with Titus' arrival, that of a family harmoniously reunited, is illustrated here too, with Domitian doing his
filial duty and responding to a greeting of his father—albeit, as
some would have it, a little coldly. The suggestion that the two men
were represented together in order to refute rumours of rivalry and
hostility between them is an attractive one;[85] and the same might
be said of Josephus' insistence on the closeness of the three.[86]
Whether both Josephus and the sculptor were influenced by passages in the imperial notebooks, or whether the idea percolated to
them in some other way does not matter: it is clear that each is
presenting things the way the dynasty wanted.

Titus' return was followed by preparations for his military
triumph, and then by the triumph itself. Josephus portrays it vividly
and elaborately, moment by moment and gesture by gesture, and
envisages it as a reflection of the empire's greatness.[87] This triumph
was another prominent motif in Flavian propaganda. Perhaps inspired by Titus' arch, art and poetry in the Flavian period shows
a fondness for triumphal scenes and victory processions, both real
and mythological.[88] Furthermore, the great day could be taken as
a celebration of the end of Rome's civil wars and the inauguration
of an era of peace. So, as we might expect, Josephus does not neglect
this implication, but looks forward to the year 75 and the dedication
of the Flavian Temple of Pax. It was this Peace Temple which was
to house, among its trophies, the Menorah from Jerusalem and the
other ritual objects represented on the arch and previously described
by Josephus as part of the procession. Thus the writer coolly depicts
the symbolic expressions of his country's ruin. The Jews are now
referred to as 'the enemy'. And it is as though the sufferings which
they had endured and over which he had expressed his grief, now

[85] J. M. C. Toynbee, *The Flavian Reliefs from the Palazzo della Cancelleria* (1957),
esp. pp. 5–6; Richmond, op. cit. (n. 45), pp. 221ff.; F. Magi, *I rilievi flavi del Palazzo
della Cancelleria* (1945), pp. 106ff. For rumours of hostility, Tac. *Hist.* 4. 51—Vespasian hurries back to Italy to curb Domitian who is in charge of Rome; Dio *Epit.*
66. 9.3; and cf. Richmond.
[86] Titus' loyalty was also suspect, with rumours that he had been building a power
base in the east: Suet. *Tit.* 5.3.
[87] *BJ* 7. 133: 'all the wonderful and rich objects displayed together on that day
... demonstrated the might of the Roman empire.' The sentiment is not reiterated.
[88] A-M Taisne, 'Le thème du triomphe sous les Flaviens', *Latomus* 32 (1973), pp.
485–504.

exist only as tableaux, themes figured in golden tapestries and framed in ivory, contributions to the triumphal pomp.[89]

Here, the balance of Josephus' writing has shifted. The splendour of the Roman generals' display cannot be appropriate to a Jew's account of his nation's downfall; Josephus' admiration must be admitted as out of keeping with the reactions he had previously evinced, and only the triumph's conclusion, the execution of Simon bar Giora as the token enemy leader, can have given him any personal pleasure in the relating. Certainly, as a subject, the Roman triumph offered fine opportunities to the literary artist to exhibit his talent, and to Greeks to read about a famous Roman custom, with its religious and topographical associations;[90] but that does not reduce the dissonance. Here Josephus can for the first time be said to glorify his patrons at the expense of his people.

Yet the historian evidently sought to redress the balance, at least to an extent; and Book 7 is noteworthy also for an increased intensity of Jewish patriotism. The triumph is followed by yet another great set-piece, the fall of Masada, with the courageous exploits and final suicides of its defenders.

It seems clear that Josephus had no direct information about the last stand of Eleazar's *sicarii* against the siege of Flavius Silva. Military activities are described entirely from the Roman sources—presumably the imperial notebooks again.[91] Information about the defenders, and the way in which the last 959 committed suicide, must have been given to the Romans by the two women of whose escape Josephus tells us; this perhaps then circulated among Romans by word of mouth. But the organisation of the Jews and the conduct of their resistance remains a closed book even after this century's excavations.[92] None the less, Josephus took an unexpected step: with an act of imagination he put himself among the defenders,

---

[89] *BJ* 7. 142–7. See also 6. 418—the tallest of the young men captured in Jerusalem reserved for the triumph.

[90] Cf. the presentation by Plutarch, *Aemilius Paullus* 32–4, (where there is more pity for the conquered in the procession than Josephus has). And note, at *BJ* 7. 123–32, the details given of the preliminary ritual and of its setting amongst Rome's public buildings.

[91] The Roman angle: *BJ* 7. 252, 275–9, 304–19. The digression on the Jewish revolutionaries, 7. 254–7, is, of course, a personal addition.

[92] See Y. Yadin, *Masada: Herod's Fortress and the Zealots' Last Stand* (1966): L. H. Feldman, 'Masada: a critique of recent scholarship', in *Christianity, Judaism and Other Greco-Roman Cults: Studies for Morton Smith at Sixty* (ed. J. Neusner), vol. 3 (1975), pp. 214–48.

and transformed that final scene into an extended dramatic narrative.

The framework of the story can safely be accepted as true. This we can say, not because archaeology has been able to confirm the events themselves—we could hardly expect this—but rather because the creation of so elaborate a fiction, either by Josephus or by a predecessor, is too hard to credit.[93] The twenty-five skeletons found by the excavators on a lower terrace of Herod's northern palace may or may not be those of survivors. The eleven *ostraka* which they unearthed and one of which appears to say ben Yair may or may not be the lots drawn by those designated to kill their comrades and families. Josephus' narrative does not stand or fall with these identifications. And the over-ingenious theory that the suicide was an apologetic invention designed to assuage Josephus' unconscious guilt, to conceal a Roman massacre or for some similar purpose, is best left to bury itself.[94]

Josephus did not invent the Masada incident, though he did embody it in a form which has given it lasting resonance, a continuing power both to inspire and to annoy.[95] And he did create two important speeches for Eleazar. For all their debt to Greek philosophy, these speeches, in so vivid a context, stand out as designed to evoke in the reader respect for the man who is made to utter them.[96] Eleazar and his companions are at the last made into virtual heroes by Josephus, and it is as though the author has forgotten his former abhorrence of such people and their ideals.

While the Roman scene of the triumph has been conspicuous for its external glitter, the Jewish episode is the more powerful. As a literary contrast, this is well-contrived. For all that, we may fancy

---

[93] The excavators are accused, sometimes unjustly, of treating their finds as a confirmation of Josephus' story, by P. Vidal-Naquet, *Flavius-Josèphe ou du bon usage de la trahison*, appx., and in *Les Juifs, la mémoire et le présent* (1981), pp. 43–72.

[94] Proposed by T. Weiss-Rosmarin in various journals: see Feldman, op. cit. (n. 92), pp. 239–43, and in a different form, by E. M. Smallwood, *The Jews under Roman Rule* (1976), p. 338 (acknowledging Morton Smith). A detailed refutation in Feldman, and brief criticisms by D. J. Ladouceur, 'Masada: a consideration of the literary evidence', *GRBS* 21 (1980), pp. 246–7.

[95] See Feldman, op. cit. (n. 92), referring to discussions of the 'Masada complex' in the consciousness of the modern Israeli; and note the irritation of Vidal-Naquet, op. cit. (n. 93).

[96] Ladouceur, op. cit. (n. 94) argues that they are meant as examples of a morbid love of death, which would be instantly rejected by those familiar with Roman philosophical and political debates; but this sophisticated Roman context is not that of Josephus. And Josephus speaks explicitly of the nobility of the action, e.g. 7. 406.

that it was not aesthetic considerations but a serious uneasiness on Josephus' part about his handling of the triumph which drew him to provide a counterweight. That he allocates a prominent position in his final book to the fate of the Masada remnant, when he could well have closed with the end of the war proper and the triumph of 71, reveals as much about his commitments as does the portrayal of the procession at Rome. And even Masada is not the very end. The *Jewish War* terminates in the death of a persecutor; there is a lurid description of the disease which afflicted the Roman governor of Libya after he had executed perhaps 3,000 (wealthy) Jews on a false charge of revolutionary activity, and had dragged others in chains to Rome. That, too, does not seem accidental.

It is characteristic of Josephus to seek to reconcile different allegiances, just as it had been the hallmark of the social group to which he had belonged. There are, of course, times when conflicting claims simply cannot be made compatible, and in Josephus the occasion of the Roman triumph is one such. But he does not give up. The pull of the Flavians is not made to supersede earlier loyalties, and adulation of the emperors is rarely close to the heart of his work. Though we cannot altogether eliminate that disturbing figure, Josephus the flatterer of the conquering emperors, this Josephus must be put in his place.

There is no doubt that his multiple-responsiveness created for Josephus problems which were ultimately insoluble, in his writing as much as in his short-lived political career. The very act of redressing with a sequel of praise for his compatriots the pro-Flavian balance which he had produced by dwelling on the triumph brings with it its own inconsistencies. For the Jews of Masada, whose story he exploits for this purpose and whom he holds up momentarily for our admiration, are among those whom he most hates. Even in Book 7 we can still find harsh condemnation of the *sicarii*, as part of the author's retrospective castigation of all the rebel groups (see p. 81). But when the year 73 is reached, and the war contains no other Jewish protagonists, animosity has to be suspended. We might see this as yet another effect of the disappearance among Jews of a political middle ground; now there was really no other position which a moderate could take. This has a counterpart: after the war, Romans too perceived Jews as of one kind only, and this emerges clearly from a grotesque incident recorded by Josephus. It was probably still in A.D. 73 that the revolt of *sicarii* from Palestine, led by a weaver named Jonathan, was suppressed at Cyrene by the local Roman governor; apart from 3,000 wealthy local Jews, notables from Alexandria and Rome were incriminated, and among them Josephus himself. Such an attack is astonishing, even if our author was later cleared, and not, like Jonathan, tortured and burned alive. Still, a vestige of the old divisions among Jews survives, emerging in the fact that, while Josephus reserves his greatest enthusiasm for the governor's appropriately gruesome end, he expresses also some satisfaction at the rebel Jonathan's punishment: his old eagerness to dissociate himself from undesirable Jews has not entirely gone (*BJ* 7.437–50; *V* 424).

Masada, then, eases one difficulty, but makes another for its narrator. And the last book of the *Jewish War*, like its predecessors, originates not in detached observation, but in intense involvement, and strong, if not particularly deep reactions. No longer, however, is the historian writing from a firm standpoint, with a clear set of political prejudices. Now contemplating the aftermath of the revolt, he is tossed to and fro, extending emotion in various directions. Along with his homeland, he has for a time lost his firm mental anchorage, and here his writing shows it. In this way it continues to be an immediate product of pressing circumstances, and to illuminate them through the strong responses expressed in it, and even through its weaknesses as history and literature.

Epilogue: The Later Josephus

The main part of Josephus' writing career was still in front of him after he had finished the *Jewish War*; and he still had some twenty years to live—exactly how many we do not know, since there is no indication anywhere of the date of his death. He had, no doubt, to continue integrating himself into his new environment. Not only was he to stay on in Rome, cut off from Palestine, with the Temple that had formed the centre of his existence now a thing of the past, but he had, increasingly, to stand on his own feet. For the assistance provided by the emperors seems to have diminished. In 79, Titus succeeded Vespasian; but by 81 he too was dead. And while Titus' brother Domitian continued to protect Josephus by punishing people who slandered him, and to remunerate him by exempting his Judaean property from tax, he does not seem to have taken an interest in his work (*V* 429). The later productions—the *Antiquities* with the appended *Life*, and *Against Apion*—had a new patron: his name was Epaphroditus, and he was probably a freedman bibliophile of Alexandrian provenance. A more remote possibility is that he was Nero's well-known freedman of that name, who assisted the emperor in his suicide and was eventually sentenced to death by another tyrannical master, Domitian, in A.D.95. But the former identification is the better since the latter makes considerable difficulties for the chronology of Josephus' works. In any case, the name Epaphroditus is certainly that of a freedman, and a freedman, however rich, would be to some extent despised by the best society at Rome. Of the bibliophile Epaphroditus we are told that he was 'big, dark and like an elephant', so that some have thought that he was in fact a negro (and also a sufferer from dropsy). If the patron was something of an outsider, the protégé, Josephus, is likely to have been too. At the same time, our author's resourcefulness had apparently not deserted him. Epaphroditus had known many

vicissitudes in his life and was interested in an unusually wide
variety of matters;[1] Josephus managed to appeal to him by carving out
for himself an original subject. He put himself forward as the man
who could set the whole of Jewish history before a pagan public.

Further than this, there is very little we can say about Josephus
the man in the latter part of his life. Only inference, and contrast
or comparison with what has gone before, provide a tenuous foot-
hold. It has become conventional to speak in terms of change and
development in the author.[2] Up to a point, this is reasonable. No
longer was Josephus at the apex of a social pyramid. The Jerusalem
priesthood had, as a group, ceased to exist: we might say that class
consciousness is less acute in the late Josephus. Then again, he had
once been a prominent politician, or on the road to becoming one.
Now the only political activity in which he engaged was of a more
oblique kind, making out through his writings the case for the
privileges of Jewish communities in the Roman empire. And even
in this cause we do not hear of any direct advocacy or diplomatic
activity of the kind that Herod's historian Nicolaus of Damascus
had performed a century earlier.[3] Certainly, there was no more
fighting for Josephus now; and we may imagine him to have been
thankful that the days of his generalship were over.

For all that, I doubt whether Josephus was a man who underwent
any radical internal alteration in the course of his life. One striking
consequence of the portrait which has evolved through the course
of this book is that leading features in the late Josephus now emerge
as already there in the early days. Thus the evidence suggested that
he really was a Pharisee from the age of nineteen: he had accepted
his family's traditional creed, after a little prevarication, and he did
not have to wait until, with the fall of the Temple, Pharisaism
became the fashionable or perhaps the only tendency.[4] Again, at

---

[1] Epaphroditus the *grammaticus*: see the Suda, s.v. 'Epaphroditus', and probably,
CIL 6. 9454. His patron, named by the Suda as 'Modestus the Prefect of Egypt',
was probably one of the Mettii prominent under Domitian. Nero's freedman, Epaphroditus, was executed not later than A.D.95; and if the *Antiquities* came out in 93
(see Appendix 3), this scarcely leaves time for Josephus to observe reactions to them,
and to follow up with the two books of *Against Apion*, while the dedicatee was still
alive.

[2] Especially under the influence of R. Laqueur, *Der jüdische Historiker Flavius
Josephus* (1920); and now see S. J. D. Cohen's *Josephus in Galilee and Rome* (1979).

[3] Nicolaus' activities both before and after Herod's death, are recorded by Josephus in *AJ* 16 and 17.

[4] See pp. 33f., and contrast the views of J. Neusner, 'Josephus' Pharisees', *Ex Orbe
Religionum: Studia Geo Widengren Oblata I* (1972), pp. 224–44.

the heart of his political position was always the conviction that co-operation and harmony were possible between Judaism and the Gentile world—especially, of course, with the Gentile power of Rome, and the administrators who represented it. The latter part of the *Antiquities* shows that Josephus continued to believe in the value to Jews of Roman protection and, more generally, in the need for good relations with those around them, wishing 'to reconcile the nations and to remove the causes of hatred'.[5] There is just a shift in emphasis: in the later phase, his Diaspora vantage point leads Josephus to concentrate more on external relations, and thus to be concerned with apologetics—the presentation of Judaism to outsiders. This brought him to be more than ever aware of the desirability of finding common ground with the Greek-speaking orientals among whom much of Jewry lived: and these, apart from his own compatriots, must have constituted the expected readership of his *Antiquities*.

Equally, there had always been awareness of the importance to Jews of the use of the Greek language: it was this which had made possible Josephus' appointment as a young ambassador from Jerusalem to Rome. All that happened after 67 was that Greek, of necessity, played a growing part in Josephus' life, and it was by a gradual development that Greek literature too became an interest.

We can detect also another change of emphasis, which could not be called a new and different direction. Once more, this is an aspect of Josephus' culture. His last published work, *Against Apion*, is a skilful demonstration of the greater antiquity and general superiority of Jewish traditions, law and practices over those of the Greeks. But it is not chauvinistic or narrow, and Josephus often makes his points by aligning Jewish history with that of other oriental peoples. He cites with approbation various middle eastern historians who had put their native records into Greek, chiefly Berossus the Babylonian astronomer and priest of Bel, Manetho the renowned Egyptian priest, Menander of Ephesus, and some Phoenicians who had drawn on the archives of Tyre.[6] He seems at home among such writers, and one has the impression that the literary world of partly Hellenized orientals to which they belonged was not alien to him.

---

[5] *AJ* 16. 175, explaining his citation of pro-Jewish decrees.
[6] *CA* 1. 75–92 (and criticism of Manetho at 1. 227–87); 1. 129–53; 1. 112–15 (Dius the Phoenician, also at *AJ* 8. 147); 1. 144 (Philostratus); 1. 116 (Menander of Ephesus); and cf. *AJ* 1. 107.

That this was a cultural milieu which had a real existence, may be proved by looking forward: a number of the Church Fathers also participate in it, and the early apologists were soon to follow in Josephus' footsteps, quarrying from those same native authors and from others like them in exactly the same way as he had done, and yet at least in part independently of him.[7] Thus, in the composition of *Against Apion*, Josephus seems, while living at Rome, to be looking eastwards. If this is so, we have identified a connection which can be traced back to Josephus' beginnings as a writer, when he had addressed that same world in its principal native language, with the first, Aramaic, version of the *Jewish War*.

Both *Jewish Wars*, the Aramaic and the Greek, had been written under stress, a personal response to events which had a strong impact on Josephus, not a neutral record, and not a version produced to satisfy others. Indeed, it would seem that a preoccupation with the revolt, and the consequent destruction, lingered on, finding expression in his return almost twenty years later to the events of A.D.67 (in the *Life*). What had occurred was truly overwhelming, and it would not be surprising if even Josephus could not put it entirely behind him.

But, of course, as an author he would move on and treat other matters. It might be said, however, that the spirit was still the same. For both the pro-Jewish apologetics of the *Antiquities* and the vituperation of the *Against Apion* are in a similar way literary responses to real problems, this time in the eighties and nineties. The evidence is too poor for us to know exactly what was happening, but various difficulties are apparent. It is clear that the years 66–73 had already produced a crisis in relations between Jews and Greeks in cities both inside and outside Palestine, and Josephus had recorded a number of conflicts which were sometimes the precursor and sometimes the consequence of the great revolt against Rome (*BJ* 2.457–98; 7.41–62 etc.). These were naturally exacerbated after the humiliating defeat of the rebels in Palestine, which will have encouraged the Greeks and destroyed the confidence of Jews of every type. Above all, Greeks were emboldened by the probability that Rome would now cease to offer her support, customary since Julius Caesar, for the maintenance of Jewish rights in the cities of the east. Thus, for example, when Titus visited Antioch in Syria,

---

[7] Theophilus, *To Autolycus*, 3. 23; Tatian, *To the Greeks* 4, 10, 40; Origen, *Against Celsus* 1. 16; 4. 11. Only some of the citations in question are from Josephus.

a mass of inhabitants greeted him, and requested first the expulsion of the Jews from the city and then, when that request fell upon deaf ears, the removal of the bronze tablets on which the people had recorded grants made to the Jews (*BJ* 7.100ff.). Antioch is also the source of a story which is not in Josephus, but which, even if fictitious, provides a symbolic reflection of the consequences of the Jewish defeat. John Malalas the later local historian has it that Titus gave Jewish spoils to the people of Antioch as a gift; and outside the city gates, on the road to Daphne, they set up great bronze figures meant to represent the cherubim from the Temple; while on the gates themselves was a bronze group of a moon and four bulls facing Jerusalem (Malalas 260–1).

It seems that imperial protection did not totally lapse under Vespasian and Titus; but Vespasian's transference of the Temple tax of two drachmas per person to the *fiscus Iudaicus*—a part of the imperial treasury—and its dedication to Capitoline Zeus effectively altered the status of the Jews from that of a privileged minority to that of one visibly treated with particular severity.[8] The succession of Titus' harsh brother Domitian made matters worse, as is suggested by the famous episode in Suetonius' *Life of Domitian* (12.2) of the examination of an old man to see if he was liable for the levy. Josephus may not have lived to see the coins issued by Domitian's successor, Nerva, claiming that abuses had been eliminated from the Jewish *fiscus*.[9]

During this whole period, with the loss of the Temple and the community of high priests and scholars which previously, from Jerusalem, had provided a focal point for Jews everywhere (whether or not they made pilgrimages, and many did), the Diaspora will have had to fall back on its own resources. The transformation of Pharisaism into Rabbinic Judaism did not occur overnight. In the interim, the establishment of a satisfactory *modus vivendi* for Jews in the cities, who now had nowhere to turn for support and sustenance, will have seemed particularly important. The Diaspora Jewish élites had had especially close social and political ties with

[8] On the *fiscus Iudaicus*, E. M. Smallwood, *The Jews under Roman Rule* (1976), pp. 376–8.
[9] FISCI IUDAICI CALUMNIA SUBLATA; see Smallwood, p. 378. The story in Eusebius, *Hist. Eccl.* 3. 12ff., taken from Hegesippus, of a large-scale Jewish persecution under Vespasian, continued under Domitian and Trajan, is greatly exaggerated, and dominated by the Christian notion that this was an attempt to extirpate the Davidic royal line.

Jerusalem high priestly families, and so they above all would be deprived. The urgency of the need for some sort of resolution of their problem can perhaps best be measured by the consequences of the failure to find one—the desperate fury of the Jewish revolts under Trajan, when during a period of about two years (115–17), in Cyrene, Egypt and Cyprus, as well as to a lesser extent in Mesopotamia, the Jews were to turn with amazing and indiscriminate violence, on civilians and soldiers, temples and property.

None the less, until the Trajanic revolt, there were still some grounds for hope, and an encouraging development was the spread of interest, among different types of people, in monotheism in general and Judaism in particular. At one level, there were Domitian's own relations, the parents of his intended heirs, Flavius Clemens the consul and his wife Domitilla: the formal cause for their execution and relegation (respectively) was a charge of godlessness, that is, disrespect for the Roman pantheon, and for Domitian's claimed divinity (Dio 67.14). At the other, the popular Stoic philosopher Epictetus is recorded as using as an example of imposture, the man who, while remaining unbaptized, toys with Judaism, so that others say of him, 'he is not a Jew, just acting the part' (*ap.* Arrian 2.9, 19–21). This proves both that Judaism was very appealing to certain types, and that it was thoroughly familiar to the general public. Likewise, Epaphroditus, Josephus' patron, must have had some sort of interest in Jewish matters, whether or not he was personally drawn to the religion.

This was the background against which the later Josephus wrote; and this explains why he thought it worth combating general ignorance of Jewish origins, and trying to make his national history acceptable and impressive to those whose taste was Greek.[10] This was why he sought to offer evidence of his own people's successes and of pagan respect. This was why, above all in the fourteenth book of the *Antiquities*, he set out a succession of documents demonstrating that Jews had traditionally been allowed both by rulers (especially the Caesars) and by city authorities, to practise their own customs unmolested and to be exempted from such public requirements as ran counter to their religion.[11]

A poor response to the *Antiquities* (*CA* 1.2–3) led him next, in the

---

[10] See the general statement at *AJ* 1. 5–6; 20. 263; and such incidental explanations of Jewish phenomena in Greek terms as *AJ* 3. 139.

[11] See especially the statements at *AJ* 14. 186–8 and 14. 267.

Against Apion, to present some of the same themes in a more aggress-
ive way, insisting now on the greater venerability and morality of
Jewish law and practice as contrasted with Greek, picking out
passages from Greek authors which seemed to recognise the antiquity of the Jewish people, criticising anti-Jewish statements made
by hostile Greek authors, and several times making the emotive
claim that the Jews were unique because, in the last resort, they
were prepared to die for their laws.[12] We may view this final phase
as a new expression of the patriotism which had underlain his
narrative of the fall of the Temple and of Masada, in the *Jewish
War*.

Here too, then, there was evolution rather than transformation.
And we find Josephus still writing, as he had done previously, with
a strong sense of purpose, convinced of the justice of his own
position. At the same time, this remained coupled, especially in the
Against Apion, with the respect for veracious historiography which
he had always professed and sometimes exemplified; and also with
a genuinely enquiring approach to the past,[13] which gives some
justification to his reputation among later readers as *philalēthes*,
lover of truth.[14]

Whether Josephus felt, in the end, that he had made a successful
case in any of his works, and that he had achieved something of
what he had set out to do; whether he died admired or ignored, we
do not know. In later days, a statue to him was to be seen at Rome
but, in all probability, it was erected not by Romans, or Greeks, or
Jews, but by Christians (Eus., *Hist. Eccl.* 3.9; Jerome, *de Vir Ill.* 13).

[12] Martyrdom: *CA* 1. 42–3; 2. 232–4, 272.
[13] The preface to *Against Apion* continues an interesting and intelligent (even
somewhat partial and boastful) contrast between the Jewish and the Greek historical
traditions.
[14] By Isidore of Pelusium, George Cedrenus and (sometimes in other words)
various others. See H. Schreckenberg, *Die Flavius-Josephus-Tradition in Antike und
Mittelalter* (1972), pp. 97, 104, 135–138 etc. Of course, the Christians had their own
reasons, and were influenced largely by the presence in their texts of the reference
to Jesus Christ known as the *testimonium flavianum*.

1. The native language of Josephus

The question of whether Josephus in Jerusalem habitually spoke Hebrew, or Aramaic, or both languages to an equal extent, cannot be resolved with any certainty. The problems are summarised here.

(1) There is no longer any doubt that Hebrew remained a spoken language down to the Mishnaic period.[1] How widely it was spoken and for what purposes is still obscure;[2] but we must envisage Palestine as, if not a bilingual or trilingual society then at least a diglossic one—one, that is to say, where two or more languages are in use for different kinds of social communication: each has its own functions, to which individual users are instinctively sensitive.[3] However, the picture of the relationship between the languages in such cases is too varied for any precise conclusions about Josephus to be deduceable from it.

(2) Josephus refers twice to something which he calls his own native language: the original version of the *War* was composed 'in his native tongue' (*BJ* 1. 3); and he was sent by the Romans to parley with the besieged Jews, 'to converse in his native tongue' (5. 361). The report of the *Jewish War* is, we have said,[4] most likely to have been in Aramaic. But there remains the possibility that He-

---

[1] For the old view, that Hebrew was no longer a language in everyday use by the first century A.D., see G. Dalman, *The Words of Jesus* (Engl. transl. 1902), col. 1. Some more recent scholarship has gone to the other extreme, making Hebrew the principal Palestinian language at the time. See, e.g., W. Chomsky, 'What was the Jewish vernacular during the Second Commonwealth?', *JQ* 42 (1951–2), pp. 193–221; H. Birkeland, *The Language of Jesus* (1954); J. Grintz, 'Hebrew as the spoken and written language in the last days of the Second Temple', *JBL* 29 (1960), pp. 32–47.

[2] See J. A. Emerton, 'The problem of vernacular Hebrew in the first century A.D. and the language of Jesus', *JThS* 24 (1973), pp. 1–24.

[3] This sociolinguistic term is applied to the relationship between Hebrew and Aramaic by C. Rabin, 'Hebrew and Aramaic in the first century', *Compendia Rerum Iudaicarum* etc. 1.2 (1976), pp. 1007–39.

[4] Chapter 7. For the general point, cf. R. H. Gundry, 'The language milieu of first-century Palestine', *JBL* 83 (1964), pp. 404–8.

brew too was a *spoken* mother tongue, and that this was what he used to address the Jews in Jerusalem.

(3) On another occasion when he talks with the Jews Josephus says that he 'transmitted Caesar's words speaking the language of the Hebrews' (6.97). Presumably this will be the same language as the one he earlier refers to as his native language, but there is nothing here to show what language that is.

(4) Related and, again, ambiguous types of expression are often used by Josephus in his Biblical etymologies. He says that he is interpreting the meaning of the word as it is 'in the tongue of the Hebrews', 'in the language of the Hebrews', or something close to this (*AJ* 1. 34, 36, 117, 146, 204, 258, 333; 3. 252; 6. 22; 7. 67; 9. 290; 11. 148, 286). Mostly it is, of course, the Hebrew word which is in question in the etymology, though in the case of the word Sabbath (1. 34) it is the form with the Aramaic termination, 'Sabbata', which Josephus gives.

(5) Again, when Josephus says that Agrippa's freedman told him of the death of the emperor Tiberius through a cryptic remark made 'in the tongue of the Hebrews', either language is possible. But in the case of the Hellenized Agrippa, Aramaic is perhaps the more likely.

(6) Twice in Josephus we find the expression 'in Hebrew'. Once it is used of the way in which the Jews from Jerusalem whom Nehemiah came across in Susa were speaking (*AJ* 11. 159). The Greek word used means simply 'in the Hebrew way'; both languages were in use at the time. The second time, the word is employed unequivocally to mean Hebrew, for there is a contrast with talking 'in Syrian', which must mean 'in Aramaic' (10. 8). There did exist, then, a specific word for Aramaic. But the incident described occurs in the reign of Hezekiah, and the Jews are represented as not understanding Aramaic at the time; the contrast is being drawn between the Jews' language and the one which did not belong to them. We may compare *AJ* 12. 15, 5, where written Aramaic is called 'Syrian letters', and explicitly stated as being very different from Hebrew. The two last examples do not exclude the possibility of 'in Hebrew' being used of speech in Aramaic in a context where it is the talk of Jews which is in question, and the contrast is with Greek, not with Hebrew.

(7) The same ambiguity surrounds New Testament uses of the above or cognate expressions. Paul spoke to the Jews in Jerusalem,

including ones from the province of Asia, 'in the Hebrew language' (Acts 21.40; 22.2). In the Gospel of John, certain names are said to be given 'in Hebrew': Bethesda (5.2), Gabbatha (19.13), Golgotha (19.17) and the appellation 'Rabbuni'. While the place-name forms look Aramaic, they could have served at the time in Hebrew speech too, if there was constant interaction between the two languages.

(8) Eusephius (*Hist. Eccl.* 3. 39.10) ascribes to Papias the statement that Matthew had written his Gospel 'in the Hebrew language' but says nothing to clarify which language he means; and it has not yet been convincingly demonstrated that our Matthew derives from an original in either one or the other.[5]

(9) Josephus uses a substantial number of transcribed Aramaic words in his description of the high priests' vestments (*AJ* 3. 151–78). He even gives the priests and the high priests themselves Aramaic appellations, *Kahanaiai* and *Anarabaches* (= *Kahana Rabba*). It is clear that this was the way he himself had been used to describe these things; but this could be because the use of Aramaic was particularly associated with the Temple ritual.

(10) We may conclude that Josephus certainly knew and used Aramaic. He calls his native language 'the Hebrews' language', however, and this kind of expression is at least sometimes used to refer to Hebrew. Its meaning seems to vary with the context, although there are very few instances about which we can be sure. Owing to its persistent ambiguity, we do not know what Josephus meant by it when he applied it to himself. But he may have meant Hebrew. In that case, he would once have spoken of Aramaic as his native language and once of Hebrew. This would imply that he was totally at home in both.

---

[5] See J. A. Emerton, 'Did Jesus speak Hebrew?', *JThS* 12 (1961), p. 202.

2. The assistant theory

Did Josephus write his own works? The view that they were the product, at least stylistically, of more than one hand was evolved by Thackeray, and has won widespread acceptance. The starting point was Josephus' statement that he had consulted helpers for his Greek.[1] Relying upon stylistic analyses (in themselves often valid), Thackeray claimed to detect the idiosyncratic styles of at least two individual 'assistants' inside Josephus. In this procedure, there are a number of methodological flaws.

(1) The activities of these assistants are traced, surprisingly, not in the *War*, for which Josephus says that he had help of some kind (yet where the style is more consistent), but in the *Antiquities*, about which he says nothing of the sort. And we have seen that it must not be inferred from Josephus' disclaimer at the end of that work that he was actually incapable of writing a long work in Greek in the eighties and nineties A.D.

(2) The assumption that unevenness of style or the marked preponderance in parts of a long work of certain mannerisms must be attributed to a division of the work among several hands, is patently false. If Josephus was, as he asserts, studying Greek authors with his own composition in view, there is nothing more natural than that the marks of authors whom he had recently been reading, or who had struck his fancy, should be apparent in certain parts of his writing.[2] Nor is this phenomenon of patchiness, whereby an expression, an idiom or a stylistic gimmick is adopted, overworked for a while, and then discarded, absent from the works of other authors.[3]

(3) Thackeray distinguishes in particular a 'Thucydidean Hack', and a 'Sophoclean Assistant'. Yet Thucydideanisms permeate

---

[1] H. St. J. Thackeray, *Josephus, the Man and the Historian* (1929). For Josephus' statement, see p. 47.

[2] Cf. B. Niese, 'Der jüdische Historiker Josephus', *Historische Zeitschrift* 76 (1896), p. 225. On Josephus' studies, see pp. 48–9.

[3] R. J. H. Shutt, *Studies in Josephus* (1961), p. 62ff.

Josephus' writings, especially the *War*. And which other model should he choose, when writing the history of a war? On some occasions, Thucydideanisms and Sophocleanisms are intermingled. A short passage in *Antiquities* 4 (89–95) will serve to illustrate this phenomenon. The passage does not fall within the main sphere of activity of either assistant according to Thackeray's analysis. But Thackeray supposes—as he must do to accommodate the evidence—that the same two men lent a hand outside this sphere too. Here we have a set-piece description of the battle between the Israelites and the Amorites. The details of the battle, not given in the Bible, have to be supplied by Josephus; and, in manner but even more in matter, he draws heavily on Thucydides—particularly, though not solely, the account in 6. 83 of the Athenian retreat to the river Asinarus. For Thackeray, this suggests the intervention of the Thucydidean assistant. At the same time, a triple alliteration which occurs in the heart of this passage reminds him of Sophocles, and makes him think that the Sophoclean assistant could be 'here at work'.[4] Are we to suppose, then, that the two assistants collaborated over the same passage? Thackeray's method of analysis does, it is true, possess some flexibility, and he elsewhere allows that the Sophoclean assistant 'does not disdain an occasional reminiscence of Thucydides'.[5] Such a statement serves only to make clear the truth of the matter: the styles of the parts attributed to the two different assistants are not unequivocally distinct, and there is a strong subjective element in Thackeray's assessment that they bear the stamp of two different hands and two different minds. To make such a claim it is not enough to discover a number of stylistic idiosyncracies specific to each part.[6]

[4] Thackeray's note, Loeb *Josephus*, *ad loc.* points out specific Thucydideanisms. He also cites three reasonably close Sophoclean parallels, with a similar type of triple alliteration. Perhaps Josephus' group of words is most reminiscent of Sophocles; but it is certainly true that other Greek poets used such alliterations to good effect. There is even an example in Homer: R. Volkmann, *Die Rhetorik der Griecher und Römer* (1885; repr. 1963), p. 515. For Aeschylus' use, see E. Fraenkel, *Agamemnon* (1960), commentary on line 268. This case illustrates Thackeray's relentlessness in the pursuit of the Sophoclean assistant.

[5] Op. cit. (n. 1), p. 115.

[6] It is unfortunate that much of the detailed information gleaned by Thackeray from those books of Josephus which he did not edit is not available. His book gives only the conclusions which he drew from those findings. His lexicon, as far as it has been published, indicates with special marks those words which are confined to the supposed provinces of each of his two assistants, but it stops at the fifth letter of the alphabet: *A Lexicon to Flavius Josephus*, parts 1–4 (1930–55).

(4) Thackeray takes the *Life* (as well as *Antiquities* 20) to embody Josephus' personal, unadulterated style, and he points out that in the *Life* (but not so much in the *Antiquities*) the word order is often unexpected, abstracts are used to excess, and the general effect is lacking in polish. This is true; but it can be accounted for by the difference in character and purpose between that work and the others. The *Life* was a polemic; and the anger and intensity of parts of it betray that it was written in the heat of the moment. The author is simply not concerned with form and style.

(5) In much of the *Antiquities*, Josephus worked with one literary source in front of him. Thackeray has overlooked the fact that his style might be influenced by that source, whichever it be at any one time. This would be feasible even if, as we learn from those cases where the source survives and we are able to make a comparison— notably, the *Letter of Aristeas*, and I Maccabees—Josephus had the tendency to replace the words of the original with ones of his own choosing. For the sentence structure of the original did sometimes survive.[7] Thus, for example, within the unit formed by Books 17, 18 and 19, whose strange, involved and tortuous style had already been noticed before Thackeray assigned them to the 'Thucydidean Hack',[8] there is one section where Josephus still has Nicolaus of Damascus to hand (17); there are parts where he seems to be using some source for Parthian history (in Book 18); and there is a large tract of narrative where it is probable that he is translating from a Latin writer (the assassination of the emperor Gaius, and the accession of Claudius in Book 19). We would wish to know whether the distinctive stylistic features of this block are to be found in equal number in all three areas of the narrative.

There are enough grave disadvantages to the assistant theory to warrant its rejection. These may be summed up by saying that it derives from a mechanical approach to literature. Thackeray does not acknowledge that the composition of a large-scale work is a complex process, and a long one, during the course of which developments in the author must occur, and different influences operate upon him. And we may add another general criticism:

[7] This is best seen in the comparative tables provided by A. Pelletier, *Flavius Josèphe adapteur de la Lettre d'Aristée* (1962), pp. 307-27.

[8] By Guilelmus Schmidt, *De Flavii Josephi elocutione observationes criticae*, pars prior (Diss. Göttingen, Leipzig, 1893), p. 26; fully in *Jahrb. f. class Philologie*, suppl. 19 (1894).

Thackeray has left out of account the literary and intellectual context in which Josephus was working. The principal reason for ancient writers to study the works of their predecessors was that they constituted exemplars worthy of imitation, as we have already observed. This is stated explicitly a number of times by Dionysius of Halicarnassus[9] in various of his works of literary criticism, and it had been the main point of his lost work, *de Imitatione*. Second-rate authors imitated their models—above all Thucydides—in a servile and ludicrous fashion, and they were castigated by Dionysius for this, and mocked by Lucian.[10] Discussions about who was the best model for a particular genre, and how far he was to be imitated, were endless. In such an atmosphere, we have no reason to be surprised by, or to draw conclusions from the fact that an author who has been applying himself diligently to the study of 'grammar', and who has every reason to be anxious to do as his cultured contemporaries were doing, shows himself to be influenced by the mannerisms of more than one exemplar. It would be natural for Josephus to try out a number of different styles in his work.

---

[9] E.g. *de Thuc.* 25; *ad Pomp.* 5.20.

[10] *de Thuc.* 2, 35, 55; and Lucian, *How to Write History*; cf. Cicero, *de Oratore* 32 (orators too imitated Thucydides).

3. The dating of Josephus' *Antiquities* and *Life*

The *Antiquities* are dated by Josephus himself to year 13 of Domitian, that is between September 93 and September 94 A.D. But the *Life*, appended to the *Antiquities*,[1] speaks of Agrippa II as dead (*V* 359), and Agrippa's death is put by the ninth-century bibliophile Photius, claiming to cite the chronicle of Justus of Tiberias, in the third year of Trajan, that is A.D. 100 (*Bibliotheca* p. 33). If we accept this date, we must find some reconciliation for the two conflicting statements—through supposing, for example, that there were two editions of the *Antiquities*, or of the *Life*.[2]

The former view, that the *Life* appeared only with the second, post 100 edition of the *Antiquities* (while the preface of the *Antiquities* was written for the first edition) gained general acceptance; but the supports upon which it rests are weak. Its first exponent, R. Laqueur, claimed to detect two separate conclusions to *Antiquities*.[3] Yet a disinterested view suggests that the supposed second conclusion, beginning 'upon this I shall conclude the *Antiquities*' (*AJ* 20. 267), is no more than a resumption of the thread from the point where Josephus had first begun to wind up the work—'here my *Antiquities* will end' (20. 259)—and had gone on to give a summary and assessment of the history as a whole (259–66). After this passage, he offers what are really to be his final words. Hence the appearance of two conclusions.[4]

---

[1] For the date, *AJ* 20. 267; on the relationship of *Life* to *Antiquities*, see above, p. 13.

[2] The second view is developed by B. Motzo, *Saggi di Storia e Letteratura Giudeo-Ellenistica* (1924), pp. 217–19.

[3] *Der jüdische Historiker Flavius Josephus* (1920) pp. 3–5. For views dependent upon Laqueur's, see D. A. Barish, 'The *Autobiography* of Josephus and the hypothesis of a second edition of his *Antiquities*', *HThR* 71 (1978), p. 62, n. 10.

[4] For a fuller examination of the supposed two conclusions, see Barish, op. cit. (n. 3), pp. 69–71.

It is more reasonable to accept that Josephus' work, that is to say the complete unit of *Antiquities* and *Life*, appeared at the date which eventually remained affixed to it. This is what the internal evidence in fact suggests: for passages from the body of both *Life* and *Antiquities* seem to imply that Agrippa II was dead when they were written;[5] and Josephus does not pay his respects to any emperor later than Domitian. Photius' date for the death of Agrippa II, on the other hand, can safely be dismissed. It is unreliable not merely in that there is a strong possibility of error about such a matter in a late author—and various types of error have been proposed to explain this case—but also because Photius is generally hasty and quite vague in his description of the work (or works) of Justus which he had seen.[6] At the same time, outside Photius, no evidence makes it necessary to hold that Agrippa was ruling after 92/3;[7] while an inscription from Auranitis and one from Trachonitis point to the cessation of his rule, at least over those parts of his kingdom, during the reign of Domitian.[8] The full evidence has now been set out with great clarity,[9] and it does not need to be scrutinised here. While it is impossible to be certain about the date of Agrippa II's death, the probability is that it occurred well before A.D.100. And there is no difficulty in putting it before 93/4, and allowing that the *Antiquities* with the appended *Life* appeared at that time.

[5] See Th. Frankfort, 'La date de l'autobiographie de Flavius Josèphe et les oeuvres de Justus de Tibériade', *Revue Belge de Philologie et d'Histoire* 39 (1961), pp. 52–8.

[6] See T. Rajak 'Justus of Tiberias', *CQ* 23 (1973), pp. 358–63, especially p. 361, n. 6 and p. 362, n. 2.

[7] Provided the coin labelled year 35 of his reign be assigned to an era beginning in A.D.56, not to the other era employed on some of Agrippa's Flavian coinage, which starts in 61. See Schurer-Vermes-Millar, p. 480, n. 43. An inscription from Batanea mentioning the year 37 = 92/3 (reckoning from 56) is the latest certain evidence of any kind for Agrippa's reign: *OGIS* 426 = *IGR* 3. 1127. cf. Frankfort, op. cit. (n. 5).

[8] See Schürer-Vermes-Millar, p. 482, no. 7. The one is dated to the sixteenth year of Domitian, the other to the first year of Nerva, without mentioning Agrippa.

[9] Schürer-Vermes-Millar, pp. 481–3, no. 47, and cf. Barish, op. cit. (n. 3), pp. 71–4.

Index